A-LEVEL YEAR 1 SOCIOLOGY FO

UNIT 2 (Researching & Understanding So

SOCIOLOGY 2 STUDY GUIDE

Published independently by Tinderspark Press
© Jonathan Rowe 2022
www.psychologywizard.net
www.philosophydungeon.weebly.com

Visit the **Sociology Robot** YouTube channel

CONTENTS

ABOUT THIS BOOK

This book offers advice for teachers and students approaching OCR A-Level Sociology, **Paper 2 Section A (Research methods & researching social inequalities)** and **Section 2B (Understanding social inequalities)**.

Study Guides for Papers 1 and Paper 3 are also available.

Paper 2 Sections A and B

Section A covers just under half of **Paper 2** in OCR Sociology. There are 4 questions worth 45 marks out of the 105 marks for the entire paper. It should take candidates just under an hour to complete this section. Section B covers more than half, is worth 60 marks and should take at least an hour to complete, with 50 minutes devoted to a 40-mark essay.

Perspectives

In Paper 1, students learned about 3 vitally important sociological Perspectives: **Functionalism, Marxism** and **Feminism. Interactionism** was introduced later to make a fourth. Other Perspectives like **Postmodernism** and the **New Right** were introduced in **1B (Options)**. On Paper 2, students will learn in more depth about **Neo-Marxism** and different branches (or 'waves') of Feminism as well as **Weberianism** as an explanation of inequality.

Research methodology introduces two new methodological Perspectives that ties in with the theoretical Perspectives above: **Positivism** and **Interpretivism**. Understanding these debates about methodology will throw new light on Functionalism, Marxism and Feminism and help students to evaluate them deeply.

Studies

The research methodology in this Study Guide is meant to be applied to research studies but isn't taken directly from them. But examples help. I start off using examples of studies from **1A: Socialisation, Culture & Identity** – notably Bourdieu's survey on taste, Parson's overview of gender roles in the American family and Willis' observation of working-class schoolboys. Later, new studies are introduced: these all feature **in Section B** and are identified with * in the text.

I hope that students revise and analyse these studies successfully after encountering them first as methodology examples that they will meet again as research into inequality.

REEARCH METHODS & RESEARCHING SOCIAL INEQUALITIES: CONTENT

What's this topic about?

In Paper 1, students were introduced to the main theoretical Perspectives in Sociology and some of the answers it proposes to questions about society. You learned dozens of 'studies' which are the results of investigating social behaviour in different settings. Now you will learn about METHODOLOGY which is how sociological research is actually carried out.

This should help you answer some important questions:

- What is the best way to investigate social phenomena? Is there a best way at all, or are all the ways flawed in some respect?

- Can sociologists be truly detached while they are investigating the society they live in? Should they even try to be detached?

- What are the limits of sociological investigation? Are some topics 'off limits' and are some ways of going about things dangerous, harmful or unfair?

Methodology

Methodology refers to the entire question of how to go about investigating society. It includes rather philosophical questions like what aspect of society should be investigated in the first place, practical questions like who should fund the research and who should carry it out, technical issues of where to do the research and how long for as well as ethical questions about how everyone involved should be treated during and after the research.

'Procedure' is another word that has a similar meaning to methodology, but 'procedure' is normally a narrower concern with the technical questions of where the research is done, who is involved, how long it lasts and what equipment is used. 'Methodology' is a wider term, taking in the issues of funding the research, publishing it, using it to influence social policy and making sure no groups are harmed or mistreated.

In **1A: Socialisation, Culture & Identity** students learned about evaluating sociological research. This often involves spotting the Perspective it comes from and discussing how rival Perspectives would criticise it. Methodology works as a powerful evaluative tool: as well as criticizing the theoretical basis of research, you can criticize or praise its methodology, arguing that it was carried out badly or well.

These methodological critiques don't just apply to the research on inequality you will meet in **2B: Understanding Social Inequalities**. When you revise the research from **Paper 1**, you should add methodological critiques to the studies there too.

CHAPTER ONE – THEORY & METHODS

Sociology tries to study society, which immediately raises the question, *How can you do that?* There are two main approaches or perspectives. One is to **imitate the way the natural sciences study the physical world** and treat social behaviour as the same sort of thing that plants or chemicals do in the lab. The other way is to **use imagination and empathy to 'put yourself in someone else's shoes'** and understand social behaviour from the inside. Neither approach is wrong, but they can lead to very different conclusions.

PERSPECTIVES

In **1A: Socialisation, Culture & Identity** you learned about the sociological perspectives based on Consensus (Functionalism) and Conflict (Marxism and Feminism) as well as the Social Action perspective (Interactionism). This section of the exam introduces methodological perspectives that direct sociologists to research things in different ways: the scientific **Positivist** approach and the more sensitive and imaginative **Interpretivist** approach (which is sometimes called Anti-Positivism).

These perspectives link together in interesting ways. **Functionalism** is usually Positivist in its approach as is traditional Marxist sociology. **Interactionism** is Interpretivist. **Feminism** and versions of modern **Neo-Marxism** often employ both methodological perspectives.

POSITIVISM

Positivism is a scientific approach. The word positivism comes from the philosophical idea that we only know things if they enter our mind through experience. This linked idea of truth being based on physical evidence experienced through the five senses is called **empiricism**. Empirical evidence is evidence that can be seen or heard or touched and empiricism is the basis for scientific proof. Empiricism is a very old idea but 'Positivism' was coined by **Auguste Comte** in the 19th century to mean the belief that society itself should be studied through physical evidence.

Emile Durkheim added to Positivism another idea: there are **social facts** which can be identified through scientific study of human behaviour and which have a *"coercive control"* over the way people act. For example, Durkheim thought that life in a big industrial city was a social fact that drove people to suicide.

For Positivists, the point of sociological research is to identify these social facts and explain the influence they have on people. This explanation takes the form of a scientific law that says that if there are certain social conditions then particular social outcomes must inevitably follow. Positivists hope that these social laws will predict upheavals in society (like riots, wars or revolutions) or social trends (such as marriages breaking up, crime waves or drug addiction).

In order to formulate these 'laws of society,' Positivists need to gather a lot of data (information) about social behaviour. This data needs to be **quantitative** (in number form) so that it can be statistically analysed. It needs to be gathered in a scientific way so that the researcher's personal biases or expectations don't influence the results. This impersonal approach is called **objectivity**.

AO2 ILLUSTRATION: DOCTOR WHO AND YOUTH CRIME

In November 2021, Conservative MP **Nick Fletcher** linked the casting of a female Doctor Who in the BBC's science fiction series to crime rates among young men. His remarks were widely mocked but they do illustrate the idea of social facts.

Fletcher complained that *"every male character or good role model"* is being given *"a female replacement,"* using examples like *Doctor Who* and *Ghostbusters*. Fletcher warned that young males would be left only antisocial role models like gangsters who *"make crime look cool"* and this would lead to *"young men committing crime."*

Role models are **social facts**: they influence you to imitate them. If you take away positive role models, it follows that people will stop imitating their behaviour. Fletcher's thinking is typically Positivist. However, it is not really based on lots of data gathered impersonally – in fact, it's based on a few anecdotes, which is the *opposite* of the Positivist approach. Nonetheless, Functionalists would accept Fletcher's broad hypothesis about how role models affect people; scientific research is needed to discover whether there are *in fact* fewer positive role models for young males (there are still a great many out there) and whether crime rates are *in fact* increasing among that group.

Other sociologists adopt the same Positivist perspective at times. It is common for Feminists to argue that violent pornography encourages crimes against women and to support this with detailed statistics about the consumption of pornography and the reporting of sexual assaults. Marxists also link increasing poverty or heavy-handed policing to rises in crime or riots. Both approaches identify social facts and support the link to social behaviour with statistical evidence.

Quantitative Data

Quantitative data means data in the form of numbers. Numerical data is much more impersonal and **objective** than words or descriptions: it's harder to misinterpret and it's less susceptible to being distorted by wishful thinking or prejudice.

Quantitative data can be expressed in **tables and graphs** which are easy to understand. Quantitative data allows for detailed comparisons of different groups and identifying trends. Quantitative data can also be used to show that *apparent* differences and trends don't really exist and that they only seem to be going on because people are focusing on a few high-profile examples (perhaps like Nick Fletcher MP, above).

Quantitative data is gathered from **structured observations** (p60), **structured interviews** (p59) and **closed questions in questionnaires** (p57).

However, quantitative data has its limitations. It can be very shallow and uninformative. It doesn't reveal feelings or motives. It is not very good for exploring individual cases or one-off events that don't reveal a pattern or a trend. Moreover, there is an old proverb that *"you can prove anything with statistics"* and numbers can easily be manipulated to support unreasonable conclusions.

AO2 ILLUSTRATION: THE BORIS BREXIT BUS

During the **2016 European Union (EU) Referendum**, the Brexit-supporting politician (and later Prime Minister) Boris Johnson organised a publicity stunt: a London bus with this message on the side:

"We send the EU £350 million a week. Let's fund the NHS instead."

Critics complained that this statistic was misleading. The figure was arrived at by taking the yearly amount the UK paid into the EU and dividing it by 52 to get a weekly figure. However, the UK also claimed a rebate back from the EU, so the real figure would have been £250 million or less. Moreover, a lot of extra costs would be incurred by leaving the EU, so the true figure was probably £130 million. Finally, even if there were savings, how could we be sure they would be paid into the NHS rather than (say) tax cuts?

Nonetheless, the figure of "£350 million" seems to have influenced voters. Like a lot of quantitative data, it's simple and memorable. An **Ipsos Mori survey (2018)** showed that 42% of people still believed the claim to be true. The **UK Statistics Authority** complained that the claim was *"misleading and undermines trust in official statistics."*

The controversy over the statistics on the Brexit Bus (source: FullFact.org)

Patterns & Trends

A great strength of Positivism is its focus on statistical patterns and trends in society. These could include rises in certain times of crime, changes in the gap between the rich and the poor or the number of women or people from ethnic minorities in top jobs.

The patterns and trends are important because Positivism is a **macro perspective** ('macro' means 'on a large scale'): it looks at society as a whole rather than individual actions and it tries to detect the social facts that are influencing people in general.

This macro perspective is sometimes called **structuralism**: the idea that society's structures dictate how people behave. It leaves very little room for **freewill or individual choice**. Functionalism and Marxism view people as shaped by their upbringing (primary socialisation) or social class. Feminism has a structuralist side to it as well, since it views Patriarchy in society as influencing people's attitudes and behaviour.

AO2 ILLUSTRATION: THE IMPACT OF CHRISTMAS ADVERTS

If you think it is unlikely that your individual behaviour could be influenced by social structures, consider Christmas adverts on TV. In 2018, John Lewis spent £18 million on TV adverts featuring the pop star Elton John. The advert had 50 million views across social media; John Lewis expects to earn back 20 times what it invests in Christmas advertising (source: BBC, 2019). UK customers spend £30 billion during the three months leading up to Christmas. However, profits dropped by 56% for John Lewis in that year, so did their popular advert really influence customers to shop in their stores? The figures back up the structuralist view (Christmas advertising encourages us to spend) but also oppose it (we don't necessarily shop in the places whose adverts we enjoy).

*If you studied **Media** as an option in **Paper 1B (Option 2)**, you will know different theories of media influence that explain how people obey media messages but also resist them.*

Screen shot of the 2021 John Lewis Christmas advert: Nathan & Skye (fair use)

The opposite of the macro perspective is the **micro perspective** that examines individuals or small groups and focuses on choice and freewill. Macro- or structuralist sociology might be missing out on the distinctive feature of human behaviour by ignoring these things.

Objectivity & Value Freedom

A crucial aspect of scientific methodology is **objectivity**, which means being neutral and impersonal, free from bias and keeping your opinions and preferences (or fears) out of the research process. It is not always easy to be objective when you are a scientist studying rocks, fossils or comets, because you might be excited by a new discovery or concerned that evidence doesn't back up your theory. It's even harder to be objective when studying people, especially when you focus on sensitive social issues (like racism, sexual assault, child abuse or poverty).

Positivists try to remain objective by following **standardised procedures**: they work out how their research will proceed beforehand and stick to that plan, ignoring interesting or concerning developments along the way. This leads to them favouring **structured observations** (p60), **structured interviews** (p59) and **closed questions in questionnaires** (p57). Objectivity is also achieved by inviting other sociologists to **replicate** your methodology to see if they come up with the same results. This is part of the **peer review process** in scientific research.

Positivists also pursue **value-freedom**, which means research that is free from values, opinions or interpretations. A value-free researcher shows no personal interest in the people being studied and has no preference for one outcome over another. Positivists use **sampling techniques** (p44) to make sure they are neutral towards their research participants, and they try to study society 'from the outside' as if they are not themselves a part of it. Critics argue that this sort of neutrality is impossible and that supposedly scientific research has values running through it.

AO2 ILLUSTRATION: DECOLONISING MATHEMATICS

Most people consider mathematics to be the most **objective** type of human thought and it is central to Positivism (the importance of **quantitative data** to identify **patterns and trends**).

However, critics argue that mathematics is **not value-free**. Mathematics is linked to the superiority of European civilisation and masculine thinking – the most famous mathematicians are males and the symbols used are Greek and Latin. Most people don't know about the huge contribution made to mathematics by Arabs (who gave us algebra, an Arabic word), ancient Egypt (fractions), India (which gave us the concept of zero) and of China. The Lebombo bone, discovered in South Africa, is the oldest known mathematical tool and it dates back to 35,000 BCE. These critics claim that mathematics must be **decolonised**, which means removing all of its associations with white, male, European superiority. Until then, mathematics will contain hidden but influential biases against other groups and cultures.

*When you study **2B: Understanding Social Inequalities** you will learn more about **Critical Race Theory (CRT)** and the project to **decolonialise** society (p155).*

Positive Views of Positivism

Sounds a bit silly, doesn't it?

Positivism tries to make Sociology as scientific as possible. This means carrying out research on **large samples**, gathering detailed **quantitative data for statistical analysis** and following standardised procedures that can be **replicated by other researchers**. This sort of research is very **reliable** (p21).

Positivist research claims to **investigate social facts** and uses them to **formulate scientific laws** about how society operates. Positivism explores **patterns and trends** in populations and makes **predictions** about where these trends are heading and what will happen if changes occur in society.

Perhaps the most important advantage of 'scientific Sociology' is the **status** attached to science. Scientific research is viewed as more credible, it is taken more seriously and it reaches a wider audience than other types of research. It is more likely to inform **social policy** (p40) when governments act on it. This is particularly important for Perspectives that want to change society through research, such as **Feminists**, **Marxists** and the **New Right**. These perspectives are known as **structuralist** for their belief that the structures of society are more important than individual decision-making.

Negative Views of Positivism

Critics argue that society isn't the sort of thing that can be studied scientifically.

The Positivist focus on statistics and large samples ignores the importance of individual experiences, choices and **freewill**. Positivism views people as **puppets controlled by society**, but people are also the creators and shapers of social forces. Positivism ignores the impact of beliefs and the power of charismatic individuals or strongly motivated groups to change the course of history. In contrast, **Social Action** perspectives focus on exactly these subjects.

The Positivist focus on objectivity and value-freedom is criticised by **Interpretivists** (p14) who claim it is **not possible to be neutral** about your own society. They argue that researchers always smuggle their own assumptions and prejudices into their research, making it **biased**. These biases might be expressed in the samples selected, the wording of questions in surveys, the choice of topics to investigate or the way that conclusions are drawn from the data. For example, Feminists point out that mainstream Sociology is actually **'male-stream' Sociology** – it is from a male point of view, reflects male interests and ignores female experiences.

Other sociologists argue that the focus on science reflects Western cultural biases. This is linked to the **Postmodernist** argument that science is not really a way of discovering truth through reason and evidence, but instead is just another **'meta-narrative'** like a religion or a cultural belief. If this is the case, then the Positivist claim to investigate social facts is mistaken and Positivism just offers a *view* of society from a Western cultural standpoint.

Historic Positivists: Auguste Comte & Emile Durkheim

The 19th century French philosopher **Auguste Comte (1798-1857)** is sometimes called 'the Father of Sociology' and it was he who coined the terms 'Positivism' and 'Sociology.' For Comte, Positivism was more than just a research method: it was a political project. Comte believed that his Positivist outlook would replace religion and he called Sociology *the Queen of the Sciences* because he thought it would enable people to build a perfect society.

Emile Durkheim (1858-1917) was born a year after Comte died but carried on his commitment to a scientific understanding of society, although he rejected Comte's political project. Durkheim believed that Positivism could predict changes in society such as unemployment or unrest. Durkheim championed the **Comparative Method** which involves comparing groups and looking relationships between different variables. Durkheim's famous book *Suicide* (1897) used detailed statistical analysis of suicide rates all over Europe to link suicide to social facts like the type of religion and marital status. Durkheim concluded that suicide was more common when people lived individualistic and stressful lives without social support, such as in big industrial cities, after divorce and where Protestant (as opposed to Catholic) Christian religion was dominant.

Contemporary Positivist: Charles Murray

You were introduced to **Charles Murray**'s ideas about the Underclass in **1A: Socialisation, Culture & Identity** and will explore them in more detail in **2B: Understanding Inequality** as part of learning about the **New Right** perspective.

Murray's book *Losing Ground* (1984) analyses trends in the rise of crime in the USA since the 1960s and compares them for trends in unemployment and in the births of children outside marriage. This is similar to Durkheim's Comparative Method. He finds no match between the patterns of crime and unemployment but he does find a match between crime and the decline of marriage. Murray claims to have identified what Durkheim would call a **social fact**: boys born to unmarried mothers grow up to be *"essentially barbarians"* who turn to drugs and crime.

Murray identifies a sort of social law that says that people are kept honest and responsible by the need to work hard to support themselves and their family. If they do not need to do this – because, for example, the state supports men when they are unemployed and supports unmarried mothers – then people do not develop a sense of responsibility. Murray paints the picture of an 'underclass' that does little or no paid work, survives on benefits and petty crime and has no sense of sexual restraint or responsibility.

Murray is accused of being selective about what statistics he makes use of in order to exaggerate a social problem. This is the same as the criticism that Positivists *claim* to be neutral scientists stating the facts but are really human beings expressing their biased point of view in scientific language.

INTERPRETIVISM

Interpretivism (or **Anti-Positivism**) rejects the idea of 'scientific Sociology' because it focuses on the aspects of human life that are not suitable for scientific study: the interior world of beliefs, motives and choices. It is also sceptical about the possibility of studying society in a scientific way even if you do focus on observable behaviour because it argues that the sociological researcher can never be truly neutral as scientific research requires.

The founding figure of Interpretivism is **Max Weber** (p19, but also p167), who rejected Positivism as a way of studying society. Weber pioneered the **Social Action** approach, which developed into the **Interactionist** perspective that you learned about in **1A: Socialisation, Culture & Identity**.

Instead of searching for social facts and formulating sociological laws, Interpretivists place importance on how people make sense of their **social world**, how they **negotiate** the social pressures that try to coerce and control them and the different ways they show **agency** (self-direction and choice) in their lives. Rather than large samples, they often focus on **individuals** or on **small groups** through the sociological method of **ethnography** (p62). Interpretivists try to understand the **meaning** of social behaviour rather than trying to predict or control it.

Relativity *by M C Escher (1953): going up or down? it depends on your point of view*

Meanings & Experiences

Weber argues that what makes behaviour 'social' is the **meaning** people give to it. For example, the difference between a brawl and a boxing match is the way the fighters and the audience interpret what is going on. Another example might be family: this is not just a biological connection between people, it is the way people interpret their relationships to each other and how they think they are supposed to treat each other; some people who are not biologically related (such as stepchildren) are considered 'family' and some people who are biologically related (such as distant cousins) might not be considered 'family.'

Interpretivism claims that in order to make sense of the social world we have to understand how people **experience** it. A single social interaction might mean different things to the people involved, depending on the beliefs they hold and the social world they inhabit. There is no single objective fact behind any social behaviour, just multiple possible interpretations. This makes it impossible to study social behaviour scientifically; sensitivity is required (*c.f.* **verstehen**, p16).

AO2 ILLUSTRATION: AZEEM RAFIQ & YORKSHIRE CRICKET CLUB

Trigger warning: the repetition of an ethnic slur is used to illustrate this point.

Azeem Rafiq is a Pakistani-born cricketer who moved to the UK at age 10 and played for the prestigious Yorkshire County Cricket Club 2008-18, becoming captain in 2012. However, in 2020 he complained of racism in the club, in particular use of the racist slur 'Paki' (henceforth 'P-word'). The Club investigated but no one was disciplined and the use of the P-word was excused as "*friendly and good-natured banter.*" Rafiq went public with his complaints and in the wider scandal the chairman of the Club resigned.

Rafiq's experience shows the importance of Interpretivist approaches. Some members of the Club regarded the P-word as 'banter' rather than racism; for Rafiq, this was a slur against his ethnicity and **not** a shortened form of his country of origin. Rafiq **experienced** racist abuse because the social interaction had a racist **meaning** for him (and would have that meaning for almost **all** British Asians). Marxists refer to this sort of language as **hegemonic discourse**: it reinforces **White privilege** by reminding non-Whites of their inferior status. Even when people use such slurs out of ignorance rather than malice, they support inequality with their language.

Second Test, Headingley (image by It's No Game)

Verstehen, Empathy & Rapport

Empathy is using your imagination to experience what another person experiences, to share their feelings and point of view. **Rapport** is a type of relationship characterised by trust, intimacy and easy communication. Both are important for an Interpretivist who tries to 'get inside another person's head' and see their **social world** as they see it.

Max Weber uses the word German word '***verstehen***' to describe Interpretivist methodology. '*Verstehen*' means 'understanding' and it involves having empathy with your research subjects and establishing a rapport with them. *Verstehen* is the opposite of the patterns and trends that Positivists focus on: it is personal insight rather than a statistical generalisation.

Subjectivity

Positivists aim to be objective (impersonal, neutral) but Interpretivists embrace the opposite of objectivity, which is **subjectivity**.

Subjectivity is often described as a bad thing: 'from your own subjective point of view' means you are not stepping back and viewing the situation in an unbiased way. However, Interpretivists claim that subjective experiences are valuable because they offer a **valid** insight into people's feelings. They also argue that the sort of objectivity Positivists aim for is in fact impossible: every view on any social situation is somewhat subjective. Instead of resisting subjectivity, it is better to embrace it and benefit from the insights you gain into **meanings and experiences** this way. This authenticity makes research more **valid** (p20).

AO2 ILLUSTRATION: OPRAH INTERVIEWS MEGHAN MARKLE

Oprah With Megan & Harry was a 2021 TV show in which **Oprah Winfrey** interviewed the Duchess of Sussex and Prince Harry. During the interview, the Duchess talked about her experiences of mental ill health due to the racism of the Royal Family and the British news media.

Oprah Winfrey is a close friend and neighbour of Meghan Markle, so a **rapport** was quickly established. When Meghan revealed racist remarks has been made about her baby, Oprah gasped in horror, showing **empathy**. Oprah used the phrase '*speaking your truth*' to describe Meghan's account: the idea of '*your truth*' (rather than '***the*** truth') draws attention to the **subjectivity** of Meghan's responses, which were the truth *as she saw it*.

The Queen later responded to the interview by saying "*Recollections may vary*" – in other words, her subjective experiences were different from Meghan's.

Critics complained that Oprah had not challenged any of the Duke and Duchess' claims and the British news media later exposed mistakes in their account. However, produced a fascinating insight into *one person's* experience of life in the Royal Family.

Researcher Imposition & Reflexivity

Researcher imposition is when the researcher imposes her own views, beliefs, prejudices or anxieties onto the research. This can be done through the **choice of topic to research** (such as Marxists focusing on class), **choice of sample** (such as young people or people from a particular neighbourhood) and even **choice of method** (such as choosing to interview people because you believe they would be too uneducated to complete a questionnaire). During the research, imposition can occur due to asking **leading questions** or guiding the participants' behaviour through **body language or non-verbal communication**.

Some research methods particularly beloved of Interpretivists, such as the **participant observation** (p61), are particularly prone to researcher imposition: you can change the behaviour of a small social group just by joining it. Studying motives and beliefs runs the risk that you project your own ideas onto your research subjects rather than discover their ideas.

One solution used by Interpretivists is **Reflexivity**. This is the process of reflecting on how you are influencing your own research. It includes acknowledging your own bias and the values and how they affect your findings. Reflexivity can be of various levels of depth and complexity:

- On a simple level, considering to what extent respondents are telling you what you want to hear – or feel inhibited from telling the truth or acting naturally in your presence or in the situation you set up. **Respondent validation** (p35) can be a solution to this problem.
- A more complex type of reflexivity is considering how your culture, gender, class or privileges might be influencing your research.
- The most complex type of reflexivity involves reflecting on your own theoretical bias, such as a Marxist focus on class at the expense of race or a Feminist focus on biological women at the expense of Trans and non-binary people.

AO2 ILLUSTRATION: KATE CLANCY'S REFLEXIVE MEMOIRS

Some Kids I Taught & What They Taught Me (2019) by Kate Clancy is an award-winning book of memoirs (an autobiography looking back on personal experiences). It is based on her career teaching disadvantaged children. However, the book was attacked on Twitter for containing discriminatory descriptions, such as referring to a Black pupil with *"chocolate coloured skin"* or two children with autism being *"jarring company."*

Clancy initially defended her writing then apologised for *"overreacting"* to criticism and said she was *"grateful"* for a chance to rewrite the book: "*I know I got many things wrong, and welcome the chance to write better, more lovingly.*"

Some critics were dismayed that an author had been bullied into rewriting her own memoirs by anonymous Twitter-users. However, Clancy's decision resembles **reflexivity** in Sociology: she reflects on how her ethnicity and other privileges (as a person without learning disabilities) have led to her supporting harmful stereotypes and she adjusts her writing based on this insight.

Qualitative Data

Qualitative data means data in the form of words. Linguistic data is much more personal and **subjective** than numbers and statistics; it's more insightful and closer to the real-life experiences of actual people. Qualitative data can explore people's beliefs, feelings and motives. It is important for understanding one-off events (like being involved in a disaster) or exploring the perspective of minority groups whose experiences get 'drowned out' in large-scale patterns and trends. It can help overcome some of the institutional biases in Sociology, such as the tendency to approach things from a White or male perspective.

Qualitative data is gathered from **unstructured observations** (p61) and **semi-structured interviews** (p59) as well as **open questions in questionnaires** (p57).

However, qualitative data has limitations. It cannot create graphs or statistical analyses, compare groups or reveal large scale **patterns and trends**. Its sheer **subjectivity** makes it **unreliable** (p21) and hard to generalise beyond the original research situation. Even if the researcher is **reflexive**, biases will be present; reflexivity itself can make the research longwinded and self-indulgent.

Positive Views of Interpretivism

Interpretivists argue that society isn't the sort of thing that can be studied scientifically. They believe that statistics offer a misleading view of human experience and they reject the Positivist idea that we are 'puppets' controlled by society. Instead, they focus on the impact of beliefs and the power of charismatic individuals or strongly motivated groups to change society.

Research: Learn about an important leader who changed history or an influential group or belief system that persuaded other people to go along with it: you could focus on the **Abolitionists** who campaigned against slavery or a famous reformer like **Gandhi** (1869-1948).

Interpretivism offers a way out of the Western and male-orientated biases in Sociology through **reflexivity**. Researchers can address their own biases while carrying out research and reflect on them in their analysis. This is an improvement on **Positivism**, where researchers believe that, since they are collecting **quantitative data**, they must automatically be **value-free**, while all the time smuggling in biases they aren't aware of. Interpretivism also links to **Postmodernism** since it rejects the idea of a single truth 'out there' that can be reached by the scientific method. It accepts that truth is always **subjective** and there might be many truths, not just one.

Interpretivism has led to the new sociological methodology of **ethnography** (p62).

Negative Views of Interpretivism

The Interpretivist focus on subjectivity and reflexivity is criticised by **Positivists** (p7) who claim it is **important to be neutral** and step back from social situations to understand them clearly. They argue that, as social scientists, researchers should try to present social behaviour as factually as possible and avoid all **bias**.

By refusing to make use of scientific methods, Interpretivism risks offering only anecdotes or opinions. This is thought-provoking but cannot be the basis of **social policies** or used to criticise social institutions, because it might be completely unrepresentative. Statistical **patterns and trends** are needed to conform whether the findings apply to society as a whole or are limited to just the individuals being studied.

Reflexivity is fine for making the researcher more self-aware and sensitive, but it takes a lot of time and it takes up a lot of space in the research report. **Johnson & Duberley (2003)** argue that reflexivity can lead to **paralysis**, with the researcher so obsessed with questioning their own assumptions that they feel unable to draw confident conclusions.

Historic Interpretivist: Max Weber (1818-1883)

Max Weber (1864-1920) is one of the 'Big Three' founding sociologists, along with Karl Marx and Emile Durkheim. In **1A: Socialisation, Culture & Identity** you were introduced to Weber as the founder of the **Social Action** perspective that gave us Interactionism; in **2B: Understanding Social Inequalities** you will learn about **Weberianism** and how his ideas apply to society.

Weber is also the founder of the **Interpretivist** perspective in sociological methods. He rejected the **Positivist** methodology of Comte and Durkheim (p13) and argued that society is influenced by people's beliefs and choices rather than people being simply the 'puppets' of social institutions. Weber argued that science is not able to capture all social phenomena or explain why all social phenomena occur. Positivists focus on objects (data) but Weber argues sociologists should focus on subjects (people).

The Protestant Ethic & the Spirit of Capitalism (1905) was Weber's book which argued that Capitalism itself came about from the religious beliefs of Protestant Christians – they valued hard work and self-denial and this led to them investing profits back into their businesses. Weber's theory shows how social change comes about from beliefs and this is best discovered through investigating **qualitative data** and using *verstehen* (understanding, p16) rather than analysing statistics.

Contemporary Interpretivist: J Maxwell Atkinson

Discovering Suicide (1968) was a book by **J Maxwell Atkinson**, an Interpretivist who criticises Durkheim's famous research into suicide rates (p13). Atkinson argues that the official statistics used by Durkheim give a misleading view of suicide rates because a death is only considered a suicide if it is ***defined as suicide*** by a medical coroner. The coroner is guided in this decision by evidence like a suicide note but, in the absence of this, by beliefs and social expectations. In Catholic communities (which regard suicide as a sin and shameful), a coroner is more likely to define a self-caused death as an accident. Therefore, suicide is **socially constructed** and it is beliefs and values, not **social facts**, that explain the different suicide rates in Europe. Quantitative data from official statistics does not necessarily reveal social facts as Positivists claim.

THEORY & METHODS: A TOOLKIT

Sociological methods can be evaluated in terms of the broad perspective they belong to: **Positivist** research (p7) tends to be highly scientific and representative but lacking in validity; **Interpretivist** research (p14) is full of insight and meaning but unreliable and hard to generalise from.

These specific evaluation issues are discussed below. The studies used as examples are those that feature in the study guide for **1A: Socialisation, Culture & Identity**. The methodological strengths and weaknesses raised here make great evaluation points for students answering the 20-mark question in **Paper 1 Section A**.

Revise: Go through the studies you learned about in **1B Options (Family, Youth or Media)**; identify whether they come from a **Positivist** or an **Interpretivist** perspective or from a combination; decide whether the are strong or weak in **validity** or **reliability**, whether their data is **representative** and whether their conclusions can be **generalised**.

VALIDITY

Validity means 'truth' or 'authenticity.' Valid research gives a true picture of social reality – of **social facts**, if you are a Positivist, or of the **social world**, if you are an Interpretivist. A valid research method will **measure or record what it claims to be measuring/record**. An invalid method will be recording something else instead.

The issue of validity is a particular problem for measuring crime. Official crime statistics *claim* to measure the number of crimes going on in the country but they *actually* measure the crimes that are reported to the police and recorded by the police. Lots of crimes never get reported or recorded. This makes official crime statistics low in validity.

Interpretivist research is usually high in validity, because it goes to the 'source' by recording individual people's personal experiences. **Positivist** research is often low in validity because it uses statistics which are more removed from direct personal experience.

Validity can be assessed by using **multiple methods** (p68), for example combining a Positivist methodology (like official statistics or postal surveys) and an Interpretivist one (like semi-structured interviews). If the results match up, then they have **concordant validity**.

Research also has more validity if the results are in line with the findings of previous research on the subject or with what would be predicted by well-established theories.

- **Respondent validation** (p35) and **triangulation** (p67) are both techniques for assessing the validity of research.

- Validity is lowered if the **sample** being studied is **unrepresentative** (p23) or if time has passed and social change has made the research **ungeneralisable** (p23) to modern life.

METHODS PROFILE: PARSONS (1959)

Talcott Parsons' *The Social Structure of the Family* **(1959)** is a classic Functionalist text on family structures, gender roles and primary socialisation. It argues that males are biologically fitted to be **instrumental role leaders** (earning money, exerting discipline) and women the **expressive role leaders** (showing compassion and caring for their family).

Parsons' conclusions have been attacked for lacking validity. They are based on broad statistical trends about the structure of American families in the 1950s, but Parsons never investigates whether men and women *want* to live that way or how they *feel* about it. Feminist **Betty Friedan** in *The Feminine Mystique* **(1963)** identifies a widespread unhappiness among American housewives that she calls *"the problem that has no name."* She argues women are trapped within unfulfilling roles.

Social change since the 1950s has further reduced the validity of Parsons' views: women in the USA and UK today are far more likely to work themselves or be the main breadwinner for their family, so Parsons no longer describes how lots of people live.

RELIABILITY

Reliability means 'consistency.' Reliable research gives the same picture of social reality every time it is carried out, assuming the situation being studied remains the same. A reliable research method will **produce results that do not vary too much**. An unreliable method will produce different results every time, even though nothing important has changed.

The issue of reliability is a particular problem for measuring beliefs and intentions, such as voting intentions. For example, polling about whether people in Scotland favour independence from the UK shows support going up and down all the time. Is this because people's views are actually changing or are their flaws in the interviews and questionnaires?

Interpretivist research is usually low in reliability, because it focuses on feelings and beliefs which are very changeable or looks at particular social situations which are hard to reproduce. **Positivist** research is often high in reliability because it uses statistics which are gathered in consistent ways according to fixed procedures.

Reliability can be assessed by using **multiple observers or scorers**, for example getting another researcher to investigate the same situation using the same instruments (e.g. the same questionnaire or the same observation schedule). If the results match up, then they have **inter-rater reliability**.

- **Pilot studies** (p33) are used to assess reliability at the start of the research process.

- Research also has more reliability if repeating the research produces the same results (or broadly similar ones). This is known as **stability** or **test-retest reliability**.

Reliability is lowered if the research involves **subjective judgments**, because the same situation can be handled differently on separate occasions. For example, an unstructured interview might question two similar people but end up getting very different data from them, because different questions were asked or the answers were interpreted in different ways.

Important: Just because a piece of research is reliable, it doesn't automatically make it valid. You could have a consistent procedure but still end up with a wildly mistaken view of society. However, if the research is unreliable then it will probably lack validity too. If your results are all over the place, then it's hard to tell which result (if any) is telling you the truth.

METHODS PROFILE: WILLIS (1977)

Paul Willis' *Learning To Labour* **(1977)** is a ground-breaking study that adopts Interpretivist methods to support **Marxist** (or more precisely, **Neo-Marxist**) theories.

Willis follows a group of 12 working class teenagers ('the Lads') from 'Hammertown Boys School' (a fictional name for a school in Birmingham) and later factory work over 2 years. He studies 'the Lads' through **unstructured observations** (p61) and **interviews** (p59) in real life settings (their classrooms and later their workplaces). The unfiltered and authentic opinions of the schoolboys make this research very **valid**.

Willis used a range of research methods which increases the **validity** of his research. However, the boys may have acted up in front of Willis and exaggerated their anti-school attitudes, especially since Willis' Marxist attitudes towards school might have influenced them.

A different researcher with a different manner might have prompted different behaviour from the boys, which makes it **unreliable**.

However, Willis' research was conducted over a two-year period. Willis argues that the boys could never have faked insincere opinions for that long. The sheer duration of the study makes the results **more reliable**, compared to studying people just once or for a short term 'snapshot' of their views and behaviour.

Modern rules about safeguarding would make it difficult or impossible for an adult researcher to study children this closely for this long, so Willis' research is unlikely to be repeated. This further lowers its **reliability**. However, Willis' general approach to studying the schoolboys pioneered **ethnography** (p62) in Marxist Sociology. Many researchers argue the problems with reliability are a price worth paying for the insights generated by this into the experience of working-class life.

REPRESENTATIVENESS

Representativeness refers to how typical the people or the situation being studied are. A representative group of participants will resemble the wider population in important ways. A representative situation is similar to many other social situations in ordinary life.

Representativeness is usually achieved through using a **sample** of the wider population (*c.f.* p44). A representative sample closely matches the **patterns** in the population as a whole.

Positivists focus on the importance of representativeness. They achieve representativeness by making sure there is a statistical similarity between the sample they study (and they usually study large samples) and the **patterns and trends** in society. The representativeness of the sample justifies Positivists' claims to identify **social facts** in their research.

Interpretivists often downplay the importance of representativeness – or the possibility of ever studying anything truly representative. They often focus on unusual groups or the uniqueness of each situation. From an Interpretivist viewpoint, the social world is ever-changing and essentially **subjective** (p16), so you cannot claim that a particular group is 'typical.' Interpretivists argue that imagination and *verstehen* (p16) are more important than statistical similarities.

METHODS PROFILE: BOURDIEU (1984)

Pierre Bourdieu's book *Distinction* **(1979)** developed his theory of **cultural capital** using data drawn from two surveys of popular taste in France. This emphasis on statistical data is very much in the Positivist tradition of **Marxism**. Bourdieu cooperated with the statistician **Salah Bouhedja**, who used correspondence analyses on the data from the 'Kodak survey' (1963) and the 'taste survey' (1967). These gathered data from 1217 respondents in Paris and in a rural French town; Bourdieu also followed the surveys up with face-to-face interviews.

The surveys were **representative** of the French population of the 1960s. However, they were less representative of other European countries (like the UK) and unrepresentative of non-European countries (like Japan). The surveys get **less representative** with the passage of time: they are now 60 years old and public tastes have changed considerably. If Bourdieu's data is not representative (or is no longer representative) then his conclusions might not be **generalisable** (*see below*) to other countries or France in the 21st century.

GENERALISABILITY

Generalisability is how a study's findings can be applied to wider society. It is related to **representativeness**: research with a representative sample or situation will have generalisable conclusions; an unrepresentative study will not have conclusions that can be generalised beyond the people or situations that were involved.

Malcolm Williams (2000) argues that there are three types of generalisability:

- **Total generalisations:** these are the sort of generalisations made in the physical sciences when situations are similar in every detail (such as the behaviour of electricity in a circuit); Williams argues that social sciences like Sociology cannot make this sort of generalisation because social situations are always unique.

- **Statistical generalisations:** these generalisations rest on a high degree of similarity between social situations and a probability that other social situations will resemble the one being studied; Williams argues that this is often used in science and is the basis for **representative sampling** (p23) used by Positivists.

- *Moderatum* **generalisations:** *moderatum* is Latin for 'restricted' and generalising *in moderatum* means arguing that **some** features of the situation being studied might apply to wider society; Williams argues this is the basis for the **subjective** research (p16) used by Interpretivists.

If research is ungeneralisable then its conclusions are not **valid** (p20) if they are applied to any group or situation other than the one that was studied.

METHODS PROFILE: MCINTOSH (1968)

Mary McIntosh wrote *The Homosexual Role* **(1968)** after conducting surveys and interviews with homosexual men in London and Leicester, especially in the Gateways club and the Gigolo Coffee Bar in Chelsea. These homosexual men cannot be **representative** of *all* homosexual men everywhere, nor of lesbians or bisexual people, and therefore McIntosh's conclusions **cannot be generalised** to other groups and situations.

However, McIntosh takes an **Interpretivist** approach, describing homosexuality as a social role that is constructed differently at other times and places. She argues that it is in fact **impossible to generalise** about homosexuality; she uses this argument to show that homosexuality should not be written off as deviant behaviour or a mental illness (as was common in the 1960s). McIntosh makes *moderatum* **generalisations** from her data, pointing to the way homosexual men who are exposed to a similar gay subculture tend to behave in similar ways, but men who are not exposed to that subculture do not.

McIntosh is another early pioneer of **ethnography** (p62) as a sociological method to understand the social world of marginalised subcultures.

EXAM PRACTICE: THEORY & METHODS

The OCR exam has four questions in **Paper 2 Section A**, based on two source items:

Source A

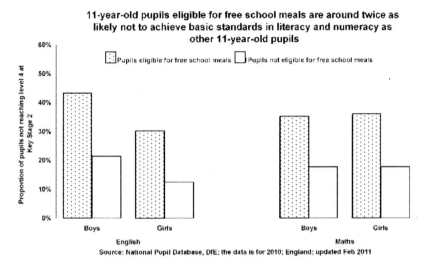

11-year-old pupils eligible for free school meals are around twice as likely not to achieve basic standards in literacy and numeracy as other 11-year-old pupils

Source: National Pupil Database, DfE; the data is for 2010; England; updated Feb 2011

Source B

Researchers investigated children's awareness of their social class and the limits it put on them in school. The children were aged eight to 13, some living on a disadvantaged housing estate and others attending a private school. The researchers carried out interviews to gather qualitative data. The more advantaged children described a much richer set of experiences in school, both inside the curriculum (i.e. in lessons and homework) and outside the curriculum (e.g. in clubs and societies). For the disadvantaged children, issues such as discipline and detention dominated the discussion.

Here is an extract from the interviews:

> Interviewer: "Is life more unfair to some children than others?"
> Girl (early secondary school) "Yes, it is. It's unfair for us because we have to just listen to teachers all the time."
> Interviewer: "But isn't that the same for all children?"
> Girl: "No. It's not, because if you're rich you get to go to a posh school where the teachers probably teach you with respect."

The children had developed clear stereotypes of 'chavs' and 'posh' children. These stereotypes were quite extreme, and the children always applied them to other children rather than describing themselves. The researchers believe this demonstrates an early awareness of social class differences. Negative attitudes were based on children lacking confidence in their own ability to do well within the system. The researchers conclude that if children had better opportunities and experiences, their attitudes to school would become more positive.

1. Summarise the data shown in **Source A**. **[4 marks: 4 AO2]**

*Make **two** points about the data. It is vital that you quote actual figures from the graph and draw conclusions from them (or you are not 'summarising' the data, only restating it). For example, about 43% of boys on FSM do not reach level 4 in English. In order to summarise, you need to say whether this is higher or lower than girls, Maths students or children **not** eligible for FSM.*

2. With reference to **Source B**, explain **two** reasons why sociologists might collect qualitative data. **[6 marks: 2 AO1 + 4 AO2]**

Write a couple of sentences about each reason. You might focus on high validity, subjectivity, or verstehen. You need to support each reason with an example from the source – a really good idea is to quote something from the source.

3. With reference to **Source A**, explain **one** advantage and **one** disadvantage of sociologists looking for patterns and trends in children's attainment at school. **[10 marks: 4 AO2 + 6 AO3]**

Write two short paragraphs, one about an advantage (such as revealing social facts, making predictions, generalising to other groups, objectivity, science) and one about a disadvantage (such as shallowness of statistics, lack of individual focus, possible subjective bias, lack of verstehen). You need to support each reason with an example from the source – a really good idea is to quote a number (or approximate number) from the graph.

4. Using **Source B** and your wider sociological knowledge, explain and evaluate using Interpretivist methods to study children's attitudes to education. **[25 marks: 5 AO1 + 5 AO2 + 15 AO3]**

*Write four paragraphs/arguments – two strengths and two weaknesses of Interpretivism would work well. Each paragraph should introduce a sociological idea with an example or comparison from **Source B**. Each paragraph should finish off with a developed evaluation (see **Chapter 4** for this). For example, you could write about Interpretivism allowing people to express their own views and drawing imaginative conclusions, but also how Interpretivist methods tend to be unreliable and can only be generalised in moderatum.*

In questions 2-3 you can pick up the AO1 marks from using sociological terminology and relating things to sociological debates (e.g. Positivism vs Interpretivism). Named sociologists and studies aren't particularly important, but **Comte**, **Durkheim** and **Weber** are relevant for questions 2-3.

Question 4 is a full essay in which you are invited to deploy *"your wider sociological knowledge"* so famous sociologists definitely belong in your answer and a comparison to **Willis'** study would also help.

CHAPTER TWO – THE RESEARCH PROCESS

Lots of people have opinions about society but they are mostly drawn from personal experience or anecdotes. Authors can use their imagination to explore society. Journalists report on events in society but with the purpose of entertainment (sensationalism) or serving the political agenda of their editor or boss. Sociology is different because it gathers **empirical** (observable) **data** to support its conclusions.

Steps in the research process are common to **Positivists** and **Interpretivists**. The studies cited here are all from **Section B (Understanding Social Inequalities, p82)**.

CHOICE OF RESEARCH TOPIC

Sociologists choose topics to research: the effect of unemployment, changing attitudes to disability, discrimination against homosexuality, the rise or fall of national identity, the impact of different family types of children, to name a few.

Some sociologists pursue a **personal interest**. **Tom Shakespeare** studies disability at least in part because he is a wheelchair-user. **Mary McIntosh** (p24) is a lesbian, and her sexuality perhaps influences her interest in homosexual identities. Other sociologists choose topics inspired by their **sociological perspective**. **Paul Willis** (p22) is a Marxist and this perhaps explains his interest in the way working class children experience education.

Often the choice of topic is dictated by the **funding body** (*c.f.* p41). Sociology is a job and researchers must earn money. If they are not being funded by a university then sociological research is funded by governments, political parties, charities (such as the **Joseph Rowntree Foundation**) and media organisations (like the **BBC**). Researchers might be influenced in their choice of topic by the possibility of publishing a book or creating a documentary and this directs them towards topics of public interest (or current fashions or moral panics).

Finally, **new developments in society** attract research interest. Elections and referendums spark research into voting patterns; shocking crimes or terrorist attacks prompt research into deviancy; new technology (such as dating apps or driverless cars) invite research into the digital world; events like the national lockdowns during the 2020-21 Coronavirus Pandemic provide opportunities to study how people react to isolation and social distancing.

Interpretivists argue that the choice of topic is a value judgment and shows that research is never **value-free** as Positivists would insist. Interpretivists use **reflexivity** (p17) to reflect on their involvement in their own research, including their starting choice of topic.

Positivists aim to be **objective** (p11) in their research and claim that the choice of topic does not introduce significant biases into their work. However, even **Durkheim** (p13) might not be as objective as he claimed: Durkheim had a close friend, Victor Hommay, who committed suicide and this may have influenced his decision to research suicide for his 1897 book.

METHODS PROFILE: SEWELL ET AL. (CRED, 2021) *p120

The **Commission for Racial & Ethnic Disparities (CRED)** is a UK government body headed by **Tony Sewell**, an educationalist who has previously researched the under-attainment of Black boys in British schools (e.g. p145). The **2021 CRED Report** is an independent investigation with the topic of structural racism in the UK. The Report's conclusions are very controversial.

The CRED Report is influenced by many factors. In 2020, protests occurred around the world under the banner of **'Black Lives Matter'** and the UK's Conservative Government promised to investigate allegations that UK society was structurally racist. In the aftermath of Brexit, the UK Government wanted to demonstrate that Britain had a bright future of equality and fairness and funded this research with that aim. Sewell and his commissioners have strong **Functionalist** principles that make them sceptical about conflict in society. It is possible that the CRED Report was commissioned specifically to disprove accusations of racist bias in British society.

This is an example of choice of topic being shaped by **new developments in society** (Black Lives Matter protests), the **funding body** (the UK Government) and **sociological perspective** (Functionalism). Critics complain that this **bias** right at the outset makes the Report's findings a foregone conclusion, despite a **Positivist** methodology that involved *"sifting through a mass of data, reading the evidence from experts and speaking to communities."*

BRITAIN'S RACE REVOLUTION

By **Daniel Martin**
Policy Editor

Landmark report says UK 'a model to world' on diversity – and finds NO evidence of institutional racism

BRITAIN is a model to the world of a successful multi-ethnic society, a major review concluded last night.

It found no evidence the UK is institutionally racist – in a rejection of the common view among activists.

The Commission on Race and Ethnic Disparities, set up by Boris Johnson in the wake of the Black Lives Matter protests, concluded that although Britain is not yet a 'post-racial society', its success should be a model for white-majority countries. Commission chairman Tony Sewell said the UK had progressed into a 'successful multi-ethnic and multicultural community' which was a 'beacon to the rest of Europe and the world'. He warned ministers must also consider the needs of the white working class, saying his report had uncovered how 'stuck' some groups were.

The landmark review found children from many ethnic minorities do as well or better at school than white pupils, which was creating fairer and more diverse workplaces. It called on firms to phase out 'unconscious bias' training **Turn to Page 2**

Daily Mail *headline, 31 March 2021: the Mail is a Conservative-supporting newspaper and approves of the CRED Report and its choice of topic*

Research: read the Introduction to the 2021 CRED Report https://www.gov.uk/government/publications/the-report-of-the-commission-on-race-and-ethnic-disparities and then research criticisms of its findings

AIMS, HYPOTHESES & RESEARCH QUESTIONS

The Topic is a broad area for inquiry. **Aims** are what the research hopes to reveal about the topic.

- **Aims** can still be quite vague (like 'finding out more' about something) but a **research question** has to be more specific. The **2021 CRED Report** (p28) seems to address the research question: 'Is racism in the UK declining?' and it comes to the controversial conclusion, 'Yes it is.'

> **Revision:** go back over your notes on the Key Studies you have learned about so far; what seems to be the **research question** behind the main ones?

- A **hypothesis** is even more specific than a research question, because a hypothesis is a *prediction*. Researchers test the hypothesis by gathering data. If the evidence goes against (refutes) the hypothesis, then the researcher needs to make changes to the hypothesis and start over. However, if the evidence supports the hypothesis then the researcher can develop a **theory**.

- **Theories** are the boldest form of sociological thought: they are accounts of how society works for different groups of people. There are Marxist, Functionalist and Feminist theories. **Induction** is the process of using evidence to build a theory out of testing hypotheses. **Deduction** is the process of making predictions based on a theory.

Positivists think that Sociology should work like the physical sciences, by proposing strict hypotheses and testing them; they refer to their theories as **social facts**. They argue that induction is an effective way of constructing theories and deductions can be made from them.

Interpretivists think that Sociology cannot and should not work like the physical sciences. They argue that induction is *not* an effective way of constructing theories because no amount of induction can ever justify an overarching theory that covers new phenomenon. This is the '**problem of induction**' which often uses the example that no amount of observations of white swans can ever justify the theory that 'all swans are white.'

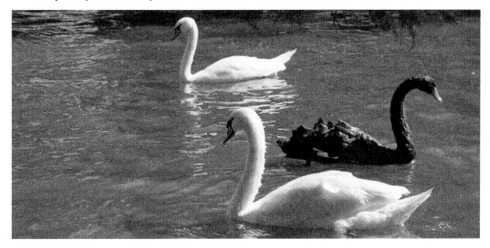

Interpretivists argue that researchers instead need to use **empathy** and *verstehen* (p16) to understand the **social world**.

Most sociologists pursue **a 'third way'** combining the scientific rigour of Positivism with the imagination and **reflexivity** (p17) of Interpretivism. They develop theories that are much more cautious than the physical sciences and do not claim to make confident deductions from them, but merely indicate possibilities that need to be explored further.

METHODS PROFILE: WILKINSON & PICKETT (2009) *p100

A controversial book in Sociology is **Herrnstein & Murray**'s *The Bell Curve* (1994) which argues that inequality in society is a product of people's innate intelligence (or lack of it). The authors conclude that inequality is a good thing (since the fear of poverty drives people to work hard) and cannot be 'fixed' by social policy.

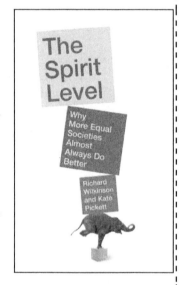

A reply to *The Bell Curve* came from two UK researchers, **Richard Wilkinson & Kate Pickett** who wrote *The Spirit Level* (2009). Wilkinson & Pickett's **aim** is to present a different view of inequality that is not unavoidable or beneficial, in the way *The Bell Curve* presented it.

Wilkinson & Pickett's **research question** is, *Are unequal societies less happy and healthy overall than more-equal ones?* They test this by measuring 11 different social problems (like drug abuse, obesity, teenage pregnancy, violence and lack of community trust) across different countries.

Wilkinson & Pickett's **hypothesis** is that these problems will increase with the amount of inequality in a country (whether there is a big gap in wealth), as opposed to whether the country is rich or poor overall.

They find that countries where there is a small gap between the rich and the poor (e.g. Scandinavian countries, Japan) suffer less from these problems, but countries where there is a large gap (e.g. the UK and the USA) do worse.

Wilkinson & Pickett build a **theory** from this: inequality makes people feel stressed and this in turn leads to things like smoking, overeating and violence which produces depression and anxiety. From this theory we can deduce that governments should try to reduce inequality in order to make the population happier and healthier.

The Spirit Level is a good example of **Positivist** research because it analyses huge samples using **statistics** to identify **patterns and trends** (p10). It points to social facts about inequality, health and happiness. It had a big effect on **social policy** (p40), with both Labour and Conservatives incorporating it into their manifesto policies during the 2010 General Election.

PRIMARY & SECONDARY DATA

Primary data is data that the researcher collects herself, specifically for the research she is doing. This data will be exactly what the researcher needs to test her hypothesis and the researcher can guarantee its **validity** (p20) and **reliability** (p21) since she collected it herself.

The main problem with primary data is time and trouble. Collecting evidence is **time consuming** and **expensive**. Gathering some sorts of data might even be **dangerous** or present **ethical problems** if you are researching children, criminals or the mentally ill.

Willis' study of 'the Lads' in *Learning To Labour* (1977, p22) is a good example or primary data and so is **McIntosh's 1968 research into homosexuals** (p24).

The alternative is to gather **secondary data**. This is data that has already been gathered by someone else. The researcher can take advantage of someone else's research by using the evidence they gathered. Obviously, there is much **less time and trouble** this way. The Internet makes it particularly easy to access secondary data.

The problem is that this data was gathered for different purposes and it might use **different categories** or **define concepts differently** (for example, defining social class or poverty). It might have biases or be invalid or unreliable. It might use an **unrepresentative sample** or be impossible to **generalise** (p23) to the situation the new researcher is interested in.

Bourdieu's use of mass surveys into French culture (p23) is a good example of using secondary data and so is **Wilkinson & Pickett**'s use of data on happiness, health and inequality (p30).

METHODS PROFILE: HECHT ET AL. (2020) *p95

Katharina Hecht and her colleagues carried out an analysis of social mobility in the UK since the 1970s. They used **secondary data**, taking statistics from a **longitudinal study** (p37) carried out by the **Office for National Statistics (ONS)** on people born in the 1950s, 1960s and 1970s.

Hecht analysed the ONS data by focusing on the **elite earners** (the top 1%) and calculates how many enjoyed **long-range mobility** (rising up from the lowest social class into the elite). She shows that those born in the 1950s had more long-range social mobility than those born later on.

The ONS data wasn't originally collected to study long-range mobility among elite earners. **Official statistics** like these won't include people who moved abroad or who were born abroad and arrived in the UK later. They won't include elite earners who hide their wealth (for example, criminals and 'tax-dodgers'). Secondary data is limited by whoever first collected it. However, Hecht would not have been able to gather such data going back so far on her own.

Hecht also collected **primary data** by interviewing 30 elite earners about how they viewed their success. This sort of **methodological pluralism** (p68) gets round some of the problems of data and also mixes **Positivist** and **Interpretivist** methodology by studying both statistics and what wealth actually means to people.

OPERATIONALISATION

Operationalisation means defining your concepts in a way that is clear and measurable. Vaguely defined concepts make research **unreliable** (because you might define things differently every time to come across them, sometimes recording them and sometimes ignoring them). Research concepts need to be operationalizable in order for another social scientist to **replicate** the methodology and see if they get the same results.

Usually, the **aim** of a study is not operationalised: it's a general statement of interest. The **research question** is more clearly defined and the **hypothesis** should be fully operationalised.

Concepts that sociologists need to operationalise include ethnicity and social class. Ethnicity needs to be operationalised so it's clear which ethnic group people fit into; for example, '**Black And Minority Ethnicity**' (**BAME**) can be a catch-all term for non-White people but many sociologists want to operationalise this more precisely, identifying whether people are Black-Caribbean or Black-African, for example. Similarly, there are several different scales for measuring social class and in **1A: Socialisation, Culture & Identity** you learned about the **Registrar General's Scale**, the **National Readership Survey Scale** and the new British Class Scale developed by **Savage et al. (2013)**.

Operationalisation is particularly important for **Positivists**, who want their research to be as scientific as possible. It is also important for **Interpretivists** who want to avoid the accusation they are too **subjective** (p16). However, some Interpretivists argue that it is operationalising concepts that actually smuggles biases into the research. For example, defining social class based on the job of the male in a household makes women less important in sociological research.

METHODS PROFILE: WILKINSON & PICKETT (2009, cont'd)*

The Spirit Level **(2009)** was introduced on p30. **Wilkinson & Pickett** try to **operationalise** a very vague concept: the health and happiness of a society. They focus on eleven social problems: physical health, mental health, drug abuse, education, imprisonment, obesity, social mobility, trust and community life, violence, teenage pregnancies and child wellbeing. They measure physical health by infant mortality rates, which is the proportion of newborn babies that die in their first year. This is a surprisingly high figure in the USA (7 per 1000), but low in Japan, Finland, Sweden and Norway (lower than 4).

Wilkinson & Pickett have been criticised for what they do *not* operationalise. For example, they do not include suicide as one of the measures of health and happiness. Finland has one of the highest suicide rates in the world (11.6 per 100,000 people; source: **OECD, 2005**).

This shows that operationalisation always involves including some things but leaving other things out. **Interpretivists** claim this is an example of **researcher imposition** (p17) that makes it impossible for research to be truly **value-free** (p11).

PILOT STUDIES

Once a study has a clearly operationalised hypothesis, it's necessary to test if it works. A **pilot study** is a 'test drive' for a research study, usually with a very **small group of participants**. The purpose is to flag up problems so that these can be corrected before the *real* research goes ahead.

Positivists use pilot studies to test that their procedures are **standardised and impartial**. At no point during the course of the study should the researcher be required to step in and make ad hoc 'fixes' to the way the study works, such as clarifying what questions mean, re-wording instructions or tweaking the list of things being observed. Once the study works without any extra input from the researcher, it's ready to be rolled out to a wider population.

Interpretivists are more likely to focus on **bias** in the way the study plays out, such as unquestioned assumptions in the questions coming to light, minority groups not being represented in the sample or the results reflecting prejudices. A pilot study is part of the ongoing process of **reflexivity** (p17) used by Interpretivists.

Positivists and Interpretivi52sts both use pilot studies to catch straightforward mistakes in the research design, especially things like **unrepresentative samples** (p23), inappropriate questions or **ethical issues** with the way participants are treated (p52).

The results of pilot studies usually don't get written up in the finished report, although Interpretivists might refer to them as part of reflexivity.

KEY STUDY: CORRELL (2017) *p104

One study that does refer to pilot studies is **Shelley Correll**'s "Small Wins Model" for removing bias from the recruitment and promotion of women in business. Correll and her team focus on educating managers and workers about bias, diagnosing where gender bias could enter business practices and developing tools that help reduce bias and inequality in a measurable way.

Correll carried out pilot studies over 3 years with medium sized tech companies around California, USA.

Image: Shelley Correll

As well as training managers in techniques to reduce workplace inequality, Correll's team listened to their feedback and made adjustments to the model. This is an example of **reflexivity** (p17) in research.

DATA COLLECTION

Data collection is also known as issues surrounding the **choice of methods**. The main issue here is theoretical: is the research guided by **Positivism** or **Interpretivism**?

- **Positivism** favours scientific forms of data collection that are **objective**, **value-free** and highly **replicable** in order to reveal **social facts**: large-scale **questionnaires** (p57), **structured interviews** (p59) and **observations** (p60), **official statistics** (p66), all gathering **quantitative data** (p8).

- **Interpretivism** favours gathering data in a more intimate and **subjective** way to explore the **meaning** of social behaviour: **ethnography** (p62), **participant observations** (p61), **unstructured interviews** (p59), all favouring **qualitative data** (p18).

Many researchers don't care about these theoretical disagreements and just use whatever methods are convenient. Some researchers deliberately try to pursue a **'third way'** between Positivism and Interpretivism, combining elements of both.

There are practical considerations, such as **time and cost**.

- **Expensive data collection** involves training researchers as interviewers or observers, recruiting large samples or hiring translators. **Time-consuming research** is expensive as well, since researchers have to be paid, so **longitudinal studies** (p37) cost a lot and don't yield results for months or years.

- **Cheap research** involves simple questionnaires or structured interviews with closed questions, structured observations and small samples; since sociologists are often based in university, this often means samples of university students. Official statistics can be obtained cheaply through the Internet. **Snapshot studies** can be carried out quickly so the costs don't spiral and the data is collected straight away. **Secondary data** (p31) reduces both time and costs.

Finally, there are issues of sensitivity in subject matter and social characteristics of researchers.

- **Sensitive subject matter** involves topics like racism, sexual or child abuse, studying the elderly or the mentally ill or where there is a danger of research causing offence or adding to the marginalisation of a group of people. These topics usually involve well-trained researchers approaching small groups of participants; time is needed to establish trust and **rapport** (p16). **Reflexivity** (p17) is important because the researcher needs to think carefully about their treatment of the research subjects.

- **Social characteristics** includes the researcher's ethnicity, gender, class and age. Sometimes it is important for the researchers to be similar to the research subjects (for example, female victims of sexual abuse should be interviewed by other women). Reflexivity encourages the researcher to reflect on how their characteristics might have caused the research subjects to feel inhibited, which lowers the validity of the study.

METHODS PROFILE: HECHT ET AL. (2020, cont'd)*

Katharina Hecht's study of social mobility since the 1970s is on p31. The study is a good example of a '**third way**' approach combining Positivist and Interpretivist styles of data collection.

Hecht's aim is to show that the UK is getting less socially mobile. She uses official statistics from the Office for National Statistics: this is **secondary data** (p31) that is cheap and quick to access and it reveals **patterns and trends** over the last 50 years.

However, Hecht also wants to explore how elite earners *feel* about the wealth and what social mobility *means* to them. To this end she uses a short questionnaire and semi-structured interviews with 30 elite earners to find out if they attribute their success to their own hard work or to their privileged backgrounds and whether they believe other people can reach their level.

Getting hold of very rich businesspeople and interviewing them about their wealth is difficult to arrange (unless you are yourself another very rich businessperson) and time consuming, so Hecht only collects data on 30 people, whereas the ONS data collects data on over 500,000 people. This illustrates the difference between **micro-** and **macro- level** data collection and the way they can be combined in a single study.

RESPONDENT VALIDATION

Pilot studies (p33) try to detect bias *before* the research is carried out in full. **Respondent validation** is a way of detecting bias afterwards. It involves getting the people who took part in the study (the 'respondents') to confirm (or 'validate') the researcher's interpretation of their views or behaviour. It is also known as participant validation or 'member checking' and it measures the **validity** of research (p20).

Respondent validation is an important part of the **reflexivity** (p17) practised by Interpretivists.

Respondent validation usually involves presenting your research participants with your findings before going on to publish them. Ideally, all the participants will study the findings and discuss them in an interview with the researcher. This gives the participants a chance to correct misunderstandings or disagree with conclusions (e.g. saying *'That's not what I meant…'* or *'You misunderstood what I was doing …'*). This is particularly important for Interpretivists who want to get **insight** into the **social world** of their participants, but it might be used by Positivists who are trying to remain **value-free** (p11).

Alan Bryman (1988) points out problems with respondent validation:

1. Getting all the participants back together to comment on the research is **difficult and time-consuming**; often respondent validation only involves a few participants (a sample of a sample) to their views might not be **representative** of the other participants who didn't take part in the validation

2. Similarly, **interviews** (p59) might be inconvenient, so validation often involves **questionnaires** (p57) which can be misleading or off-putting
3. Sociological research is often written in **technical language** and involves difficult concepts. Unless they are educated in a particular way, respondents might struggle to understand the researcher's conclusions. In particular, they might interpret the research as criticising them.

METHODS PROFILE: JONES ET AL. (2010) *p125 vs HECHT ET AL. (2020)*

Ian Jones, Miranda Leontowitsch & Paul Higgs interviewed 20 men and women who were top managers in the UK about their decisions to take early retirement. Their aim was to explore whether retirement was a positive or negative change in life.

The researchers refer to their participants as **quasi-subjects**. This is a term developed by **Ulrich Beck (2004)** to describe participants who *partly* represent an institution they belong to (such as their job, age group and social class in this case) but who *also* have freewill and individuality and can speak for themselves. This makes it important to investigate to what extent the participants are speaking as 'typical' members of their age group and social class and to what extent they are unique individuals with their own personal agenda.

Respondent validation is important in this example. For example, Jones et al. conclude that their quasi-subjects felt grateful and privileged to be able to take early retirement; they were aware that people in previous generations weren't able to do this and their own children and grandchildren might not be so fortunate either. This is the sort of conclusion that needs to be validated by the respondents themselves – and since the quasi-subjects were an educated group they were able to understand the researchers' aims and conclusions and confirm that this was indeed how they felt.

Katharina Hecht's study of social mobility since the 1970s is on p31. Hecht's aim is to show that the UK is getting less socially mobile. She interviews 30 elite earners who report that they earned their top positions by hard work and merit. However, Hecht contrasts their views with official statistics since the 1970s which tell another story: compared to people in the past, these elite earners started out with more advantages (wealthy parents, good education, etc). Hecht identifies the **'meritocratic paradox'** which is that, as society gets more unfair, the people who benefit believe it has treated them fairly.

However, Hecht's 30 participants would *not* agree with her conclusions. In Hecht's research, they are not quasi-subjects but simply **subjects**: they are treated as people who cannot see past their own circumstances to understand what's really going on. It's rather typical of **structuralist** (and especially **Marxist**) research to treat participants as subjects. Marxists often argue that people suffer from **'false consciousness'** that stops them from appreciating how unfair Capitalist society really is. False consciousness means that respondents often will not validate Marxist research.

LONGITUDINAL STUDIES

Most sociological research takes the form of **'snapshot' studies** that give a picture of social facts (for Positivists) or the social world (for Interpretivists) at a particular moment in time. Sometimes this is exactly what the researcher wants; for example, a researcher's aim might be to study people's reaction to a terrorist attack or a sporting victory or how crime rates change after a new law is brought in.

Often, these 'snapshots' are **unreliable**. Participants might be 'having a bad day' or there might be stress or changes going on in their lives that make their responses **ungeneralisable** (p23).

Image: Ryan McGilchrist, 2008

Longitudinal studies take place over a long period of time: usually weeks or months but sometimes years. The participants in a longitudinal study are known as a **cohort** and the researcher follows the cohort over time, measuring their attitudes, relationships or behaviours at regular intervals.

- A **prospective longitudinal study** identifies a cohort who share something in common (such as being born in the same year) and follows them over time as they age, observing changes that happen to them. The biggest problem with this is **sample attrition**, which is where participants drop out of the study. Often, the participants who leave the study are the most interesting (e.g. they moved abroad, went to prison or died unexpectedly) and their departure can make the cohort **unrepresentative** (p23). The longer the study lasts, the worse sample attrition becomes.

- A **retrospective longitudinal study** identifies a cohort who all share a common outcome (such as ending up in prison or being a victim of crime) but then works backwards in time, identifying factors in their life history that brought them to this point. Sample attrition isn't a problem but **incomplete data** is: there might be no record of the background of some of the participants, especially if they have had unusual lives (moved around a lot, changed their identity, been homeless).

The advantage of longitudinal studies is that they reveal **patterns and trends** over time (p10) which is why they are popular with Positivists. However, they can also explore a person's entire **life course**, which is a concept that Interpretivists think is important.

The disadvantage of longitudinal studies is that they are **expensive** (since the researchers and perhaps the participants need to be paid). If the researchers become too close to the cohort they will lose their **objectivity** (p11). However, these problems are reduced in retrospective studies.

METHODS PROFILE: MESSNER & COOKY (2021) *107 VS HECHT ET AL (2020)*

Michael Messner & Cheryl Cooky carried out a 30-year **prospective longitudinal study** but the cohort was not a group of people but a selection of TV channels: this is a **content analysis** (p65) where researchers study the content of media documents. Starting in 1989, the researchers recorded 3 two-week segments of sports coverage from 3 Los Angeles TV networks and repeated this procedure every 5 years, bringing in the sports highlights show on ESPN (a digital sports channel) in 2004. Their aim was to find out how women's sports were being presented.

Messner & Cooky are able to chart the proportion of time given to men's and women's sport (95% devoted to men in 2019) and how this changes over time – or rather, how it *hasn't* changed much in 30 years. They identify changes in the style of presentation. For example, in the 1990s TV coverage often sexualised women sports players but in 2019 this switched to **'gender-bland' reporting** which doesn't treat the women as sex objects but does present their sports as boring, with none of the passion and excitement that characterises the way male sports are presented.

Hecht et al (p31) also make use of a longitudinal study carried out by the **Office for National Statistics**. The cohorts are people in the UK born at certain times: the first cohort was people born 1955-61; these people were surveyed in 1971 aged 10-16 and again in 1991 aged 30-36. Hecht compares them to cohorts born 1965-71 (surveyed in 2001) and 1975-81 (surveyed in 2011). The ONS survey records where the cohorts lived and their social class as well as where they were born and their social class at birth.

INTERPRETATION OF DATA

Once data has been collected, sociologists have to make sense of it. There are two main methods: **quantitative methods** and **qualitative methods**.

Qualitative data interpretation makes use of **qualitative data** (descriptions in words, *c.f.* p18) by putting these descriptions into categories; this creates **categorical data**. The process to do this is called coding. Usually, a researcher will go through a written version of the data (a **transcript**) and apply codes to certain phrases, statements, attitudes or behaviours. Categorical data can be shown as **percentages** and put into **pie charts** or **histograms**. The **mode** is an important measure for categorical data: it shows the most popular category or the most frequently occurring code.

Qualitative data is also interpreted through **semiotics**. Semiotics is the study of signs and symbols, which for a sociologist can mean the language people use, the way they dress and act and the meaning behind body language and gestures. Semiotics is an important technique for Interpretivists, but it has been adopted by many **Neo-Marxists** who use semiotics to show how ordinary language or behaviour is actually a symbolic form of oppression or resistance to Capitalism.

METHODS PROFILE: MESSNER & COOKY (2021, cont'd)*

Messner & Cooky (p38) use **codes** to analyse the qualitative data taken from recorded TV sports programmes. The codes include gender of sport (men's, women's, neutral), type of sport (basketball, football, golf, tennis, etc.) and competitive level of the sport (professional, college, high school, etc.). Codes also include production values such as the use of music, the use of graphics, and the inclusion of interviews and/or game highlights.

The researchers also use **semiotics** to analyse what sports commentators are saying and what TV cameras focus on. They conclude that in the 1990s, TV commentary focused on women sports players' bodies, especially their sexual characteristics. However, they observe that this is less common now, but that women's sports are covered in a 'gender-bland' way that lacks passion and excitement.

Quantitative data interpretation analyses **quantitative data** (p8) and creates **numerical data**. Usually, a researcher performs statistical analyses looking for **patterns and trends**. Important measures for this sport of data are the **mean** and **median** (which are **measures of central tendency**, revealing the data that is 'in the middle') and **standard deviation** (showing how much scores typically vary above or below the mean).

A more complex type of statistical analysis is **regression analysis**. Regression analyses measure relationships between different variables, taking as-yet-unknown factors into account. A regression analysis will show how one variable changes depending on how other factors alter. This is useful for showing things like how poverty or crime alter when unemployment goes up or down, more or less is spent on policing and benefits are increased or decreased.

A **linear regression** showing how a clear pattern emerges from random data points

METHODS PROFILE: HECHT ET AL. (2020, cont'd)*

Katharina Hecht's study of social mobility (p31) uses a longitudinal study carried out by the Office for National Statistics. Regression analysis shows whether people are more or less likely to improve their social class (social mobility) in different cohorts when they have similar class backgrounds or levels of education to start with. Hecht also looks at other influencing factors like receiving private education or moving to London. The results show more mobility in the older cohorts (surveyed in 1971) than the younger ones (surveyed in 2001 and 2011).

RELATIONSHIP TO SOCIAL POLICY

Social policy means the laws and programmes created by the Government. They include things like making behaviours illegal (or legalising things that used to be banned) as well as changing benefits and healthcare, altering the curriculum taught in schools and controlling immigration.

Most social policy is intended to solve social problems. **Peter Worsley (1977)** defines a **social problem** is any behaviour that causes *"public friction or private misery."* Crime and poverty are obvious examples but so are domestic violence, school failure, drug abuse and racist discrimination.

Sociology can contribute to social policy in three ways:

1. **Descriptive research:** This is research that aims to describe the nature and scale of a problem, such as how much inequality there is, whether it is growing and who is worst affected by it. **Hecht et al. (2020)** conduct descriptive research by showing that social mobility is less common as elites 'pull away' from the rest of us (p31) – however they do not suggest what should be done about this.
2. **Explanatory research:** This research aims to reveal the causes of social problems – and usually to suggest solutions too. For example, **Wilkinson & Pickett (2009)** conducted explanatory research in their book ***The Spirit Level*** (p30) by showing that a lot of social problems that are ordinarily thought of as quite separate (such as obesity, violent crime and teenage pregnancies) are in fact related to inequality in society. They suggest that social policies to reduce inequality will reduce these problems too as a 'knock-on effect.'
3. **Evaluative research:** The aim is to research *existing* social policies to see if they are working and make suggestions as to how they can be improved. For example, **Sewell et al. (2021)** produced the **CRED Report** (p28) which found that social policies to reduce ethnic inequality in the UK have been successful, although they make 24 recommendations including changing the way the police deal with minorities and the way ethnic minority children are treated in schools.

Sociological problems are issues that fascinate sociologists but might not be widespread enough to be considered social problems or they might be viewed as not a 'problem' in the normal sense of the word.

Durkheim's fascination with suicide (p13) might be a sociological problem rather than a social problem. Another sociological problem might be **Jones' et al.**'s research into why successful people choose early retirement (p36): taking early retirement isn't a problem (in fact, it sounds rather nice) but it's puzzling for sociologists why some workers choose to do it but others don't.

There is a link to **choice of topic** (p27) because researching social problems often attracts funding, whereas it is much harder to find someone to fund research into sociological problems that don't have a clear link to social policy.

AO2 ILLUSTRATION: WHO FUNDS SOCIAL RESEARCH?

The Office for National Statistics (ONS) funds research into the UK population and publishes data to advise governments on social policy. Since 2008 it has been a **non-ministerial department**, independent of government. This is a huge boost to its credibility as a provider of unbiased data (very important for Positivists) and also a boost for the credibility of Government social policies that are based on ONS-provided data.

Government departments also fund research into areas they manage, such as the **Department of Health & Social Care (DHSC)** or the **Department for Education (DfE)**. This research can have a direct effect on social policy, but these are ministerial departments headed by a politician, so their research is sometimes criticised for being politically biased. The **Commission on Race & Ethnic Disparities (CRED)** was set up in 2020 by the Prime Minister, so the findings of **Sewell et al. (2021**, p28) was seen by critics as politically biased and invalid.

Outside of Government, there are charities and think-tanks that fund research into social problems. The **Centre for Policy Studies** is a Right Wing think tank linked to the New Right. **The Joseph Rowntree Foundation (JRF)** funds research and programmes to reduce poverty in the UK and it claims to be politically neutral. **The Sutton Trust** funds research into improving social mobility. Both were created by millionaire businessmen who were **philanthropists** (people for use their wealth for public good) and this makes some Marxist sociologists question whether they are truly politically neutral.

Research can also be funded by universities – through the **Economic & Social Research Council (ESRC)** – or by media organisations like the **BBC**. These bodies are more likely to fund research into interesting sociological problems that aren't related to social policy.

Positivism vs Interpretivism

Positivism was developed by **Auguste Comte** (p13) with the explicit intention of helping governments arrive at the right social policy. Positivism aims to present policymakers with clear statistics about **social problems** and policy recommendations that are completely unbiased (**value-free**, p11). Because Positivism claims to discover the underlying causes of social behaviour (**social facts**), it focuses on explanatory research that is **macro** in scale.

Interpretivists are sceptical about Positivist claims of value-freedom and discovering social facts. They point out that research can never be unbiased and so-called social facts are really just the unexamined assumptions of researchers imposed onto the data. They tend to focus on **sociological problems** rather than social problems and their independence from government funding leaves them free to conduct **micro-** scale research and engage in **reflexivity** (p17), even if that sometimes gets in the way of clear findings and concrete solutions.

Consensus vs Conflict

Functionalism and the **New Right** are both consensus perspectives and they tend to take a Positivist view of the relationship between research and social policy. **Charles Murray**'s book *Losing Ground* **(1984**, p13**)** was very influential on Right Wing governments in the USA and the UK. Murray employed statistical analyses of crime rates, birth rates and unemployment to demonstrate a social fact that lone parents unwittingly contribute to the growth of an unemployed and semi-criminal underclass. Murray recommends cutting benefits and support for lone-parent families to encourage a return to married parents and working fathers. Since then, the New Right has had a big influence on UK social policy.

Marxism and **Feminism** are conflict perspectives that have a more mixed view of Positivism and social policy. Marxists view the Government as part of the **ruling class** and Feminists often view it as a force for **patriarchy**: both are sceptical about whether social policy can make any difference to the social problems they care about (the exploitation of the poor and of women). Some of them argue that, with all its flaws, the Government is still the best institution for solving social problems; this approach lies behind **Wilkinson & Pickett**'s *The Spirit Level* **(2009**, p30**)** which encouraged a Left Wing UK Labour Government to focus on inequality.

Other conflict sociologists see their role as being a 'gadfly' (a stinging insect) that criticises the Government and shows the flaws in social policy. These sociologists seek funding from charities and political think tanks that given them more freedom to criticise. **Hecht et al. (2020**, p31**)** was funded by the **Sutton Trust**, an educational charity which invests £4 million every year in research and programmes to improve social mobility.

Structuralism vs Social Action

Functionalists, the New Right, Marxists and Feminists all tend to be **structuralists**: they view individuals as shaped by the social structures around them rather than having freewill and independence. Structuralists take a keen interest in social policy because they don't view people as individuals or small groups having the power to change things without help from the Government.

Social Action sociologists see individuals and small groups as able to 'rise up' and challenge or change social structures. They often take **Max Weber** (p19) as an inspiration. **Jones et al. (2012)** share **Ulrich Beck**'s view that research participants are **quasi-subjects** (p36) who partly reflect the social structures around them but also partly forge their own path in life.

Social Action tends to adopt **Interpretivist** methods and focus on **micro**-scale research that has little connection to social policy. However, some **Feminists** and **Neo-Marxists** have adopted Social Action theories – especially the ideas of **labelling theory** – and focused on minority groups and subcultures. The research by the **Centre for Contemporary Cultural Studies** into 1970s **Punks** is a good example of this. This research tends to be into **sociological problems** but it can be used to challenge popular stereotypes about (for example) ethnic minorities or youth subcultures.

Strengths & Weaknesses

There are two big incentives for carrying out research that relates to social policy: **(1)** your research will be studied by policymakers and might make a difference to people's lives and **(2)** your research has a better chance of being funded, since there are lots of government bodies, think tanks and charities interested in social policy too.

The main disadvantage to such research is that with funding comes interference – and even if the funder does **not** interfere with your research, there may be a suspicion that your research is biased because of who funded it. Research for ministerial departments or politically-motivated think tanks like the **Centre for Policy Studies** always comes with the suspicion of political bias. Some charities, such as **JRF** or the **Sutton Trust**, claim to be politically neutral and have great credibility, but even they get criticised for political bias sometimes.

Avoiding social policy means researchers can investigate without political interference (or accusations of it), but it also means there is less funding and less of a readership for the findings. The **ESRC** funds a lot of research into sociological problems rather than social problems, simply for the sake of furthering our understanding of society. However, this sort of funding is limited and it still tends to follow 'fashions' in universities – for example, research into inequalities affecting ethnic minorities and LGBTQ groups is popular right now because of the attention drawn to these issues by protest organisations like **Black Lives Matter** or **Stonewall**.

Revision: revisit your notes from **paper 1** on Consensus, Conflict and Social Action to add social policy as an evaluation issue

THE RESEARCH PROCESS: A TOOLKIT

We have covered the research process in general, but some aspects of research need closer analysis and a consideration of strengths and weaknesses.

THE SAMPLING PROCESS

A **sample** means the people who participate in research. Research has a **target population** which is all the people the research is investigating and trying to describe. The target population might be as small as *'the boys in this school's Sixth Form'* or as large as *'all the working-class adults in the UK.'* The sample is a small selection of that larger population.

- A **small and tightly defined target population** is quite easy to sample, but the conclusions from the research often won't generalise to other populations. If your target population is boys in your school Sixth Form, the sample might not tell you much about boys of a similar age in other schools. **Interpretivists** (p14) are usually happy with this sort of population.

- A **large target population** means the research's findings will apply to a lot more people, but it's hard to select a sample from such a population. **Positivists** (p7) usually try to study large populations through sampling but they have to use careful sampling techniques to get a sample that is truly **representative**.

A **sampling frame** is a list of everyone in the target population. Sometimes it's easy to acquire a sampling frame; every school will keep a list of all the students enrolled there. However, sometimes there is no complete or reliable sampling frame; there's no 'master list' of everyone who lives in the UK or everyone in a town who is working-class.

Positivism aims to conduct **macro**-level research on large target populations. A sampling frame helps them to gather a sample that is **representative** (p23) – in other words, it is a miniature version of the target population. This enables Positivist researchers to **generalise** conclusions about the sample back to the target population.

Interpretivism aims to conduct **micro**-level research on small target populations. The sampling frame is less important for this sort of research. Interpretivists hope to gain **insights** into the behaviour and attitudes of people involved – and into their own behaviour and attitudes too if they use **reflexivity** (p17). They are less interested in **generalising** to a wider population to propose patterns or trends.

Terminology: Subjects, Participants, Respondents

Older research often refers to the people taking part as the **'subjects'** of research. This term is unfashionable now. It implies that the people involved are like lab rats or guinea pigs being investigated by superior social scientists. Some Positivists really believed research to be like this in the past, but not so much anymore.

Participants is a better term, since it refers to people actively participating in research rather than being studied from above. **Respondents** is another term which focuses on how people respond to the questions and situations that the researchers study.

The replacing of the Positivist term 'subjects' with the more Interpretivist-friendly terms 'participants' and 'respondents' might indicate a shift in methodology going on in Sociology as a whole.

SAMPLING TECHNIQUE: OPPORTUNITY

Opportunity sampling means using the people who are available in a certain place at a certain time. This group of people is termed 'an opportunity sample.'

Opportunity sampling is the **easiest and quickest** sampling technique. It does creates **unrepresentative samples**. People who are all present at a certain place at a certain time typically share characteristics in common (like working in the same job, studying the same subjects). People who don't share these characteristics are unlikely to be present.

Imagine gathering a sample of students from the student lounge during break – but students who have break time duties or meetings won't be present.

Opportunity sampling is also at risk from **bias**, since the researcher might approach people that seem friendly or helpful and avoid people they find threatening or view as boring.

Positivists avoid this technique, because it is unrepresentative and biased, and they aim to be **value-free** (p11). Interpretivists are less critical of opportunity sampling, since they don't put some much emphasis on representativeness, and they can reflect on issues of bias through **reflexivity** (p17).

SAMPLING TECHNIQUE: PURPOSIVE

Purposive sampling means deliberately selecting particular people because they have the characteristics the research is interested in. A 'purposive sample' might be a group of people who are specially invited to take part in research.

Purposive sampling is different from opportunity sampling because it doesn't just use anyone to hand; instead, the researcher goes out and tracks down **special individuals**.

Imagine tracking down students who took part in a demonstration or sit-in because you want to know what motivated them. You will have in mind exactly the people you want to study and no one else will do.

Positivists rarely use this technique, because you **cannot draw patterns and trends** from unusual individuals. This is a technique usually associated with Interpretivists who want to increase their understanding (*verstehen*, p16) of the **social world** of unusual people.

METHODS PROFILE: WILLIS (1977, cont'd)

Paul Willis' *Learning To Labour* (p22) studies a group of 12 working-class schoolboys ('the Lads'), but how did Willis recruit them? Willis describes how they were selected because they were likely to leave school as soon as was legal (aged 16 in the 1970s) and were part of **an anti-school subculture**. Presumably, Willis shared with the teachers the sort of students he was interested in researching and they suggested 'the Lads' as matching this description (*cf.* **gatekeeping**, p50).

Notice how this **purposive sampling** gets round the problem that 'the Lads' would never *choose* to get involved in research. The boys were unusually rebellious even for a tough working-class school: they are the special individuals that purposive sampling can locate and recruit.

SAMPLING TECHNIQUE: SNOWBALL

Snowball sampling is when the researcher makes contact with one person (or a few people) and asks them to recruit other individuals who would be suitable. It is a special sort of **purposive sampling** because the respondents go out and recruit each other rather than all being invited by the researcher. The sample size grows like a snowball as each new recruit recruits more people.

Imagine tracking down a few students who took part in a demonstration and asking them to invite other students whom they know helped organise things behind-the-scenes – as the researcher, you wouldn't know about these other people's involvement.

Snowball sampling is particularly useful when there is **no sampling frame** – particularly if the target population is doing something criminal or which attracts social stigma, so they are unlikely to respond to **volunteer sampling** but they might get involved if someone they trust invites them. Because the respondents recruit more respondents, snowball samples often contain people the researchers would never make contact with by any other method.

As with purposive sampling, which it resembles, this is popular with Interpretivists who want to **understand behaviour on a micro-level**. It is not used much by Positivists, because if you do not recruit your own sample, you **cannot know whether it is representative** of your population.

METHODS PROFILE: HECHT ET AL. (2020, cont'd)*

Katharina Hecht's study of social mobility (p31) mixes Positivist and Interpretivist approaches. She gathered a sample of 30 'elite earners' some of whom were multi-millionaires. Hecht discovered their names in the *Sunday Times Rich List* or because they were well-known figures in the London financial industry. Some of them went on to invite other elite earners that they knew to join in – so this is **snowball sampling technique**.

The response rate was 40%. Hecht reflects that her own class background and her education at the London School of Economics (a prestigious university) made the initial respondents more likely to agree to help: this is an issue of **access** to a hidden group (p50).

SAMPLING TECHNIQUE: VOLUNTEER

Volunteer sampling is when the researcher **advertises the research** and waits for people to volunteer themselves to take part; it is also called **self-selecting sampling** and the group that is recruited this way is a **volunteer sample**.

Volunteer sampling is similar to **purposive sampling** because the researcher can advertise for a particular type of person (or advertise in places or media that this type of person uses). However, it is different because the researcher cannot control exactly who is recruited.

The sample will be biased, but not because of the researcher's biases but rather because of the biases in the participants themselves. Some people are more likely to volunteer (e.g. people interested in Sociology, people with free time, people who need money if the volunteers are being paid) but volunteers are less likely if the research looks embarrassing, boring or dangerous.

Imagine recruiting students who took part in a demonstration by putting up a poster in the student lounge asking everyone who took part in throwing eggs at the Principal's car to come to room 13 at lunch – why would actual demonstrators not turn up?

A common approach is to send the invitation out in the mail or through email. Sending mass surveys through the post is volunteer sampling because anyone who returns a completed survey is volunteering to take part.

Volunteer sampling is useful when there is **no sampling frame** but it is more popular with Positivists than **purposive** or **snowball sampling**, because you can recruit large samples this way from big target populations.

SAMPLING TECHNIQUE: RANDOM

Random sampling is a technique to **remove all bias** from the selection of participants. A group selected in an unbiased way will be a random sample.

IMPORTANT: 'random' in popular language means 'unplanned' or 'surprising' (as in, you watched a random YouTube video or talked to a random person at a party). THAT IS NOT WHAT IT MEANS IN SOCIOLOGY. **Random means 'selected without bias'** *– your YouTube video was not really selected randomly (YouTube's algorithm put it in front of you based on things you had previously watched) nor was the person you talked to at the party truly random (you* **chose** *to talk to them and there were other people you chose not to talk to). Walking into the student lounge and picking the first dozen people you see is not random sampling – it is opportunity sampling.*

To remove all bias, a **randomisation technique** is needed. This could be the classic **'names from the hat'**: write everyone's name on a separate piece of paper, put all the names in a box or bag, draw out a number of pieces of paper until you reach the sample size you want then recruit those people. Computers apps also produce a randomised sample from a list of names.

The important thing to understand is that it is essential to have a **complete sampling frame** in order to create a random sample.

Creating a random sample of boys from the school Sixth Form is easy because there is a complete sampling frame – the school register. Creating a random sample of teenage boys in a city is not possible because there's no up-to-date master list kept anywhere.

The main problem with randomised sampling is that it **doesn't necessarily create a representative sample**. For example, drawing names from a hat could produce a sample made entirely of boys from one ethnic group. This problem is more likely to occur with small sampling frames. Positivists only use random sampling when they have access to very large sampling frames (like the **UK Census**, *see below*).

Random sampling can also include **inappropriate respondents** who are difficult to track down, who don't want to be in the research or who are unsuitable for studying (perhaps because they don't speak English or have health problems). Interpretivists usually want respondents who will engage with their micro-level research, so they tend to avoid random sampling.

METHODS PROFILE: HECHT ET AL. (2020, cont'd)*

Katharina Hecht's study of social mobility (p31) mixes Positivist and Interpretivist approaches. Hecht uses the **ONS Longitudinal Study** to get data on social mobility in different decades. The **Office for National Statistics** (p41) uses the **UK Census** as its sampling frame. The Census is a survey carried out every 10 years to gather data on every household in the country (*c.f.* p58). The ONS then takes a random sample of 1% of the sampling frame: about 500,000 people in each cohort. The sheer size makes it likely that the sample is **representative**.

The Census doesn't include *everybody* in the country – you won't appear on the Census if you are homeless or an illegal immigrant. However, Hecht was only interested in data from the ONS Longitudinal Study about people moving into the 'elite earners' group and most of these people will be on the Census (they have homes and they are not in the country illegally).

STRATIFIED SAMPLING

This is an improvement on **random sampling** and makes use of randomisation but it also makes sure the sample contains the right amounts of the right sort of people.

Stratified sampling involves dividing your target population into groups (or 'strata') and making sure your sample has the same strata in the same proportions. Once the strata have been decided upon, they are filled by random allocation, just like random sampling.

Creating a stratified sample of boys from a school Sixth Form involves identifying the strata in the target population – such as 60% in Year 12 and 40% in Year 13, perhaps 30% doing Science courses – then using school registers to randomly select students for each strata.

Stratified sampling requires a **complete sampling frame** and also a lot of **information about the target population** and that information might not be available – for example, you might want a strata of students from particular class backgrounds but the school wouldn't keep data like that on record.

Stratified sampling is the 'holy grail' of Positivist research because as well as being **unbiased** it creates **highly representative samples**.

However, Interpretivists argue that the strata themselves conceal **researcher imposition** (p17). This is because the choice of what strata include or leave out reflects researcher bias; for example, a researcher might not bother to include 'religion' as a strata but assuming that religion isn't relevant to social behaviour is a biased assumption. Since there are an infinite number of strata, researchers can never know if they are ignoring important strata or not (should you have a strata for handedness? how about star signs?) and trying to include every strata you can think of 'just in case' would make the research time consuming and over-complicated.

SAMPLING TECHNIQUE: SYSTEMATIC

Systematic sampling is a variation on **random sampling**. Instead of randomising the sampling frame, the researcher goes through the sampling frame selecting every n^{th} person from the list (e.g. every 5th or 10th or 100th person). This produces a systematic sample.

Systematic sampling has the same strengths and weaknesses as **random sampling**. In particular, it requires a **complete sampling frame**. Counting out every n^{th} person guarantees that the sample will be more spread out, whereas a randomly selected sample could draw from people who are 'clumped together.' This makes a systematic sample more representative than a purely random one if the sampling frame is arranged in a particular order (say, ordering people by age would produce a systematic sample of all ages).

SAMPLING TECHNIQUE: QUOTA

Quota sampling is an alternative to **random sampling** and an improvement on **purposive sampling**.

A quota sample is recruited by filling strata that match the target population, just like a **stratified sample** (*see above*). However, you do not fill each strata randomly. Instead, you fill each strata using a non-random method, like **opportunity**, **purposive** or **volunteer sampling**.

Quota sampling is useful when you want your sample to be **representative**, but you **do not have a complete sampling frame**. Because the respondents are either volunteering themselves or being chosen specially by the researcher, some **bias** is inevitable.

Quota sampling is often used by companies trying to gauge public opinion – for example, approaching people in the street with clipboards to carry out surveys, but making sure to get data from a certain number of men, women, minorities, age groups, etc.

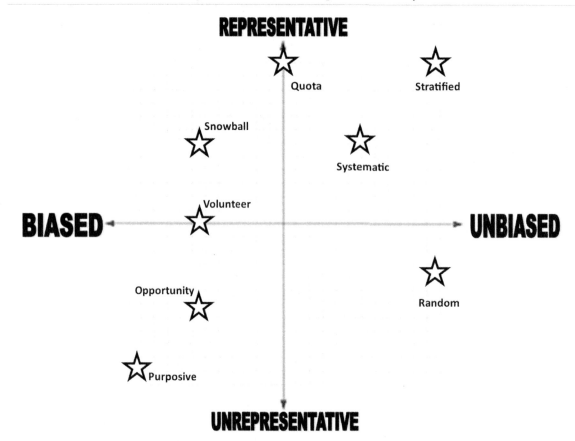

This chart might help you visualise the way different sampling techniques relate. **Positivists** aim to use unbiased procedures to gather highly representative samples (top right quadrant); **Interpretivists** are comfortable with biased procedures so long as they are reflexively addressed and they often don't care about generalising conclusions from a representative sample.

ACCESS & GATEKEEPING

Access means the ability to make contact with potential respondents and recruit them into a sample. There are several problems with access faced by sociologists:

- **Protected groups:** Some groups are protected from researchers, often because of safeguarding issues. For example, children, the mentally ill, victims of abuse and people inside 'closed institutions' like prisons or women's refuges. In order to get access to these groups, a **gatekeeper** (e.g. a parent, head teacher, doctor or prison governor) has to allow it.

- **Hidden groups:** These groups are hard to locate and make contact with; some live 'off the grid' or have a language barrier, others deliberately avoid contact with the authorities (e.g. deviants). A **gatekeeper** is often needed to put the researcher in touch (e.g. a community leader, translator or gang member). Wealthy people can also be hard to gain access to (*c.f.* **Hecht et al.**, p46)

- **Hostile groups:** These groups are easy to find but they don't want to take part in research; this often includes subcultures who are suspicious of outsiders as well as criminal gangs or religious sects. **Gatekeepers** might be members who can vouch for the researcher and make introductions.

Snowball sampling (p46) is particularly useful for gaining access to hidden or hostile groups once initial contact has been made. **Volunteer sampling** (p47) is particularly ineffective with these groups (it's not obvious how to advertise to hidden groups and hostile groups don't want to volunteer).

Gatekeeping means managing access to groups. With protected groups, the gatekeeper is someone in authority whose permission is needed to recruit respondents. The gatekeeper will be concerned about the rights and wellbeing of respondents and won't want them to get involved in research that might be stressful or expose them to stigma, abuse or stereotyping.

With hidden or hostile groups, the gatekeeper is someone who can put the researcher in touch with respondents, perhaps by translating or vouching for the researcher's good intentions. This sort of gatekeeper is a 'friend on the inside.'

Gatekeepers often have access to a **sampling frame** (a list of all the members of the group).

METHODS PROFILE: GENTLEMAN (2009) *p129

Amelia Gentleman is a journalist who spent 4 days observing 26 elderly residents in a care home (Monmouth Court in Ipswich, p51). She carried out **overt observations** (p61) and **unstructured interviews** (p59) with residents and staff and published her findings in *The Guardian*.

The care home is a closed institution, and the elderly residents are a protected group: some are ill, confused or depressed and not in a position to **consent** (p52) to participate in research; there is a danger a journalist could misrepresent the care home as an evil place, make the residents look foolish or a burden on others or make the staff look uncaring.

The Matron is the **gatekeeper** and she allows Gentleman to visit the public areas of the care home (the day lounge) and interview selected residents and staff. This makes the sample a **purposive sample** (p45) carried out in negotiation with the gatekeeper.

ETHICS

The **British Sociological Society (BSA)** lays out a set of ethical guidelines for researchers to follow. Breaking these guidelines can create distrust, which lowers the **validity** of research (p20) as well as making it harder for future researchers to gain **access** to respondents (p50). Sociologists need to be in good standing with the BSA to work in universities and get their research published, so breaking the ethical guidelines can ruin a sociologist's career.

There are six ethical guidelines:

1. **Consent:** Respondents should be aware that they are involved in a research project and its purpose; they should give **informed consent** to taking part.

    - Some respondents cannot give informed consent: children are considered too young and people with mental health problems are not competent to do this. A parent or carer could consent on their behalf.

    - Some groups have to be studied without their consent, because they wouldn't be doing what they are doing if they knew they were being studied (e.g. criminals) or else would not respond truthfully to questions.

2. **Deception:** Researchers should not lie to respondents about the purpose of the research or their own identity. They should not feign friendship in order to gain data.

    - Sometimes deception is unavoidable if the researcher has to keep their identity secret (e.g. **covert observations**, p61). The data gained from 'going undercover' can be so valuable (e.g. to **social policy**, p40) that it justifies deception.

3. **Confidentiality:** Research should not be intrusive. Respondents should have their true names and backgrounds concealed – many researchers use pseudonyms (fake names) for respondents. Promising **confidentiality** can increase trust, leading to respondents giving more **valid** data.

    - Confidentiality includes not revealing locations or institutions that might identify the respondents.

    - Confidentiality can come into conflict with **integrity** (*below*) if the respondents do or reveal something illegal or immoral.

4. **Protection:** Respondents should be protected from harm. This includes not being asked distressing questions or being put in stressful situations. It also includes not being exposed to ridicule or punishment (such as losing your job) when the research is published. **Respondent validation** (p35) is an opportunity to make sure that everyone agrees with what is being published.

    - Not everyone agrees on the definition of 'harm.' For example, asking questions about experiences of abuse or crime can trigger anxiety. Gaining **informed consent** (*above*) is important for justifying this.

5. **Integrity:** Researchers should not carry out illegal or immoral acts while pursuing research. If they come into possession of 'guilty knowledge' (e.g. a respondent confesses to a crime) then they should report it to the police or other authorities.

   - This can come into conflict with **privacy** when the researcher promises to keep identities confidential and **protection** when researchers suffer sanctions (get arrested, relationships end, fired from their job) because of what was revealed during the research.

6. **Safety:** Researchers should not put themselves or their research assistants in danger.

   - Some research is unavoidably risky, such as observing criminals. Other research can create anxiety, such as studying people who are dying or listening to testimonies of abuse. This links to **choice of topic** (p27) because the risks of some topics have to be justified by the benefits to be gained (e.g. informing **social policy**).

> **Research:** visit the British Sociological Society website (https://www.britsoc.co.uk/ethics) and read the ethical guidelines yourself – notice the extra guidelines on digital research that will be important for **3A: Globalisation & the Digital Social World.**

METHODS PROFILE: WILLIS (1977) vs GENTLEMAN (2009)*

Paul Willis (*c.f.* p22) observes 12 schoolboys in lessons and with their teachers, parents and later their employers. He gains **consent** from their teachers and (we assume) their parents to do this; later, he gains consent from the boys themselves once they turned 16. There was no deception and Willis keeps their identities **confidential**, referring to their school by the fictional name of Hammertown Boys School. There are no issues with protection or safety, but Willis' **integrity** could be questioned: he witnessed 'the Lads' carrying out acts of vandalism (setting off fire extinguishers), bullying and racist abuse, but did not intervene or report anything. Of course, if he *had* intervened, he would have lost the trust of the boys.

Amelia Gentleman (*c.f.* p51) observes 26 elderly residents in a care home over 4 days. Most of the residents are depressed and some suffer from dementia; several are dying: Gentleman needs **consent** from the Matron (and probably family members) on behalf of the residents. Gentleman's article states '*Names of residents have been changed and some details have been altered to obscure identities*' – this ensures **confidentiality** and **protection**. There is no problem with **deception** and **integrity** but **safety** is an issue: Gentleman reports residents who are dying and carers with tragic financial problems; she finds the atmosphere "*dispiriting*" and the research must have taken an emotional toll on her.

NB. Amelia Gentleman is a journalist, not a sociologist, and doesn't need to be a member of the BSA or follow its guidelines. However, there is a similar journalistic code of ethics.

EXAM PRACTICE: THEORY & METHODS

The OCR exam has four questions in **Paper 2 Section A**, based on two source items:

Source A

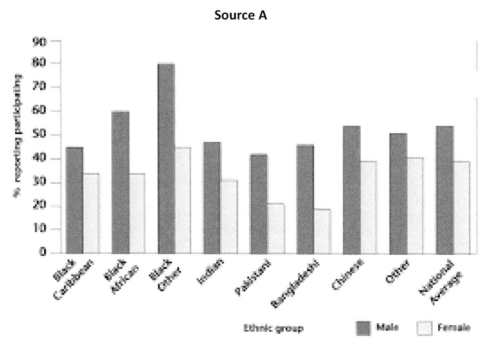

Source: Sport England's Sports Participation & Ethnicity in England – National Survey 1999/2000

Source B

Dr William Tantam spent more than a year in Jamaica studying amateur football or 'pick-up ball' in a rural community. For 14 months he played football every weekday with the same group of players. He socialised with them and conducted interviews to discover what role football played in their lives. 'Pick-up ball' could be dangerous, since it is played in the street with cars passing.

One team was of younger (20s-30s), poorer men; the other of older (40s-50s), wealthier men. Most had participated in an annual inter-school tournament. Those from poorer backgrounds had 'skipped class' to concentrate on football, hoping to win scholarships – after gaining poor qualifications, they had taken up low-paid and precarious jobs. Those from wealthier backgrounds had been discouraged from participating in schoolboy football – later they migrated to get a better education then returned to Jamaica for well-paid jobs as doctors or teachers.

The rural community was divided along lines of wealth and class, but football offered a way for the men to interact as equals. The younger players were less interested in winning a match; more interested in demonstrating creative or skilful moves. Due to the pressure of 'playing for a scholarship,' they had developed an individualistic form of football . The older group focused on team play and winning matches. While the two teams shared a field, they were playing two very different games with different aims.

1. Summarise the data shown in **Source A**. **[4 marks: 4 AO2]**

*Make **two** points about the data. It is vital that you quote actual figures from the graph and draw conclusions from them (or you are not 'summarising' the data, only restating it). For example, only 20% of Bangladeshi women report participating in sport. In order to summarise, you need to say whether this is higher or lower than Bangladeshi males or women from other groups.*

2. With reference to **Source B**, explain **two** reasons why sociologists might have problems with access to research participants. **[6 marks: 2 AO1 + 4 AO2]**

Write a couple of sentences about each reason. You might focus on hostility, access to wealthy groups or gatekeepers. You need to support each reason with an example from the source – a really good idea is to quote something from the source.

3. With reference to **Source A**, explain **one** advantage and **one** disadvantage of sociologists gathering primary data. **[10 marks: 4 AO2 + 6 AO3]**

Write two short paragraphs, one about an advantage (such as revealing social facts, operationalising your own concepts, relationship to social policy) and one about a disadvantage (such as problems with access and gatekeeping, time and expense, sampling problems, ethical problems). You need to support each reason with an example from the source – a really good idea is to quote a number (or approximate number) from the graph.

4. Using **Source B** and your wider sociological knowledge, explain and evaluate ethical issues in researching differences between classes. **[25 marks: 5 AO1 + 5 AO2 + 15 AO3]**

*Write four paragraphs/arguments – two ethical strengths and two ethical weaknesses would work well. Each paragraph should introduce a sociological idea with an example or comparison from **Source B**. Each paragraph should finish off with a developed evaluation (see **Chapter 4** for this). For example, you could write about the importance of establishing trust through consent, honesty and confidentiality, but the problems of misrepresenting poorer people as failures or losers or the safety issues of street sports.*

In questions 2-3 you can pick up the AO1 marks from using sociological terminology and relating things to sociological debates (e.g. Positivism vs Interpretivism). Named sociologists and studies aren't particularly important.

Question 4 is a full essay in which you are invited to deploy *"your wider sociological knowledge"* so famous sociologists definitely belong in your answer and a comparison to **Willis**' study would help (he looks at class differences between schoolboys) as would **Hecht et al.** (Hecht used her university background to get access to a wealthy group).

CHAPTER THREE – RESEARCH METHODS

Now that you are familiar with the theoretical basis of the research process, it's time to look at research methods themselves.

Structured/Controlled Methods

These methods involve planning everything beforehand. Questionnaires will have closed questions, interviews will be entirely scripted, observations will take place in artificial environments that the researcher has set up and use pre-written checklists.

The advantage of doing this is that it gives the researcher control over what happens. This is important for **Positivists**, who want to be as **scientific** as possible (p7). It helps the researcher study a **sampling frame** and recruit a **randomised sample** from it (p47). In particular, it enables the research to **operationalise** what they are studying (p32) in a way that can be measured or counted – and that leads to the **interpretation of quantitative data** (p38).

The disadvantage of this sort of preparation and control is that the research can become rigid, superficial and unrealistic: questions don't probe deeply, interviews become stilted and one-sided, observations become artificial. It's difficult to **generalise** (p23) the findings of such research to real life, where behaviour is messier, more unpredictable and more varied. Interpretivists complain that this sort of research doesn't reveal much about the **meaning of the social world** (p15).

Unstructured/Naturalistic Methods

These methods involve not planning everything beforehand, in favour or more realism, authenticity and spontaneity. Questionnaires will have open questions that can be answered in ways the researcher doesn't predict, interviews will be unscripted, observations will take place in real-life settings and abandon checklists in favour of trying to share what ordinary people are experiencing.

It's important to appreciate that this sort of research isn't careless, 'anything goes' or fly-by-the-seat-of-your-pants. A lot of preparation has to go into it. Imagine interviewing someone without pre-written questions: you would have to give a lot of thought to what this person is like, what they might say, how you might react.

The advantage of doing this is that it helps the researcher understand (*verstehen* – p16) the social world. It leads to the **interpretation of qualitative data** (p38) which is much more meaningful. This is important for **Interpretivists**, who value a **subjective but personal understanding** of social behaviour. Moreover, the research is authentic and can be **generalised** (p23) to real life.

The disadvantage is the lack of **scientific objectivity** (p11). In particular, the research lacks **reliability** (p21). Qualitative data is more likely to show **bias**, it doesn't reveal **patterns and trends** (p10) and it is less easy to analyse in a way that can help inform **social policy** (p40).

RESEARCH METHODS: A TOOLKIT

There are three main methods for gathering empirical data: **questionnaires, interviews** and **observations**. 'Empirical' means based on first-hand experience and the evidence of the five senses. **Ethnography, content analyses** and **statistical data** are best understood as variations of these methods. For example, content analyses are really a type of observation focused on a media document while statistical data is often taken from large-scale surveys involving questionnaires.

METHOD: QUESTIONNAIRES

Questionnaires are also known as **surveys** or **self-reports**. A questionnaire is a set of written questions and the respondent has to write their answers.

- **Closed questions** are questions that force the respondent to choose from a set of possible answers. The simplest closed question is the yes/no question; other examples include multiple-choice questions and checklists. These questions produce **quantitative data** (you can count the number of people who choose each answer or assign a different score to each answer) which can be turned into **statistical data** (p38).

- **Open questions** are questions that allow respondents to answer in any way they like. The simplest open question is *'Explain in your own words …'* This allows respondents to offer their own unique viewpoint, but it produces **qualitative data**. There is also the risk of answers being unclear or illegible and of better-educated respondents writing in more detail than less-educated ones.

The main advantages of questionnaires is they can be distributed to very **large samples** (through the mail, online, etc) and **do not require trained research assistants** to administer them.

There are many disadvantages to questionnaires. They require the respondent to be able to read and often read to quite a high standard – lengthy questionnaires with technical language can be very off-putting. They might have to be translated into other languages.

Writing a clear, concise questionnaire is not easy to do. Questions can be muddled or interpreted in ways the researcher didn't intend. Another problem is **leading questions**: questions which are worded in a way that encourages a particular answer. A related problem is **affirmation bias**, which is the tendency for respondents to answer *'Yes'* to any question rather than think deeply about it. However, a **pilot study** (p33) could identify these problems in advance.

A lot of people **don't like filling out questionnaires** unless they are being rewarded in some way which is way a lot of consumer surveys come with a free pen or offer to include the respondent in a prize draw. However, because **people are unsupervised while they complete questionnaires** you cannot know if they are taking it seriously or even *who* precisely is answering the questions.

AO2 ILLUSTRATION: NATIONAL SURVEYS IN THE UK

The biggest national survey in the UK is the **Census** which happens every 10 years (recently in 2021, or 2022 in Scotland). The Census provides the UK Government with data about the **demographics** (population make-up) of the UK. The results are published by the **Office for National Statistics** (**ONS**, p41) and are used by sociologists.

Every household has to return a Census form (by post or online) and there is a £1000 fine for failing to do so or returning false information about the people in your household. People who don't have a household (e.g. the homeless) might not appear in the Census. Only one question in the Census is optional and this is the question asking '*What is your religion?*'

Based on 2001 data, about 94% of people complete the Census and data on the rest is either gathered in follow up surveys or statistically calculated from tends. The final results are considered to represent 100% of the UK population.

Other national surveys include the **British Social Attitudes Survey** (3000 respondents every year to gather data on changing norms and values), the **Crime Survey for England & Wales** (CSEW, asks 50,000 respondents about the experience of crime in the previous 12 months) and the **Labour Force Survey** (gathers data about employment from 44,000 households every quarter).

Research: Find out more about these surveys and visit the YouGov.co.uk site (despite its name, not a government-run organisation)

METHODS PROFILE: MARTIN & BLINDER (2020) *p118

Nicole Martin & Scott Blinder published *Biases At The Ballot Box* (2020) which was an investigation into the way political candidates are supported or penalised based on their ethnicity.

The researchers emailed a web-based questionnaire to members of the public who had been part of an online **YouGov survey** into voting intentions in the 2017 UK General Election. This was a **quota sample** (p49) of 7903 respondents that was quite representative of British voters.

The questionnaire provided a profile of two (fictional) political candidates, including their views on immigration and law & order: the candidates were either White, Black Caribbean or Pakistani. The question was: '*Which of these candidates would you rather have as your MP*?' which is a **closed question**.

The researchers used this quantitative data to assess the popularity of political candidates based on their ethnicity of the candidate, the candidate's policies and the ethnicity and gender of the respondents. They found that Pakistani candidates were less popular than White ones offering the same policies, which can be **generalised** to show racist biases in UK voting.

METHOD: INTERVIEWS

Interviews are like questionnaires but are conducted face-to-face (or over the telephone or Internet). The interviewer asks the questions and the interviewee answers them.

- **Structured interviews** are essentially questionnaires that are read aloud, with all the questions scripted in advance. This is much slower than a questionnaire and more expensive, but the interviewer doesn't have to be particularly well trained and might be able to explain questions the interviewee doesn't understand. Because the questions are always the same, they are **reliable** (p21).

- **Unstructured interviews** do not have pre-scripted questions. They resemble a normal conversation, with questions arising out of the previous answer. This is good for establish trust, **empathy and rapport** (p16). It's ideal for sensitive topics, because questions can be phrased differently to avoid distressing the interviewee (which is important for **ethics**, p52). However, the interviewer must be well-trained, and this method is **unreliable**, since every interview will turn out very differently.

- **Semi-structured interviews** combine the two previous approaches: the interview proceeds like a conversation but there are pre-scripted questions that must be asked. This produces an interview which is **quite reliable** and allows the interviewer to ask follow-up questions and pursue topics that the interviewee brings up. As with unstructured interviews, the interviewer must be well-trained.

Interviews don't require the respondent to be able to read – although the interviewer and interviewee must share a language so translators might be needed. **Trained research assistants** are needed for interviews, although the training needed to administer a structured interview is pretty basic.

Interviews have the same problems with leading questions as questionnaires. There is an additional problem of **investigator effects**: this is when the interviewer influences the answers through their tone, facial expression or body language (probably without realising it). Training interviewers not to do this is quite difficult, but **pilot studies** (p33) help identify the problem.

A related problem is when the researcher has **social characteristics** that might influence the interviewee, such as being a different race, gender, age or social class.

The main disadvantage of interviews is that they are **time-consuming**, which means they can't be used with large samples the way that questionnaires can.

The main advantages are the **detailed qualitative data** they gather and the **naturalistic and authentic** way they do this. An unstructured interview can be so naturalistic that the interviewee doesn't even realise they are being interviewed (though there are **ethical issues of deception** with this, p52). The scripted questions in a structured or semi-structured interview can be **closed questions** (p57), which means that interviews can gather quantitative data too.

METHODS PROFILE: HECHT ET AL. (2020)* vs GENTLEMAN (2009)*

Katharina Hecht's study of social mobility (p31) includes interviews with 30 elite earners. Hecht conducts **semi-structured interviews**. She encourages the interviewees to discuss their attitudes to their jobs, money and fairness in society. Hecht also asks pre-planned questions about whether they consider themselves to be high-earners, whether the view inequality as fair and whether they regard their wealth as a reward for their talent or hard work.

Amelia Gentleman's research into care homes for the elderly (p51) includes interviews with the residents and the staff. These are **unstructured interviews**, because Gentleman wants the respondents to offer their own views based on their own experiences: Violet describes having to sell her flat to pay the bills at the care home, Miranda wants to talk about her childhood in the 1930s. The staff offer their perspectives: an Iraqi student nurse is surprised that the British abandon their elderly relatives in care homes and is dismayed how rarely those relatives visit. A set of pre-written questions would not have produced these spontaneous responses.

METHOD: OBSERVATIONS

Observations are different from questionnaires and interviews, because instead of respondents telling you about their experiences, relationships or attitudes, you observe their behaviour and from this you can draw conclusions about their experiences, relationships or attitudes.

In some ways, observing behaviour is *better* than respondents telling you about things: respondents might exaggerate or conceal the truth or else they might not know what's going on.

In other ways, observing behaviour is *worse* than respondents telling you about things, because your interpretation of their behaviour might not be accurate (**valid**) and this is particularly likely if the people you are observing are from a different class, culture or subculture.

- **Controlled vs naturalistic observations:** Controlled observations are more common in Psychology than Sociology, because they take place in artificial conditions. Naturalistic observations are more common in Sociology and take place is a **real-life situation**, with the participants going about their ordinary business (e.g. employees in a workplace, students in a classroom, shoppers in a mall).

- **Structured vs unstructured observations:** Structured observations have a pre-prepared **checklist** (or **observational schedule**) and only behaviour on the checklist is recorded; this can be tallied later to produce **quantitative data** (p38). Unstructured observations use a blank notepad or recording device and the researcher records **qualitative data** as the situation unfolds. With unstructured observations there's a greater risk of missing things or focusing on the wrong things, but the researcher is free to focus on interesting developments even if they didn't plan for them to happen.

- **Participant vs direct observations:** In a participant observation the researcher joins in the activity with the people being observed, but in a direct observation the researcher stands back and concentrates on observing. It's easier to pay attention during direct observation but participant observation might produce more insight into the people being observed, making it less likely you will misinterpret their behaviour (greater **validity**).

- **Overt vs covert observations:** Overt observations are obvious and announced: the researcher is clearly visible and it's known that she is observing behaviour. Covert observations are secret: the researcher is hidden from view or appears to be just another member of the public. People are more likely to change their behaviour if they know they are being observed (**reducing validity**) but there are **ethical issues** (**consent** and **deception**) with covert observations and sometimes practical problems too (how can you hide the fact that you are making notes on what people do?).

Observations have greater **validity** than questionnaires/interviews, because you are seeing what people actually do in a situation, rather than recording their attitudes or intentions. Electoral polls show that there is a big difference between the way people *say* they are going to vote in surveys and the way they *actually* vote on the day of the election.

On the other hand, there is a problem of **misinterpretation** with observations. **Interpretivists** argue that the solution is for the observer to embed himself in the culture or community of the people he is observing and understand it 'from the inside' (*c.f.* **ethnography**, p62).

Observations are **time consuming** and require **trained researchers**, especially the sort of 'embedded' observations recommended by Interpretivists. Observations are limited to quite **small samples** and, except for controlled observations that sociologists rarely use, **it isn't possible to randomise** the samples either. This leads to criticism (especially from Positivists) that the samples are **unrepresentative and biased**.

METHODS PROFILE: GENTLEMAN (2009, cont'd)*

Amelia Gentleman's research into life in a care home for the elderly (p51) was a **naturalistic observation**, because it took place in a real care home with real residents and staff going about their day-to-day business.

It was also an **unstructured observation**: the researcher went in with an open mind rather than a checklist of things she expected to see.

It was a **direct observation**: Gentleman did not join the staff in washing and feeding residents and cleaning their rooms; she did not join in the conversations and card games of the residents. She stood back and recorded what she saw and heard.

It was an **overt observation**. Everyone knew that Gentleman was a journalist from *The Guardian* who was writing an article on them. The staff might have pretended to be busier than usual and the residents might have been tense and self-conscious. Gentleman noticed how *"dispiriting"* the *"joyless inertia"* of the day room was with no one speaking to each other – she attributes this to the culture of the care home, but it might just be a reaction to the presence of an outsider. This lowers the **validity** of her conclusions.

On the other hand, Gentleman visited the care home over 4 days, which is time for people to get used to her presence.

METHOD: ETHNOGRAPHY

Ethnography means writing about culture, but it specifically refers to a distinctive **Interpretivist** methodology. Ethnography is not a separate way of gathering data from the ones previously described; instead, it means carrying out **interviews** and **observations** in a certain sort of way.

The original ethnography involved researchers going to live with unusual communities for long periods of time, until they developed a deep understanding of the culture 'from the inside' and understood its norms and values like a native member. **Margaret Mead**'s 1935 fieldwork among the tribes of New Guinea that you learned about in **1A: Socialisation, Culture & Identity** is this sort of ethnography. Mead lived with the Arapesh, Mundugumor and Tchambuli tribes, learned some of their language and took part in the festivals and meetings. She used the insights to reflect on sex and sexuality in her own American culture afterwards.

Ethnographers today don't have to live with isolated tribes on remote islands. Ethnography now means **a systematic attempt to participate in a group, community or subculture in order to understand it**:

- **Participant observations:** it's important for ethnographers to take part in the culture they are studying and be a member of the community, not an outsider looking in

- **Unstructured interviews:** ethnographers use naturalistic methods and want to engage with the people they are studying in the way that these people treat each other, such as normal conversation

- **No questionnaires:** surveys remind everyone that the researcher is an 'expert' seeking information and the respondents are providing her with data; ethnography usually avoids this artificial and divisive approach

- **Longitudinal design** (p37): Ethnography is not about taking a 'snapshot' of a community, but rather experiencing how the community reacts to changes over time; most ethnographic research will last for weeks or even years.

- **Reflexivity** (p17): Ethnographers should reflect on how their presence in a community might affect it as well as how joining a community affects them and teaches them to view their own culture in a new light

Is **Gentleman (2009**, p51**)** an ethnographic study? Gentleman visits the care home over 4 days and carries out naturalistic observations and interviews. However, she doesn't participate in the community she is studying: she doesn't get a job there working undercover as a nurse or disguise herself as an elderly resident. She isn't really there long enough to get 'inside' the culture of either the staff or the residents. So, there are ethnographic *aspects* to Gentleman's research, but it falls short of being 'proper' ethnography.

You can evaluate ethnography by writing about the strengths and weaknesses of **participant observations** (p61) and **unstructured interviews** (p59) and **qualitative interpretations** (p38).

Ethnography has strengths of its own. The idea of getting 'inside' a culture and experiencing the social world the way the natives do is very appealing for **Interpretivists**: it focuses on **understanding** (*verstehen*, p16) and **empathy and rapport**. It can be very useful for dispelling myths about other cultures or subcultures and this can have implications for **social policy** (p40).

However, ethnography **takes a long time** (and expense) and demands a lot of **commitment and training** for researchers (who might need to learn another language). Joining a community 'in disguise' has **ethical implications** (**consent** and **deception**, p52) and this causes problems if the researcher forms friendships with the people being studied without telling them who she really is. Ethnographers prefer **overt observations**, hoping that the sheer amount of time they spend with the community will make them familiar and accepted, but some groups cannot be studied overtly (e.g. criminal gangs).

A final criticism is that **the sort of understanding ethnographers seek might actually be impossible**. It might be that no amount of time spent in another culture ever really gives you the outlook of someone who grew up in it. Researchers risk imposing their own ideas and beliefs onto the group they are studying. For example, **Derek Freeman (1983)** accuses Mead of describing norms and values in the tribes she lived with that didn't really exist. Mead very much *wanted* to find different gender roles and sexual attitudes in these non-Western cultures and convinced herself that she had.

ETHNOGRAPHY VS ETHNOMETHODOLOGY

Ethnography is in the OCR Specification, and it is described above. **Ethnomethodology** sounds similar but it isn't in the Specification and won't feature in the Exam. Ethnomethodology is focusing on how people make sense of their social world.

METHODS PROFILE: MOORE & CONN (1985) *p131

Patricia Moore & Charles Conn wrote *Disguised: A True Story* **(1985)** about 27-year-old Moore's experiences of going through life disguised as a 85-year-old woman ('Old Pat').

Moore carried out a **covert unstructured participant observation**; she put on makeup to make her look wrinkly, wore glasses that blurred her vision, wrapped bandages around her body so she was hunched over, plugged her ears so she couldn't hear well, and wore uneven shoes so she was forced to walk with a stick.

Over a 3-year period between 1979-82, Moore played 'Old Pat' in 114 US cities in 14 States, as well as 2 Canadian Provinces. She was robbed, beaten and left for dead by a street gang. People would shout, assuming she was deaf, and push in front of her in queues – and her own self-esteem suffered as she started viewing herself as less important.

This has many features of **ethnography**, such as Moore getting so involved with the experience of the elderly that she came to view herself the way they do. It demonstrates the **commitment** that ethnography can demand – and there are extra ethical issues like **safety** here – but also the insights that come from it. Moore used these experiences in her career as a designer, making appliances to make life easier for the elderly.

METHOD: CONTENT ANALYSIS

So far, we have looked at methods of studying people 'in real life' but sociologists also study the **artifacts** (cultural objects). Artifacts include **media documents** (like books, newspapers, magazines, films, TV programmes and adverts) and **communications** (like diaries, letters, Twitter feeds or transcripts of conversations).

A content analysis involves creating a **schedule** like the schedule used in a **structured observation** (p61, i.e. a checklist). The researcher goes through the artifact counting the number of times certain words, phrases, images or concepts occur. This produces a **quantitative interpretation** (p38) of the artifact. The researcher can also use **semiotics** to carry out a **qualitative interpretation** of the artifact.

Content analyses can **reveal the values and beliefs of the person or culture** that created the artifact. For example, a content analysis of a newspaper reveals our society's preoccupations with sex, violence, money and celebrity. If content analyses span a period of time (i.e, a **longitudinal study**, p37), you can analyse **changing social attitudes** in the rise and fall of certain concepts or images in the media. The artifact can be re-read or re-played many times, making this a very **reliable** method.

Because content analyses don't deal with actual people, there are **no ethical issues** of trust, consent and protection. However, there may be issues of **confidentiality** if you are analysing private communications (such as discussions on social media or private letters).

The main criticisms of content analyses are that they are **subjective interpretations**. For example, a researcher might focus on references to race but not think to look for references to disability or sexuality. This might misinterpret the artifact by over-emphasising something unimportant and missing content that's more important. Similarly, the analysis only reveals **the values and beliefs of whoever created the artifact**, which might not be typical of society. There's a danger when analysing historical artifacts of **imposing modern ideas on the past**, which has **poor validity**.

METHODS PROFILE: MESSNER & COOKY (2021, cont'd)*

Michael Messner & Cheryl Cooky (p38) carried out a **content analysis** of men and women's sports on 3 Los Angeles TV channels and the digital channel ESPN. The researchers recorded 3 two-week segments of sports coverage. The **schedule** included gender of sport (men's, women's, neutral), type of sport (basketball, football, golf, etc.), competitive level of sport (professional, college, high school, etc.) and time given over to the segment (minutes/seconds). **Codes** quantified production values such as music, graphics and game highlights.

It was a **longitudinal study** over 30 years, with an analyses every 5 years. This shows changes from the highly sexualised representation of women's sports in the 1990s to the 'gender-bland' reporting today. It also shows that overall coverage of women's sports has not grown significantly despite calls and pledges to represent more women in sport.

METHOD: STATISTICAL DATA

Statistical data is usually **secondary data** (p31) gathered by non-sociologists but used by sociologists in their research. It is always **quantitative data** (p8) and is particularly valued by Positivists for revealing **social facts**.

- **Official statistics:** This data is gathered by government agencies – in the UK, this usually means the **Office for National Statistics** (**ONS**, *c.f.* p41) and includes data sets with huge samples, like the **UK Census** (p58). Because the government tends to use the same categories and collects data every year, official statistics are a great source of **patterns and trends over time** and can be used in **longitudinal studies** (p37). However, they are subject to **political manipulation** (sometime called 'massaging' the figures) – for example, it might be embarrassing for a government if crime or unemployment goes up, so categories can be redefined to make it look like this isn't happening. For example, raising the school leaving age (ROSLA) reduces unemployment figures.

- **Non-official statistics:** This data is gathered by agencies that aren't the government, such as newspapers, TV shows, charities or market research companies. They tend not to have the enormous **sample sizes** of official statistics and often **don't date back** as far into the past. However, they are **free from political massaging**. The disadvantage is that they can be **methodologically flawed** – for example, people might vote more than once in a newspaper poll or TV phone-in (this is called 'voodoo-polling').

The main advantage of all official statistics is that the data is **easy to access**, often **free** and **up-to-date**.

Interpretivists point out a problem that all statistics are **socially constructed** (*c.f.* Atkinson's criticism of Durkheim, p19). This means statistics do not paint an objective picture of society because they are based on assumptions, definitions and biases by the people who create them. For example, most of us think of unemployment as being out-of-work for any reason, however official government statistics do not count students as unemployed, even though they might be out of work during the long university holidays. Similarly, official crime figures only cover crimes recorded by the police, but lots of crimes are not reported so the real figure is much higher.

AO2 ILLUSTRATION: POLLING COMPANIES

Polling means surveying the public for their views on things. There are several companies that carry out national and international polling.

YouGov in an online polling company based in the UK and founded in 2000. Its surveys usually have samples of 1500-2000 people, but of course its statistics cannot include the views of people who do not have access to the Internet.

Ipsos MORI is another UK polling company based in the UK and dating back to the 1990s. It uses online questionnaires, face-to-face **structured interviews** and computerised telephone surveys.

Gallup and Pew Research are American polling companies that carry out worldwide surveys. Pew was founded in the 1990s but Gallup is over a century old. Gallup specialises in gathering data through telephone interviews.

These companies all provide non-official statistics, however on a very large scale. Since they are businesses, their statistics are not always made free to everyone. However Pew Research is a not-for-profit organisation and has a particular focus on reporting religious attitudes.

Research: visit the YouGov FAQ site and investigate the company defends its polling methods from criticism: https://yougov.co.uk/about/panel-methodology/research-qs/

MIXED METHODS: TRIANGULATION

Most research uses more than one method. **Triangulation** means approaching the same social behaviour from two or more angles. It is a way of checking the **validity** (p20) of findings. The results of one method should be backed up by the results of a different method.

- **Internal triangulation** means using different approaches within a single method, such as **open and closed questions** (p57) in a single questionnaire. **Semi-structured interviews** (p59) are a type of internal triangulation.

- **External triangulation** means using two (or more) completely different methods, such as an interview followed by an observation. Interviewing people about their intentions and then observing them to see if they act on those intentions. If they don't do what they said they were going to do, then the interview was **invalid**. The research into care homes by **Gentleman (2009**, p51**)** mixes an observation with interviews.

- **Data triangulation** is when primary and secondary data is combined, such as interviewing people and seeing if their responses match up with the results from official statistics about trends in the country as a whole. The research into social mobility by **Hecht et al (2020**, p31**)** mixes official statistics with Hecht's own interviews with elite earners.

- **Investigator triangulation** is when different observers or interviewers are used, usually from different backgrounds (e.g. different ethnic groups or genders), to see if the social characteristics of the researcher are affecting the respondents or if the researcher's biases are affecting the way they interpret the data.

The main advantage of triangulation is that the **strengths of one method can complement the weaknesses of another**. For example, the big picture from official statistics can make up for the small sample of an interview.

However, triangulation van make research more time consuming and expensive. It does not remove the drawbacks of any of the methods it uses; it just balances them with the strengths of a different one. This is why **Tim May (1993)** states: *"while triangulation might appear attractive, it is not a panacea* [a magical cure] *for methodological ills."*

MIXED METHODS: METHODOLOGICAL PLURALISM

Methodological pluralism is very similar to **triangulation** and the two concepts blur into each other. Triangulation is about checking the validity of research but methodological pluralism is about **deepening and enriching** the data and the conclusions that can be drawn from it.

Case Studies

Case studies are a sociological method that is (weirdly) absent from the OCR Specification, but deserve mention here. Instead of a normal sample group, a case study focuses either on **one unusual individual** or else on **a small group connected by a shared experience** (e.g. a family, a friendship group, people in a workplace, protestors at a demonstration).

This narrow focus can make case studies **hard to generalise** from. However, the advantage is that the researcher can gather **rich in-depth data**. Case studies make use of methodological pluralism to examine the focus individual or group from all angles.

Interpretivists value case studies because you can have immense **empathy** (p16) for the person and view their life history in context. Case studies are often **longitudinal studies** (p37), following a person over a long period of time. However, this intense focus can lead the researcher to become **over-involved** with the person being studied, which is why **reflexivity** is important (p17).

KEY STUDY: WILLIS (1977, cont'd)

Paul Willis' *Learning To Labour* **(1977**, p22**)** is a case study of 12 working-class 'Lads' that Willis follows through their last year of school and into the workplace.

Willis **observes** the boys in their classrooms and in meetings with their teachers and parents. He **interviews** the boys and their teachers and later their employers. Willis uses this detailed and sympathetic data to question a popular sociological view that working-class boys develop an anti-school subculture because they are frustrated by their lack of success. Willis finds that the boys have no interest in educational success and only want to join the adult workforce.

Willis can be criticised for becoming **over-involved** with the 'Lads': he sometimes seems to excuse their bullying, racist attitudes and destructive impact on other students' learning.

METHODS PROFILE: GENTLEMAN (2009, cont'd)*

Amelia Gentleman spent 4 days observing 26 elderly residents in a care home in Ipswich (p51). She **observes** the residents and **interviews** residents and staff. She paints a distressing picture of the way the elderly are abandoned by their relatives.

Gentleman's 4-day stay is too short for her to become **over-involved** with the residents but perhaps it is also too short for her to build up a deep understanding of what life in the care home is really like (for instance, she does not witness anyone die).

EXAM PRACTICE: THEORY & METHODS

The OCR exam has four questions in **Paper 2 Section A**, based on two source items:

Source A

Views of disabled men & women on how disabled adults are treated compared to non-disabled in the UK

YouGov survey of 1008 men and women living with a disability (2018)

Source B

Researchers from the Glasgow Media Group (a group of sociologists linked to Glasgow University) compared and contrasted media coverage of disability in five papers in 2010-11 with a similar period in 2004-5. The papers were *The Sun, The Mirror, The Express, The Mail* and *The Guardian* – including Left and Right Wing political views. The news stories were coded and dominant themes were statistically identified.

They found a significant increase in the reporting of disability (713 articles in 2004-5 compared to 1015 in 2010-11). There was a drop in negative terms like 'cripple' and the presentation of disabled people as victims or sufferers declined. However, there was an increase of reports about disability benefits fraud (2.8% rising to 6.1%) and an increase in negative terms like 'scrounger' and 'skiver' for people on disability benefits (54 examples in 2004-5 going up to 142 in 2010-11).

The researchers recruited focus groups of 6-8 people who were interviewed about their attitudes to disability. They stated that they believed disability fraud was 70% higher than it actually was and cited news articles as evidence for this belief.

Source: Briant, Watson, & Philo (2011) Bad News for Disabled People: How the Newspapers are Reporting Disability

1. Summarise the data shown in **Source A**. [4 marks: 4 AO2]

*Make **two** points about the data. It is vital that you quote actual figures from the graph and draw conclusions from them (or you are not 'summarising' the data, only restating it). For example, about 46% of women disabilities think disabled adults are treated much worse than other people. In order to summarise, you need to say whether this is higher or lower than males or other opinions.*

2. With reference to **Source B**, explain a strength and a weakness of using triangulation in sociological research. [6 marks: 2 AO1 + 4 AO2]

Write a couple of sentences about each evaluation. You might focus on measuring validity, complementary strengths and weaknesses, time & effort and weaknesses still being present – a really good idea is to quote something from the source.

3. With reference to **Source A**, explain **one** advantage and **one** disadvantage of sociologists using non-official statistics as secondary data. [10 marks: 4 AO2 + 6 AO3]

*Write two short paragraphs, one about an advantage (such as absence of political massaging) and one about a disadvantage (such as shallowness of statistics, smaller samples, methodology problems). You need to support each reason with an example from the source – a really good idea is to quote a number (or approximate number) from the graph. Make sure that both points link to **non-official statistics**, not just statistics in general.*

4. Using **Source B** and your wider sociological knowledge, explain and evaluate using content analyses to study inequality in society. [25 marks: 5 AO1 + 5 AO2 + 15 AO3]

*Write four paragraphs/arguments – two strengths and two weaknesses of content analyses would work well. Each paragraph should introduce a sociological idea with an example or comparison from Source B. Each paragraph should finish off with a developed evaluation (see **Chapter 4** for this). For example, you could write about content analyses revealing trends over time and wider social values and norms, but also how content analyses only reflect the views of the writers and are limited by the codes the researchers decide to use.*

In questions 2-3 you can pick up the AO1 marks from using sociological terminology and relating things to sociological debates (e.g. Positivism vs Interpretivism). Named sociologists and studies aren't particularly important, but knowledge of polling organisations like YouGov is relevant for question 3.

Question 4 is a full essay in which you are invited to deploy *"your wider sociological knowledge"* so famous sociologists definitely belong in your answer and a comparison to other content analyses (like **Messner & Cooky**) or disability research (like **Tom Shakespeare** from **1A: Socialisation, Culture & Identity**) will help.

CHAPTER 4 – EVALUATION

In **Paper 2 Section A**, questions 2, 3 and 4 assess **AO3**/evaluation and only questions 3 and 4 require developed evaluation.

As well as the evaluative points you can find in the preceding chapters, here are some evaluative positions candidates can adopt:

"This is scientific" / Positivism strengths

You can evaluate research for being scientific if it gathers quantitative data, analyses data statistically, uses structured research methods or official statistics, recruits randomised samples and/or studies very large samples and target populations.

Positivism favours scientific research and scientific research has many strengths. It is objective, so it is not interfered with by bias, imagination or wishful thinking. It is evidence-based, which makes it reliable, credible and persuasive. It can predict future trends and patterns, so it is useful for social policy. Since it explains social facts, it can be used to change society for the better, which is also useful for social policy.

To evaluate these ideas, point out examples of scientific research and the influence it has: the way operationalises hard-to-pin-down concepts in measurable ways, the way it can challenge purely anecdotal or personal evidence with a more impersonal view and the way it can offer explanations for things that otherwise look like chance or coincidence.

To elaborate on these ideas, address some flaws in scientific research. It can be narrow and superficial and lacks empathy into what makes people tick. It is often not as objective and value-free as Positivists would like to think. It can view participants as lab rats or guinea-pigs, which leads to ethical issues.

It's important not to be formulaic. Say *why* science is like this: give an example of research and what came out of it. Using ONS data is scientific *because it is drawn from a nationwide sample like the UK Census*. Not all mass surveys are scientific *because they can have unrepresentative samples, such as YouGov ignoring people who don't have Internet access*.

"This is insightful" / Interpretivism strengths

You can evaluate research for being insightful if it gathers qualitative data, analyses data thematically, uses unstructured/naturalistic research methods, uses ethnographic methods and/or studies very small samples and focused target populations.

Interpretivism favours insightful research and Interpretivism has many strengths. It is reflexive, so it addresses its own biases and subjectivity. It explores the social world of ordinary people, so it is generalisable to real life. It uses ethnography to study groups that are often ignored or viewed as deviant. It sees the research participant as important in their own right, so it tends to be ethical and high in validity.

To evaluate these ideas, point out examples of insightful research and the influence it has: the way it encourages case studies, its importance for studying deviant or excluded groups, the way it helps overcome bias and prejudice.

To elaborate on these ideas, address some flaws in Interpretivist research. It can be limited in scope with little to say about society as a whole. It is often subjective and mixes fact and opinion too freely. Is focus on reflexivity can make it wordy with unclear conclusions.

It's important not to be formulaic. Say *why* Interpretivism is like this: give an example of research and what came out of it. Using case studies is insightful *because it challenges stereotypes about the working class, like Willis' study of 'the Lads.'* Not all ethnography is insightful *because researchers can see in cultures only what they want to see, as Freeman criticises Margaret Mead*.

"This describes society" / Structuralism strengths

You can evaluate research for being structuralist (**macro-scale**) if it gathers data about large samples and generalises the findings to society as a whole, discovering patterns and trends.

Structuralism favours large-scale research and large-scale research has many strengths. It is likely to have a representative sample of participants and their behaviour can be generalised to wider society. These conclusions can be expressed statistically and, because they ignore individuals and freewill, they can make predictions about future trends, which is useful for social policy.

To evaluate these ideas, point out examples of structuralist research and the influence it has: the way it dominates official statistics, the influence it has over politicians and voters in elections, its importance for policies like combating crime or unemployment.

To elaborate on these ideas, address the flaw in structuralist research. It ignores the importance of freewill and the social action of individuals or small groups.

It's important not to be formulaic. Say *why* structuralism is like this: give an example of research and what came out of it. Hecht et al's study shows social mobility is reducing *because it draws on data from the UK Census over 40 years*. However, it ignores individual action *because some talented people will still become high earners in spite of this*.

Structuralism is very similar to science/Positivism, and you can often use one to evaluate the other: most scientific studies are also structuralist in scope and outlook; most structuralist research uses scientific procedures. Both share a high respect for statistical data.

"This describes personal relationships" / Social Action strengths

You can evaluate research for being Social Action (**micro-scale**) if it gathers data about small samples and focuses on choice and freewill.

Social Action favours small-scale research and small-scale research has many strengths. It is easier to achieve understanding (*verstehen*) of the participants' social world because you can have empathy and a rapport with them. It is likely to be more ethical because you consider the participants' perspective on things.

To evaluate these ideas, point out examples of Social Action research and the influence it has: the way it sheds lights on groups that are ignored or considered deviant and uses qualitative data to show people resisting social pressures.

To elaborate on these ideas, address the flaw in Social Action research. It exaggerates the importance of freewill and ignores the role that powerful structures like class, race, gender and age play in social behaviour.

It's important not to be formulaic. Say *why* Social Action is like this: give an example of research and what came out of it. Jones et al's study shows people choosing early retirement *because they find it empowering and fulfilling*. However, it ignores social structures *because people from working class backgrounds won't have the option to do this for finabncial reasons*.

Social Action is very similar to insight/Interpretivism and you can often use one to evaluate the other: most Interpretivist studies are also Social Action in scope and outlook; most Social Action research uses Interpretivist procedures. Both share a high respect for qualitative data.

"This is generalisable" / Sampling strengths

You can evaluate research for being generalisable if it is based on representative and/or unbiased sampling.

Representative sampling has many strengths. It is usually stratified (stratified or quota sampling) and draws a large sample group to avoid the risk of unusual participants influencing the findings. Unbiased sampling is usually randomised (random or stratified sampling).

To evaluate these ideas, point out examples of good sampling and the effect it has: the way Positivists can use representative samples to identify patterns and trends in society.

To elaborate on these ideas, address alternative sampling approaches. Sometimes it's important to target a very specific group or a narrow target population that you cannot randomise or no sampling frame exists for (e.g. a criminal gang, homeless people, drug users, illegal immigrants). Sometimes access and gatekeeping force researchers to use a particular sampling technique.

It's important not to be formulaic. Say *why* a particular sample is necessary or undesirable: give an example of research using this sort of sample and how it might be done differently. Willis' sample of schoolboys is not randomised *because he was looking for a very specific group of working class boys with anti-school attitudes*. Hecht et al's purposive sample is justified *because it's difficult to persuade elite earners to take part in research unless you seek them out specially*.

"This is consistent" / Reliability strengths

You can evaluate research for being reliable if it delivers consistent results, has standardised procedures that always work the same way or has been tested with pilot studies or over a long period of time.

Reliable research has many strengths. It is unlikely to be a fluke or one-off result. It can be tested by other researchers or replicated with new samples or in new situations.

To evaluate these ideas, point out examples of reliable research and what makes it so valuable: the standardised procedures that can be followed over and over, longitudinal studies that can test a cohort again and again at regular intervals, clearly operationalised concepts that can be put to use in new situations.

To elaborate on these ideas, address some flaws that make research unreliable. It can focus on a one-off event or unusual groups of people in a situation that will never be repeated. Alternatively, it might have a procedure that is unstructured, so that it never happens the same way twice: unstructured interviews and observations are good examples.

It's important not to be formulaic. Say *why* reliable or unreliable research is like this: give an example of research and how it could be different. Gentleman's research in a care home is unreliable *because she didn't ask standardised questions in her interviews*. Messner & Cooky's content analysis is reliable *because they decided what codes to use and applied the same coding system to different sports TV shows every 5 years*.

"This is unbiased" / Validity strengths

You can evaluate research for being valid if it delivers authentic results, is free from bias or controls in place that prevent interference or distortion of data.

Valid research has many strengths. It is likely to be true and reflects real life. It produces findings that the participants will agree with and other research can confirm.

To evaluate these ideas, point out examples of valid research and what makes it so valuable: the unbiased and value-free stance taken by the researcher, the objective measures being used, techniques like respondent validation and triangulation in use and qualitative data explored in a reflexive way.

To elaborate on these ideas, address some flaws that make research invalid. It can treat statistics in a superficial way. Alternatively, it might have a procedure or sample that is artificial, so that it doesn't reflect real life: structured interviews and observations are can be like this.

It's important not to be formulaic. Say *why* valid or invalid research is like this: give an example of research and how it could be different. Gentleman's research in a care home is valid *because she took an unstructured approach that allowed the residents and staff to express their own views*. Messner & Cooky's content analysis is low in validity *because they focused on a handful of TV shows and ignored sports coverage on radio, in newspapers and on the Internet that might represent women's sports better*.

"This is practical" / Time-cost strengths

You can evaluate research for being practical if it leads to techniques and strategies that can be used by other researchers or the public; in particular, research can have implications for social policy.

Positivism favours practical research and practical research has many strengths. It is credible and persuasive – probably because it has a scientific methodology, a large sample and/or presents statistical data that reveals patterns and trends. However, some research is practical because it has procedures that are cheap and quick to carry out.

To evaluate these ideas, point out examples of practical research and the influence it has: the important sociological concepts and tools that some research introduces or the wide interest by politicians in some sociological ideas.

To elaborate on these ideas, address some flaws in practical research. It can promote social policy that is divisive or destructive; sometimes the data is accused of being politically biased or 'massaged' to suit political agendas.

It's important not to be formulaic. Say *why* practical research is like this: give an example of research and what came out of it. Wilkinson & Pickett's work is practical *because it used official statistics that were already available to show that unequal societies are unhappy*. Not all practical research is beneficial *because Charles Murray's statistical analysis of unemployment in the underclass inspired New Right governments to cut benefits for the poor*.

"This is official" / Official statistics strengths

You can evaluate research for being official if it uses official statistics provided by the government, especially by the Office for National Statistics (ONS).

Official data has many strengths. It has the 'seal of approval' of government statisticians and the ONS is independent from politicians themselves. The data goes back years and is drawn from nationwide surveys like the UK Census. It is available for free through the ONS website.

To evaluate these ideas, point out examples of research using official statistics: the way it can draw attention to patterns and trends affecting the whole country or happening over decades.

To elaborate on these ideas, address some flaws in official data. It can be politically biased or 'massaged' to suit political agendas and its wide scale doesn't suit Interpretivists.

It's important not to be formulaic. Say **why** official data is like this: give an example of research and what came out of it. Hecht's research is official **because it uses the ONS Longitudinal Survey to show social mobility dropping from the 1970s onwards**. Not all official data is trustworthy **because Charles Murray's statistical analysis of unemployment in the underclass is accused of serving a New Right agenda to blame the poor for social problems**.

"This is ethical" / Ethical strengths

You can evaluate research for being ethical if it respects the rights of its participants and preserves the safety of researchers.

There are many ways for research to be ethical. It makes sure that participants give informed consent, are treated honestly, are protected and are guaranteed confidentiality. It ensures the safety of its researchers and doesn't put them in dangerous situations

To evaluate these ideas, point out examples of ethical research and the steps it takes to do the right thing: the way it briefs participants beforehand or explains things to them afterwards, the way it hides true identities and only uses fictitious names and the way it is careful not to break the law.

To elaborate on these ideas, address some problems with ethical research. Sometimes research is ruined if the participants know exactly what it going on or what the researcher is looking for. A certain amount of risk or stress is unavoidable in some real-life situations that sociologists want to study. There are contradictions between keeping your word to participants and reporting crimes to the proper authorities

It's important not to be formulaic. Say **why** ethical research is like this: give an example of research and what came out of it. Willis' study of 'the Lads' is ethical **because he concealed their true names and changed the name of their school to Hammertown Boys School, so as not to ruin its reputation**. Pat Moore's research into old age has ethical problems **because she put herself in danger, as when she was beaten nearly to death by a street gang in New York**.

EXAM PRACTICE: SECTION A

The OCR exam has four questions in **Paper 2 Section A**, based on two source items:

Source A

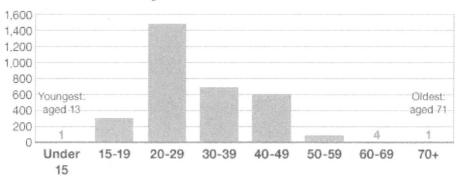

Source: ACPO, 2010

Source B

Geoff Pearson studied football hooligans by carrying out a covert participant observation of Blackpool Football Club supporters between 1995 and 1998. He did this because he had found interviews with supporters to be unreliable, because fans brag about their troublemaking but also hide their worst offences.

The other supporters believed he was a Law student at nearby Lancaster University but did not know he was researching them. Pearson attended 78 games and would meet up with a group of supporters in the pub before or after a match. He did not live in the area, so he could not observe the supporters outside of a football context.

Over time, Pearson became known as a regular fan and he built up a knowledge of the game, the club and the supporters. He found he had to commit 'minor offences' during the research to avoid attracting suspicion. He made a point of only carrying out offences (e.g. pitch invasions) that other supporters did regularly and avoided more serious offences (e.g. violent assaults). Pearson found that his willingness to engage in minor offences gave him the reputation as "*a bit of a nutter*" even though he never took part in anything serious. Nevertheless, he did witness serious assaults.

Pearson concludes that football hooliganism is not 'mindless' and it is not about the violence so much as a sense of community and the excitement of challenging the police.

1. Summarise the data shown in **Source A**. **[4 marks: 4 AO2]**

*Make **two** points about the data. It is vital that you quote actual figures from the graph and draw conclusions from them (or you are not 'summarising' the data, only restating it). For example, 20-29 year-olds receive the most banning orders from football matches, but compare them to other age groups who are similar or very different.*

2. With reference to **Source B**, explain **two** ethical problems with covert participant observations. **[6 marks: 2 AO1 + 4 AO2]**

Write a couple of sentences about each reason. You might focus on deceiving people or the integrity or safety of the researcher. You need to support each reason with an example from the source – a really good idea is to quote something from the source.

3. With reference to **Source A**, explain why respondent validation would be useful to understand this data better. **[10 marks: 4 AO2 + 6 AO3]**

Write two short paragraphs, one about a problem with the validity of the data (such as fans believing they were only bystanders when someone else carried out an offence) and one about how respondent validation could alter the findings. You need to support each reason with an example from the source – a really good idea is to quote a number (or approximate number) from the graph.

4. Using **Source B** and your wider sociological knowledge, explain and evaluate using ethnography to study groups in conflict with the police. **[25 marks: 5 AO1 + 5 AO2 + 15 AO3]**

*Write four paragraphs/arguments – two strengths and two weaknesses of ethnography would work well. Each paragraph should introduce a sociological idea with an example or comparison from Source B. Each paragraph should finish off with a developed evaluation (see **Chapter 4** for this). For example, you could write about ethnography allowing the researcher to empathise with the group being researched and see through bragging, but also how ethnography tends to be subjective and time consuming.*

In questions 2-3 you can pick up the AO1 marks from using sociological terminology and relating things to sociological debates (e.g. Positivism vs Interpretivism, ethical conflicts). Named sociologists and studies aren't particularly important.

Question 4 is a full essay in which you are invited to deploy *"your wider sociological knowledge"* so famous sociologists definitely belong in your answer and a comparison to **Mead**'s ethnography or **Weber**'s theories would also help.

KEY RESEARCH

The studies in this guide are taken from material already presented in **1A: Socialisation, Culture & Identity** or else material that will be introduced in **2B: Understanding Social Inequalities**. The material from 2B is indicated by the * symbol. For each study, I include the key terms, a Perspective (if relevant) and the particular topics it is linked to.

Bourdieu (1984): *Distinction*, cultural capital, habitus; **Positivism**, questionnaire; p23

Correll (2017)*: Small Wins Model; gender equality in work; pilot studies, reflexivity; p33

Durkheim (1897): *Suicide*; comparative method, Functionalism, **Positivism**, statistics; p13

Gentleman (2009)*: study of care home for the elderly; **Interpretivism**, case study, observations, interviews; p51, 53, 60, 62, 68

Hecht et al (2020)*: *Elites Pulling Away*; social mobility, meritocracy; **Mixed Methods**, official statistics, longitudinal, interviews; p31, 35, 36, 38, 40, 46, 48, 60

Jones et al (2010)*: early retirement, quasi-subjects; **Interpretivism**; p36

Martin & Blinder (2020)*: *Biases At The Ballot Box*; racist bias in voting; **Positivist**, questionnaire; p59

McIntosh (1968): *The Homosexual Role*; **Interpretivism**, questionnaires, interviews; p24

Messner & Cooky (2021)*: women in TV sports, longitudinal, quantitative & qualitative; **Positivist**, content analysis; p38, 39, 65

Moore & Conn (1985)*: *Disguised: A True Story*; disguised as 'Old Pat'; **Ethnography**, observation, longitudinal; p64

Murray (1984): *Losing Ground*; unemployment, underclass, New Right; **Positivism**, statistics; p13

Parsons (1959): *The Social Structure of the Family*; gender roles, Functionalism; **Positivism**; p21

Sewell et al. (2021)*: *Commission for Racial & Ethnic Disparities*; social policy, Functionalism; **Positivism**; p28

Weber (1905): *The Protestant Ethic & the Spirit of Capitalism*; Social Action, Interactionism, **Interpretivism**, p19

Wilkinson & Pickett (2009)*: *The Spirit Level*; inequality & happiness, social policy; **Positivism**, statistics; p30, 32

Willis (1977): *Learning to Labour*; social class, education, employment, Marxism; **Ethnography**, observation, case study; p22, 46, 53, 68

FURTHER RESEARCH

These studies are less central to any argument. Some of them just reference a useful piece of terminology or a quote.

Atkinson (1968): *Discovering Suicide*; criticises Durkheim's statistics for being socially constructed, p19

Bryman (1988): problems with respondent validation; p35

Comte (1848): coins the terms 'Positivism' and 'Sociology'; p13

Freeman (1983): criticises Mead (1928) p64

Friedan (1963): *The Feminine Mystique*; criticises Parsons' view of gender; p21

Johnson & Duberley (2003): argues reflexivity leads to paralysis, p19

May (1993): triangulation is not a *"panacea,"* p67

Mead (1935): *Sex & Temperament in Three Primitive Societies*; pioneers ethnography; p62

Williams (2000): three types of generalisability; p24

Worsley (1977): defines social problems as causing *"public friction and private misery,"* p40

UNDERSTANDING SOCIAL INEQUALITIES: CONTENT

What's this topic about?

This introduces you to the main sociological theories about inequality and differences in society, in particular why inequalities exist, what can be done about them and how they should be defined and measured.

This should help you answer some important questions:

- What is Inequality in society: is it a fact of life that drives people to excel, a necessary evil or something that makes all our relationships oppressive and unjust?
- Why is there Inequality: does it derive from people's innate differences or is it something imposed on people in order to secure privileges for some people at the expense of others?
- What should be done about Inequality: do we need to accept our differences or is this a social evil that must be removed at any cost?

Inequality & Difference

Difference refers to the qualities and abilities that some people have but others don't. Some people are tall, some short; some people have perfect eyesight, others need spectacles; some people are the children of wealthy parents but others are born into poverty.

Inequality is a **social construction** applied to these differences. For example, having or not having freckles is a difference, but no great social meaning is attached to it; no one loses their job or gets turned away from shops because of freckles. Being intelligent is a difference that has great social meaning attached to it and opportunities are given to people who can demonstrate their intelligence (through their qualifications) and doors are closed to people who cannot. Wealth is a social construct too, since society decides what can be bought and how much money matters to your status in other people's eyes.

You can see that inequalities are socially constructed because the differences that societies values vary from culture to culture. In India, the caste system is a very powerful source of inequality, but that system does not exist in America. In tribal cultures, who your ancestors are affects how others judge you; in individualist cultures, like the UK, you are more likely to be judged on your job, your qualifications and your social class.

Because culture is the way it is, there is a tendency for people who share a culture **to view inequalities as natural differences**; for example, in the UK we tend to assume that school and university qualifications distinguish people who are naturally intelligent. Sociologists question whether these inequalities really *are* based on natural differences or whether they are **social constructs** – for example, unintelligent people who go to top schools and benefit from expert tutors can get qualifications, but clever people without those advantages might not.

CHAPTER FIVE – PATTERNS & TRENDS

This first part of the course is called '**What are the main trends in social inequality & difference?'** so the first task is to think about some definitions. This is done through the broad Perspectives of Consensus, Conflict and Social Action introduced earlier in the A-Level.

Inequality of Outcomes

This refers to the way wealth and material goods are distributed unequally. For example, some people earn big wages while others are on the minimum wage. Some people are homeless or live in slums while others live in big mansions.

A common response to this is that some people **deserve** those big salaries because they do important or difficult jobs and other people **deserve** to live in those mansions because they bought them with money that had saved up over the years. This is a common response to inequality, which is to claim it is **justified** because it reflects important differences. Some people are talented and hard-working, other people are lazy and unskilled: that's a **difference in ability** that results in unequal living conditions.

> **Research:** You should recognise this as the argument for a **Meritocracy** put forward by **Davis & Moore (1945)** – c.f. **1A: Socialisation, Culture & Identity**: look back on your notes and link the ideas; also c.f. p136

AO2 ILLUSTRATION: THE GLOBAL NORTH & SOUTH

A global example of the inequality of conditions is the divide between the 'Global North' which is wealthy and the 'Global South' which is not. The divide is roughly along the equator (in fact, about 30° North of the equator – see the **Brandt Line**, *below*), with the Northern Hemisphere containing the world's rich countries and the Southern Hemisphere the poor ones (with Australia being the big exception). The North contains just a quarter of the world's population but generations 80% of its income and owns 90% of its manufacturing industries.

In the 21st century, **globalisation** has led to economic growth in the BRICS countries (Brazil, Russia, India, China, South Africa) of which three (Brazil, India, South Africa) are in the Global South. India is still home to the largest concentration of poor people in a single country but it has a large and well-off middle class and a very rich elite. These complications prompt critics to argue that the Global North/South distinction no longer reflects reality.

*Looking ahead, you will study **Globalisation** as part of **3A: Globalisation & the Digital Social World**: make sure you refer to the emergence of the BRICS countries in that part of the Exam and use the research from Paper 3 as part of your study of Inequality.*

RESEARCH PROFILE: BRANDT (1980)

The former German Chancellor **Willy Brandt** chaired a committee that produced the **'Brandt Report' (1980).** The Report argues for a huge gap in the standard of living between the Global North and South. Brandt argues for more cooperation between North and South so that we can *"build a world in which sharing, justice, freedom and peace might prevail."*

Brandt calculated the GDP (Gross Domestic Product, the amount of money generated by businesses) in each country and drew the 'Brandt Line' to show the difference between the high-GDP North and the low-GDP South (excluding wealthy Australia and New Zealand).

The Brandt Line (1980)

The Brandt Line is still used to illustrate the North-South Divide although China is considered to be north of the line today. China is predicted to become the world's largest economy by 2030 with India in 3rd place behind the USA (source: **Centre for Economics & Business Research (CEBR), 2020**).

Inequality of Opportunities

This refers to the way **life chances** (p99) are unequally distributed. Some people receive a top education, enjoy good medical services and a healthy diet and are treated fairly by the criminal justice system. Other people have poor schools – if they have the option of going to school at all – and face disease and malnutrition or else discrimination and harassment.

A common response to this is that inequality of opportunities can be addressed by **redistributive taxation**. This means wealthy people pay more tax and prosperous countries give more aid and this is spent to improve the **life chances** of less fortunate people (e.g. through benefits, state healthcare and through foreign aid programmes). However, there's no agreement on how much money should be redistributed this way and, in any event, money might not be the only problem.

A major cause of inequality of opportunities is **discrimination** and people can be discriminated against for their social class, race, gender or age as well as things like their disabilities, sexuality or religion. Discrimination doesn't just involve holding negative attitudes; it includes practices and processes in the way institutions work that favour some people and disadvantage others, such as offering medical advice only in English or not offering promotions to women who have taken time off to have a baby.

Research: You can link this to the idea of **Social Reproduction** proposed by **Pierre Bourdieu** (**1984**, *c.f.* p23): look back on your notes and link the ideas to inequality.

AO2 ILLUSTRATION: THE OLD SCHOOL TIE

The 'old school tie' refers to the distinctive ties worn by students at the prestigious British Public Schools like Eton, Harrow and Westminster. These are fee-paying schools that attract children from the wealthiest families. Former-students tend to recognise and respect each other, so 'the Old School Tie' takes on another meaning of the ties that bind these former-students together and make them do each other favours. It is also called 'the Old Boys Network.'

The advantages of this sort of elite education go beyond good grades. Public school students are 1000 times more likely to get into Oxford or Cambridge University than students on **free school meals (FSM)**. Only 6% of the UK population attend such schools but they make up 74% of judges and 32% of Members of Parliament (MPs); they earn 7% more on average than people who went to state schools. In 2019, Boris Johnson became the 5th Eton-educated Prime Minister since 1945 and 64% of his cabinet were privately educated too (*c.f.* p118).

Aerial view of Eton College (prestigious UK public school)

RESEARCH PROFILE: RIVERA (2015)

Lauren Rivera studied the 'Old Boys Network' in the USA in *Pedigree: How Elite Students Get Elite Jobs* **(2015)**. Rivera interviews 32 university students applying for top jobs in **banking, consultancy and law** (the 'elite professional services' or **EPS** jobs) and 120 interviewers from those firms who discuss with her what they are looking for (anonymously).

She also carries out a participant observation by joining the human resources (HR) department at a top consultancy firm, which she gives the fictional name of Halt Halliday.

Rivera discovers a **'double filter'** in operation to exclude candidates. Candidates are not considered unless they come from Ivy League universities (the top American colleges, similar to Oxford & Cambridge in the UK) and the Ivy League universities favour students from the top private schools. Rivera quotes one law firm interviewer saying: *"Number One people go to Number One schools."*

The second filter is recruiting candidates who *"fit"* which means sharing similar hobbies, interests and outlooks to the interviewers. This tends to exclude applicants who are female, non-White and who did the 'wrong' extra-curricular activities. However, female and Black applicants who made it to the interview stage tended to be offered *higher* salaries.

Rivera's research was carried out before the **Global Financial Crisis** of **2008** and does not take into account the new EPS employers who are **Tech companies** and who tend to focus on ability rather than cultural background. Her findings link to **Weber**'s idea of **social closure** (p166).

The 40-Mark Essay

You need to make 5 discussion points in your 40-mark essay, but the distinction between inequality of outcomes and opportunities can *always* be the first one – and possibly the first two (making a point about inequality of outcomes then a second about inequality of opportunities).

You need to relate your point specifically to the question, which might be about inequalities relating to **class** (p91), **ethnicity** (p111), **gender** (females or males, p102) or **age** (the elderly or the young, p123).

The **Global North vs South** is a great AO2 point for addressing class (the South is poor) or ethnicity (the South is non-White). The **Old School Tie** is good for addressing class (expensive schools are for the wealthy) as well as gender and ethnicity (Rivera finds women and non-Whites are disadvantaged by the double filter).

You then need to evaluate your point. Fortunately, inequality by outcome works as a criticism of opportunities and inequality of opportunities works as a criticism of focusing on outcomes. The Global North vs South can be criticised for being simplistic and out-of-date, given the economic rise of the BRICS countries; **Rivera's study** is out of date since the research was carried out before the **Global Financial Crisis (GFC) of 2008** and might not generalise to new elite Tech jobs or elite employers in other countries.

PERSPECTIVES ON PATTERNS & TRENDS

Views on the meaning of patterns and trends vary from Perspective to Perspective.

CONSENSUS PERSPECTIVE: FUNCTIONALISM & NEW RIGHT

Functionalism (p134) tends to focus on **differences** rather than inequalities, mostly because Functionalists believe that biological differences between humans influence social behaviour. This means where critics would see the inequality in some people earning more money than others, Functionalists see a difference in talent and hard work resulting in some people *deserving* more money than others.

Functionalists aren't entirely blind to inequality: they recognise that life isn't fair. However, Functionalists usually focus on **inequalities of opportunities** (p83) and argue that something should be done about housing, healthcare and education so that everyone gets the same chance to succeed. They recognise that, because of differences in ability, there is nothing to be done about **inequalities of outcome** (p82).

The **New Right** (*c.f.* p141) can be viewed as an offshoot of Functionalism that focuses on how a strategy to fix inequalities of opportunity – the Welfare State and benefits paid to the unemployed – has backfired to create a delinquent **Underclass**. Supporters of the New Right tend to be much more hostile to attempts to 'fix' inequality by state benefits, which they see as creating a 'Benefits Trap' that only deepens inequality and makes it permanent.

This broad Perspective supports the idea of **Meritocracy** (p135) but opposes **positive discrimination** (p88) and government interference generally.

> **Research:** You were introduced to the **New Right** and **Charles Murray**'s views on the Underclass back in **1A: Socialisation, Culture & Identity** and in **1B** if you studied **Families** or **Youth Subcultures** – refer back to those notes.

AO2 ILLUSTRATION: GRAMMAR SCHOOLS

Grammar Schools are a type of **selective school** in England & Wales that only admit pupils who can pass an entrance exam known as the **Eleven Plus** (because most students are aged 11 when they sit it). The exam is supposed to measure innate academic ability and students need to score 80-85% to pass. Grammar Schools have a particular focus on preparing students for university.

With the focus on innate academic ability, Grammar Schools are often supported by Functionalists and the New Right as being a very **meritocratic** approach to education. Although they are a minority now, Grammar Schools were common in the 1950s and '60s. This was a time of great **social mobility** in the UK and Grammar Schools have been linked to this trend.

Supporters argue that bringing back Grammar Schools would increase social mobility, because bright children from disadvantaged backgrounds could pass the Eleven Plus and get a superior education from these *"beacons of excellence."* Critics argue Grammar Schools deepen inequality, because middle class families are better able to get their children into Grammar Schools (e.g. hiring tutors to prepare their children for the exam) so the poor do not really benefit from them.

Critics argue schools like this should be scrapped

CONFLICT PERSPECTIVE: MARXISM & FEMINISM

The Conflict Perspective distrusts the idea that social inequalities are rooted in biological differences. Instead, they argue that **inequalities of outcome** are created entirely by **inequalities of opportunity**, so if the opportunities could be shared more equally, the outcomes would be equal too. This means the current inequalities of outcome mean that the UK is an unjust place.

Marxists (*c.f.* p148) view the idea of **meritocracy** as a dangerous myth – it is **ruling class ideology** to persuade people that the inequalities going on are justified and necessary. For example, poorer students who cannot get into Grammar Schools regard themselves as stupid and do not see their failure as a problem with the system.

Feminists (*c.f.* p158) are particularly opposed to the idea that gender differences (e.g. the **Gender Pay Gap**, p102) are due to biological differences between men and women. They argue that Patriarchy **subordinates women** and offers them fewer life chances (e.g. the **Glass Ceiling**, p103).

Marxists and Feminists recommend tackling inequalities of outcome directly – *making* everybody equal rather than just giving them equal chances. Policies like **positive discrimination** (known in the USA as **affirmative action**) force companies or universities to take on a proportion of people (a 'quota') who are female, from poor backgrounds or from ethnic minorities.

AO2 ILLUSTRATION: POSITIVE ACTION VS POSITIVE DISCRIMINATION

Positive discrimination is controversial because it is still a type of discrimination, just in favour of a group that normally suffers negative treatment. For example, a university might have two candidates for a course, one with good grades from a Grammar School or Public School but the other with worse grades from an ordinary state school: positive discrimination would give the place to the *weaker* student. This reduces **inequality of outcome** but critics argue this is unfair and point out that the weaker student is more likely to fail a course they were not suitable for.

Positive action involves choosing between candidates for a job or a course in a fair way, but helping candidates with **protected characteristics** (e.g. disability, ethnicity, gender, religion, etc.) overcome their obstacles. For example, this includes offering translation services, childcare facilities or disabled access. The **'extra time'** some candidates get in exams is a type of positive action. This reduces the **inequalities of opportunity** by creating a 'level playing field.'

For some people, life is an uphill struggle (photo: stumayhew)

Research: Find out examples of positive discrimination, quotas and positive action today

SOCIAL ACTION PERSPECTIVE: WEBERIANISM

You were introduced to the Social Action Perspective in **1A: Socialisation, Culture & Identity** in the form of **Interactionism** and learned that **Max Weber (1864-1920, p165)** pioneered this idea in Sociology. Weber's ideas resemble Marx's ideas in some ways (such as focusing on the **importance of social class** and the **destructive effects of Capitalism**) but Weber argues that individuals have a lot more **autonomy** (individual power) than Marx gives them credit for.

Weber introduces the phrase **'life chances'** to describe **inequalities of opportunity** so **Weberianism** (*c.f.* p165) focuses on the factors that increase or decrease a person's life chances, including things like their own talents as well as their social network and **market situation** – how easy they find it to get paid for their abilities.

You could view Weberianism as a sort of 'half-way house' between Functionalism and Marxism. Weber accepts that individuals have talents and skills (which are meaningful **differences**) but recognises that your social circumstances affect whether or not people can leverage those abilities to improve their situation (which produces **inequality**).

Weberianism is also a **micro-Perspective** (micro means small) which focuses on how small groups of people or individuals can make a difference and bring about change, as opposed to Consensus and Conflict which are **macro-Perspectives**, focused on how individuals are defined by their membership of large groups and shaped by social structures beyond their control – the macro-Perspectives (macro means large) are sometimes called **structuralist Perspectives** in contrast to Social Action.

AO2 ILLUSTRATION: THE TRADE UNION MOVEMENT

Organised labour is when people working in the same job combine together to influence their employers, usually to demand better wages or better working conditions. Since the 18th century, workers have formed organisations called **Trade Unions** to help do this. The greatest power of a trade union is to call on all its members to **go on strike** until the employer meets their demands.

Throughout history, trade unions have been banned by some governments and strike action met with brutal force. On the other hand, trade unions themselves have sometimes behaved aggressively, such as picket-lines showing hostility towards strike-breakers (workers who continue to go to work during a strike, nicknamed 'scabs').

The peak of trade union membership in the UK was in 1979. In that year, known as the '**Winter of Discontent**,' strikes closed hospitals and led to rubbish piling up in the street. The Conservative Government of **Margaret Thatcher** (p141) entered a violent conflict with the National Union of Miners and passed laws to limit the power of unions to call strikes. In 2020, trade union membership in the UK stood at half what it was in 1979.

Trade unions are important for a **Weberian** view of inequality, because they enable individuals with little power to band together as a **'party'** (p166). The decline in trade union membership could be interpreted as part of increasing inequality (since workers have less power) or as a result of decreasing inequality (since workers don't feel the same need to band together in this way).

Trade Unions are also supported by the Marxist Perspective as a way for working class people to **resist** Capitalism and Feminists support them when they campaign for the rights of women in the workplace. Functionalists are more suspicious of trade unions as a disruptive force, but even they recognise that workers need to have representatives in their negotiations with employers.

Research: Find out more about current trade unions, the Winter of Discontent or the 1980s strikes and the Thatcher government's action against strikers

A picket discourages strike breakers from going to work (photo: Roger Blackwell)

The 40-Mark Essay

The difference between two Perspectives can often be a good discussion point (of the five you need to make) in a 40-mark essay. For example, the difference between Consensus and Conflict on whether patterns of inequality reflect social injustice or differences in ability; or the difference between Social Action and Conflict on whether individuals are being ignored by just focusing on patterns of inequality for large groups.

You need to relate your point specifically to the question, which might be about inequalities relating to **class** (p91), **ethnicity** (p111), **gender** (females or males, p102) or **age** (the elderly or the young, p123).

Grammar Schools make a great AO2 point for addressing class (linked to social mobility) and age (since school students are young). **Positive Action and Positive Discrimination** can be applied to class, gender, ethnicity or age, if you have a good example. **Trade Unionism** applies to discussions of class.

You need to evaluate your point. Fortunately, the Perspectives all criticise each other. **Functionalism** argues that the other Perspectives ignore genuine (and biological) differences in ability which reflect a successful **meritocracy** (p135). **Marxism** and **Feminism** argue that the other Perspectives overstate the importance of individuals and their talents compared to the structural injustice that affects everyone. **Weberianism** draws attention to how individuals need a supportive social network to achieve equality, but that network is made up of individuals with their own autonomy.

PATTERNS & TRENDS: A TOOLKIT

You are expected to know about four main types of patterns/trends and could be asked to focus on **work and employment** (the economic side of inequality), **social life** (such as exclusion, discrimination and abuse) and **life chances** (the opportunity to improve your situation, including social mobility).

- **Work & Employment:** includes the chances of getting a job, the wages you get paid, the working conditions you have to put up with and your chance of getting a promotion; in a true **meritocracy** (p135) these conditions should reflect your talent, qualifications and hard work, with the best qualified people getting the nest jobs and the hardest and most talented workers getting the promotions.
- **Social Life:** includes your freedom to travel and join social groups without being excluded, harassed or discriminated against; it includes aspects like mental health, marriage and family life – ideally everyone should have access to all of these things unless they deliberately forfeit them (e.g. by committing crimes or behaving antisocially).
- **Life chances:** includes your access to good healthcare, good education, safe and secure accommodation as well as things like healthy diet and exercise; without these things, your chance of having successful employment or social life goes down.

INEQUALITY OF SOCIAL CLASS

Social class is a type of **social stratification**, which means a way of separating people in a society into a hierarchy of power and importance, with the (supposedly) most valued members of society at the top and going down to the least valued at the bottom. Social class divides people into groups (classes) based on the type of work they do, which also impacts on their income, their housing and their education.

Karl Marx original divides society into a small but powerful **ruling class** (the **bourgeoisie**) and a large but exploited **working class** (the **proletariat**). Marx also added the **petite bourgeoisie** (or **petty bourgeoisie**) who were shopkeepers and small business owners with enough wealth to rise above the rest of the ruling class, but not enough power to join the true ruling class. This led to the tripartite distinction of **upper class**, **middle class** and **working class** which is still influential.

Research: You were introduced to social class and different ways of measuring it back in **1A: Socialisation, Culture & Identity**, including the Great British Class Survey and the 21st century social classes proposed by **Savage et al. (2013)** – refer back to those notes.

Social class is **socially constructed** and, according to the writer **George Orwell (1941)**, the UK (and specifically England) is *"the most class-ridden society under the sun."* Class is indicated by signs such as dress and hair style, accent, pastimes (including the sports you prefer, such as middle class rugby and cricket compared to working class football) and shopping habits.

Max Weber (p166) uses the term **social closure** to describe how classes try to prevent outsiders from entering their group and enjoying their privileges and features like accents help enforce social closure by marking out people who 'don't belong.'

AO2 ILLUSTRATION: ACCENTS & SUPERMARKETS

British people often judge social class by someone's accent. 76% of UK employers admit to discriminating against applicants based on accent (source: **Chartered Institute of Personnel & Development, 2016**). **Helen Magowan (2016)** ranks accents in a 'pyramid' with the **Queen's English** at the top: an accent with a lot of status but spoken by very few people. Beneath that is **Received Pronunciation (RP)**, which is the accent of most TV presenters and politicians: it is still in the minority, but it carries a lot of status. **Regional accents** come next so long as they are not too strong, then the many **local accents** are at the bottom, firmly indicating the place a person comes from and their working-class links.

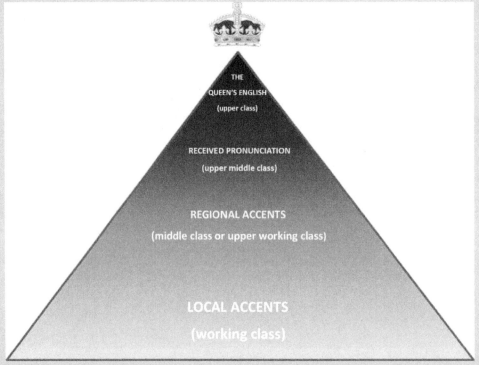

Class is so ingrained into British culture that even our supermarkets follow the class system. At the posh end, Waitrose has 47% of customers from the A/B classes (of the **NRS Scale**), followed by Sainsbury's (34%), Marks & Spencer (22%) and Tesco (21%), whereas Lidl has 54% of the D/E classes with Somerfield (50%) close behind (source: **Verdict Research, 2004**).

You might think this is the same everywhere, with some chains offering expensive goods for posh customers and others offering cheaper versions, but apparently not: in France, chains like Carrefour, Leclerc and Leader Price aren't associated with different classes of customers.

Social Class: Work & Employment

Marx argues that the class system originates in work, with the ruling class owning the land and the factories and the working classes labouring on the land or in the factories for a wage. Functionalists instead see a **meritocracy** (p135), with the majority of jobs requiring little skill or responsibility and therefore being poorly paid, but as jobs get more demanding fewer people can do them and the wages go up.

Some jobs certainly do seem to require skills that not many people have (e.g. brain surgeons) but it isn't clear that there are rare skills involved in being a banker or the CEO of a big company to justify the huge salaries. Similarly, some poorly paid jobs are unskilled (like stacking shelves) but many low-wage jobs actually require a lot of skill (like hairdressers) or involve unpleasant duties that few people are willing to do (like abattoir workers).

Despite this, 1% of UK adults earn 14% of the nation's income and this share has grown steadily since the 1980s, when it was only just over 6% (source: **Institute for Fiscal Studies, 2019**).

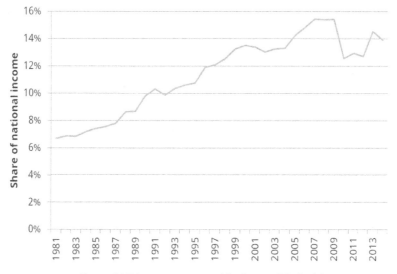

Share of UK income accounted for by top 1% of adults

To be in the top 1%, you need a taxable income of £160,000 a year (in 2019). To be in the top 0.1% you need to earn £650,000 – and of the top 0.1%, a half live in London.

The gap between the rich and the poor is widening by other measures too. In 2020, the median household income in the UK was £29,900 and this was a rise of 7% since 2011. However, the poorest fifth of the population did not keep up and their income fell by 3.8% per year between 2017-2020. Meanwhile, the income of the richest fifth increased between 2011-2020 by 0.7% a year, to a median household income of £62,400 (source: **Office of National Statistics, 2020**).

Research: Find out where you and your family fit in on national income by visiting
https://ifs.org.uk/tools_and_resources/where_do_you_fit_in

At the other end of the scale is **poverty**. Poverty can be measured in different ways:

1. **Subsistence poverty:** not having enough money to feed yourself and your family. However, this measure doesn't take into account **what** you are eating (for example, is someone subsisting if they can feed themselves, but only by living on stuff that is cheap but unhealthy, like Pot Noodles?).

2. **Relative poverty:** not having as much money as most of the rest of the population; in the UK, you are in relatively poverty if you earn 60% less than the median household income (whatever that is at the time). However, this is not a stable measure (a family might go in and out of poverty as the national average changes) and doesn't reveal standard of living (if the national average is very high, a family in poverty might still be pretty comfortable).

3. **Perceived poverty:** not having enough money to own or do things that are perceived as essential; this is based on **Mack & Lansley**'s *Poor Britain* **(1985)** which uses survey data to calculate what British people perceive as essential and defines poverty as being forced to 'exist' rather than 'live.' However, this is also an unstable measure (e.g. the invention of smart phones suddenly created a new 'essential' that placed a lot of people in poverty if they couldn't afford one – you will consider this as part of the **digital divide** in **3A: Globalisation & the Digital Social World).**

4. **State minimum poverty:** this is defined as the minimum amount of money the state pays out on benefits, so this ought to be the lowest income anyone in the country gets. However, it ignores people who aren't eligible for benefits or are homeless as well as the question of whether the state minimum is actually enough to support people.

Using measures of **relative poverty**, 14 million people are in poverty in the UK – more than one in five of the population, up by 400,000 and 300,000 respectively over the past five years. Poverty is linked to **unemployment**, but there is a growing problem of **in-work poverty**: families which experience poverty despite at least one member being in work. 56% of people in poverty in the UK are in working families, compared to 39% 20 years previously; working single parent families account for 3 in 10 of households in poverty (source: **Joseph Rowntree Foundation, 2018**).

AO2 ILLUSTRATION: FOOD BANKS

Food Banks are run by charities and religious groups. They collect donations of food from the public and from businesses. Food is prepared as food parcels to be collected by families. To take advantage of a Food Bank, you normally need a voucher, issued by schools, social workers or health visitors or through Citizens Advice. The biggest network of food banks is the **Trussell Trust**.

Food Banks are increasing and there are more Food Banks in the UK than McDonald's restaurants (source: **FullFact, 2019**). The 2020-21 Coronavirus Pandemic increased the need for food banks and the Trussell Trust handed out 50% more food parcels in 2020 than the previous year. Food Banks are reporting more use by middle-income families (i.e. those with mortgages and cars) as low wages place working families in '**food poverty**.'

RESEARCH PROFILE: HECHT ET AL. (2020)

Katharina Hecht and her colleagues examine **social mobility** in the UK through an analysis of a **longitudinal study** (p37) by the **Office for National Statistics (ONS)** going back to the 1970s. Social mobility is the rate at which people move between class; specifically, the proportion of people born into working class backgrounds who end up as middle class adults. Hecht's paper is called *Elites Pulling Away* and she claims that *"in the mid-1970s, the UK was among the most equal countries, but became one of the most unequal of the rich nations by the early 1990s."* The top 1% almost doubled their share of national income from 7% in 1981 to 13% in 2015.

The ONS originally studied a number of cohorts, the oldest born 1955-61 and first surveyed in 1971, aged 10-16, and again in 1991, aged 30-36.

Hecht defines the elite as the richest 1% in terms of income. She examines **'long range mobility'** (i.e. reaching the top 1% from being born into the poorest backgrounds) and finds that 1 in 5 men with elite occupations who were born 1955-61 benefited from long range mobility, only 1 in 8 of those born 1975-81 did so. She finds that London is *"a crucial arena for elites"* but that people who join the London elites after coming from outside London are likely to have been born into a privileged background anyway.

Hecht conducted a **mixed methods** study of 30 top-earners, using interviews and a short questionnaire, and notes that they view themselves as upper middle class (54%), rather than upper class (6%). They believe strongly in meritocracy and link their success to hard work rather than background, despite the fact that increasingly they come from privileged backgrounds. She calls this the **'meritocratic paradox'** that growing inequality is accompanied by a shift towards *more* meritocratic beliefs.

The study seems to reveal **social closure** taking place and links to similar findings from **Rivera**'s study of recruitment into elite jobs (p85) and a **Weberian** explanation of inequality (p165).

Research: Find out about food banks in your community and the opening or closing of local businesses that affect the livelihoods of working-class people

Social Class: Social Life

Social class doesn't only affect your earning and social mobility. It can affect other areas of social life, leading to **social exclusion**, which is when people are unable to participate fully in society because of their background. Social exclusion is often due to **economic deprivation** – taking part in social activities often costs money – but it can also be due to **discrimination**, lack of **awareness of opportunities** or a **sense of unworthiness** ("I'm not good enough to go there and do that").

The OCR Specification expects students to consider evidence *"from a range of areas of social life"* so we will look at differences in **marriage and divorce**, **travel and leisure** and **participation in democracy**.

Marriage & Divorce

Marriage is declining and divorces has increased. Marriages between opposite sex couples have declined by 42% since 1972 and the divorce rate is 33%, based on all marriages since 1964. Although divorces have been reducing, 2019 saw over 100,000 divorces, the largest rise since 1972 when 'no fault' divorces were introduced (source: **ONS, 2020**).

Alongside these overall trends, a clear **'Marriage Gap'** is emerging between working class and middle class families. 53% of births are to married parents, but 87% of those births are to high income families, compared to 24% to low income families. This gap opened up in the 1990s and has remained largely unchanged since (source: **ONS, 2015**). This means that children from poor backgrounds are much more likely to be born into single parent families while children from wealthy backgrounds tend to have both parents still married.

Of course, 'unmarried' doesn't necessarily mean that a child grows up without a father and 'married' doesn't necessarily mean **happily** married: children can be neglected or mistreated by married parents and raised with love and attention by single parents. Nonetheless, this difference in family background has an impact on **life chances** (p99) and is a central argument for the **New Right** (p141).

Another trend has been in **who** people choose to marry: 38% of women born in 1958 'married up' (e.g. by marrying their boss) but this fell to 16% among women born 1976-81, of whom 56% married into the same class and 26% a lower class (source: **IPPR, 2012**). Picking a partner who is from the same background as yourself is known as **assortative mating** and it makes sense during periods of economic stress and uncertainty – marriages are more likely to be happier when the couple share similar backgrounds – but it contributes to **social closure** (when the elites marry among themselves, p166) and reduces **social mobility**.

*The IPPR data is useful for evaluating **gender inequality** too (p102) because this change in marriage trends coincides with the arrival of 2nd Wave Feminism in UK culture.*

Travel & Leisure

Alcohol consumption varies by social class, with people from lower socio-economic groups consuming more alcohol, especially men (source: **WHO, 2020**). Excessive alcohol use leads to physical and mental ill health, which in turn affects **life chances** (p99).

Sport is another indicator of class differences. **Grant Jarvie (2006)** finds that the most popular sports among the AB social classes are cricket, skiing and tennis; among the DE classes the most popular are snooker/pool, fishing and walking; AB are most likely to participate in golf (33%), but C1 in football (32%); sports such as squash seem to be extremely elitist (39% for AB for only 5% for DE) whereas swimming and cycling are more democratic. **SportEngland's Active Lives Survey (2019)** reveals that people in lower socio-economic groups (LSEGs) are most likely to be inactive (33%); by contrast, people in professional or managerial jobs are the moist likely to be active (72%). This difference impacts on physical and mental health and has an effect on **life chances**.

When it comes to holidays, social classes ABC1 account for 69% of the domestic holidays taken in the UK, but DE just 12% (source: **Statista, 2019**).

For holidays abroad, visiting the USA is divisive, with 15% of C2DE respondents wanting to go there, but only 9% of ABC1 (source: **YouGov, 2016**). The popular destinations for people earning over £100K turn out to be China (15%) and India (8%) – but also Antarctica (5%). However, the most popular overseas destination by far for UK holidaymakers is Spain – 18 million UK tourists in a typical year and popular with working class families and young adults.

Holidays are a good indicator of **cultural capital** (*c.f.* **Bourdieu**'s theory in **1A: Socialisation, Culture & Identity**) and links to physical exercise, with the wealthy able to travel further and engage in more active and culturally prestigious pastimes.

Participation in Democracy

Social classes DE are more likely to vote Labour (47%) and AB vote Conservative (also 47%, source: **Ipsos MORI, 2017**). This is likely because Labour favours policies of increasing taxes on the rich and redistributing wealth through the Welfare State, which would benefit less economically successful groups; the Conservatives favour cutting taxes, which would benefit high earners who do not depend on the Welfare State.

Voter apathy is a problem. In the 2019 general election, only 67.3%% of the adult population voted – a big drop from regular turnout of over 80% in the 1950s. Significantly, the biggest drop in voting is among the poor. In the 2019 election, voting among the DE classes was 53% compared to 68% for the ABs (source: **Electoral Commission, 2019**).

An important feature of voting is that you must first be on the electoral register. Since the form to register is posted to your address, homeowners are much more likely to register to vote than renters, because people who rent move home more frequently. People who leave school without continuing in education are more likely to be unregistered.

It's not just voting. Poorer people are disengaged from other sorts of political activity, like creating or signing petitions, joining a protest, contacting their MP or boycotting products for political or ethical reasons.: 83% of ABs do these things but it drops to 41% for the DE social classes (source: **Hansard Society, 2019**).

This represents political disengagement of the working classes which risks becoming a vicious circle – as fewer working-class people vote, they see more politicians elected by the rich, so it seems there's less point in voting in the future. It is also a problem for the Labour Party, since the Conservatives have supporters who are much more likely to vote on the day of the election. **Paul Webb (2013)** argues the working classes are more likely to be **'stealth democrats'** who are disillusioned with mainstream politics but are more likely to get involved in **direct action** (e.g. street protests).

Research: Find out about online forums for democratic participation, such as petition sites like **38Degrees.org.uk** or **Change.org** – or about local politics, councillors, and MPs in your area

AO2 ILLUSTRATION: THE SPANISH PACKAGE HOLIDAY

In the 18th century, wealthy families sent their teenage sons on **'the Grand Tour'** of Europe to visit the sites of great civilisations and acquire **cultural capital**. In the 19th century, working class mill and factory workers had a (unpaid) holiday each summer called the **'Wakes Week'** and used it to travel to new seaside resorts like **Blackpool**. In the 1930s, all-inclusive holidays at parks like **Butlins** appeared, where poorer holidaymakers could be accommodated with entertainment on site. By 1975, most workers had a least a fortnight of paid holiday and 1979 was the first year where British people spent more on overseas holidays than holidaying in the UK.

Spain was the favourite destination, especially the **'Costas'** (the coasts, famous for their attractive beaches, most of which were named by travel companies!). Package tours, which include flights, food and hotels in one purchase, made these holidays affordable for working class tourists, whose UK money was valuable in relatively impoverished Spain. This led to **'British cantonments'**: resorts dominated by British tourists, British bars and restaurants and British culture, at the expense of Spanish culture (this is **cultural homogenisation**).

RESEARCH PROFILE: PRIETO-ARRANZ & CASEY (2014)

José Prieto-Arranz & Mark Casey carried out a **qualitative content analysis** (p65) of a popular TV sitcom **Benidorm** which began in 2007. The show features the lower working-class Garvey family who fund a holiday to Benidorm through benefit fraud: good-natured slob Mike Garvey, his sensible wife Janice, his foul-mouthed and over-tanned mother Madge, hyperactive son Michael and teenage daughter Chantelle who is a single mother.

The researchers analyse how the show represents working class families and the 'sun & sand' culture of the Spanish tourist industry. The Garveys are shown as lacking **cultural capital** (they ignore the local Spanish culture and treat Benidorm as *'Blackpool with sun'*). The Garveys are contrasted with a middle-class couple, the Weedons, who seek the authentic Spanish culture which is viewed with suspicion and incomprehension by the working class characters.

During the first 4 seasons, the working-class characters become more likeable; for example, Chantelle starts taking her responsibilities as a mother seriously. The show reinforces stereotypes about the culturally impoverished working classes but in other ways it celebrates their lifestyle as attractive and sincere compared to the unhappily married and dissatisfied Weedons.

The analysis only covers the first 4 seasons of ***Benidorm*** but the show continued for another 6 seasons, introducing new characters and plots. Moreover, the show was unexpectedly cancelled in 2018, so the analysis cannot explore later representations of class or where the creator, **Derren Litten**, intended to take the show.

Social Class: Life Chances

Max Weber introduced the concept of life chances. **Stephen Aldridge** (2004) suggests *"Life chances refer to the opportunities open to individuals to better the quality of life of themselves and their families."* People with more life chances get better jobs, experience freedom from discrimination, harassment and crime and live longer. People with few life chances end up stuck in dead end jobs, experience victimisation and suffer shortened life expectancy.

Life chances are connected to **employment** and **earnings** as well as factors like physical exercise and alcohol consumption. **Poor education** affects life chances as it restricts the type of jobs school leavers can do as well as their skills in other areas (such as using computer technology, speaking other languages or knowing their rights). A useful measure of whether a student comes from a deprived background is being eligible for **Free School Meals (FSM)**. According to the **Education Policy Institute (2020)**, children who are FSM for 80% of their time at school ('persistently disadvantaged') lag 20 months behind other students in their educational level and this gap has not closed since 2011.

During the 2020-21 Coronavirus Pandemic, school students were educated from home during lockdowns. 15% of teachers from deprived schools reported that more than a third of students lacked electronic access to school work compared to 2% at schools with more wealthy intake (source: **Sutton Trust, 2020**).

Life chances are also affected by health. People living in the most deprived 10% of areas spend nearly 20 fewer years in good health than those living in the wealthiest 10% and spend nearly a third of their lives in poor health, compared with only a sixth for people living in wealthy areas (source: **Public Health England, 2017**). There is a higher concentration of deprived areas in the north, creating a 'North-South Divide' in health inequalities and related life chances in England. The trend for health and life expectancy to improve with the wealth of your neighbourhood is known as the **'Marmot Curve'** (after the **2010 Marmot Review** that revealed it).

Mental health is important for life chances but harder to measure. Nevertheless, 86% of homeless people report mental health problems and this group is 14 times more likely to die by suicide than the general population (source: **Homeless Health Needs Audit, 2020**).

AO2 ILLUSTRATION: HOMELESSNESS

People become homeless for lots of reasons. There are social causes, such as poverty and unemployment; but also life events which push people into homelessness, such as when people leave prison, care or the armed forces with no home to go to. Women who escape a violent or abusive relationship may find themselves homeless as can children running away from abuse or neglect. A lack of life chances makes homelessness more likely, but homelessness also reduces life chances, since the homeless cannot easily claim benefits or apply for jobs and are at risk from crime, violence and exploitation.

According to the homelessness charity **Crisis**, the average age of death for the homelessness is 45 for men and 43 for women. People sleeping on the street are almost 17 times more likely to be victims of violence. Crisis carries out an annual survey to measure **core homelessness** (rough sleeping, living in sheds and garages, sofa surfing and being put up in hostels and B&Bs) and estimates the number of homeless peaked in England before the 2020-21 Coronavirus Pandemic, going up from 207,600 in 2018 to over 219,000 at the end of 2019.

RESEARCH PROFILE: WILKINSON & PICKETT (2009)

The Spirit Level (2009) is a book by **Richard Wilkinson & Kate Pickett** with the subtitle: *Why More Equal Societies Always Do Better*. The authors argue that inequality has negative effects on society: *"eroding trust, increasing anxiety and illness, encouraging excessive consumption."*

The researchers measure 11 health and social problems, such as drug abuse, obesity, teenage pregnancy, violence and community trust and they conclude that outcomes for these are significantly worse in unequal societies. Crucially, these patterns hold true whether those societies are rich or poor. They conclude that inequality makes humans feel stressed, leading to depression, smoking, overeating and violence. Conspicuous consumption includes buying fancy cars and luxury clothes, which serves no purpose except reassuring anxious people about their place in the hierarchy. *"In a more unequal society people are more violent, less public spirited, less likely to trust each other or to be involved in community life."*

Before the 2010 General Election, 75 MPs signed an 'Equality Pledge' to "support the case for policies designed to narrow the gap between rich and poor" and the Labour and Conservative leaders both cited the influence of *The Spirit Level* on their policies.

Wilkinson & Pickett were criticised by **Christopher Snowdon (2010)** for 'cherry picking' their data. For example, they ignore countries like South Korea (unequal but healthy) and they don't include charity donations or suicides, which would not fit their trends. For example, suicide rates are higher in more equal societies.

The 40-Mark Essay

You could be set a 40-mark question on inequality related to social class. However, you could also be set a question about inequality related to **work & employment**, **social life** or **life chances**, which would let you bring in ethnicity, gender and age as well. Finally, a question could be set about a Perspective on inequality and social class would be relevant to that (especially a question on **Functionalism**, **Marxism** or **Weberianism**).

An important evaluation issue for social class is the distinction between **inequality** and **difference**. 'Difference' is morally neutral: it's a statement of fact. 'Inequality' carries a moral judgement that a state of affairs is wrong and unjust and ought to be improved.

When you studied **1A: Socialisation, Culture & Identity**, you were introduced to **Davis & Moore (1945)** who argue that there is **stratification** in society, with people being matched to the jobs they are capable of and being paid according to their skills. This is the idea of a **Meritocracy** (p135), with the best qualified and most talented people being highly rewarded. If Davis & Moore are right about stratification, then the simple fact that people are paid differently for the work they do or have different educational outcomes is ***not*** proof that there is inequality going on.

According to this view, the gap between the rich and the poor doesn't matter so long as everyone is being appropriately rewarded for what they do and so long as the poorest people are earning enough to avoid misery.

This argument can be supported. Benefits for the poorest people increase over time, child mortality is dropping, lifespans are growing, exam results are improving; poor people are better fed, better housed and better educated than they were 50 years ago by most measures. Moreover, it's common for even the poorest families to have access to the Internet, own mobile phones and enjoy relatively low levels of crime. The number of people in **subsistence poverty** (p94) is dropping and it could be argued (e.g. by Right Wing critics) that **relative poverty** and **perceived poverty** aren't really 'poverty' at all – just people feeling unhappy with their lives because they're not as rich as they'd like to be.

The wealthy pay most of the taxes: a third of the entire UK tax revenue is paid by the 380,000 people who earn over £150,000 per year (source: **HMR&C, 2017**).

The **New Right** (p141) has a powerful argument that all efforts to fix inequality through the Welfare State have in fact made the life of the poorest people worse rather than better.

The argument against this is that the wealth of the rich is largely unearned (it is often based on owning property) and the jobs they do don't involve skills or talents that poorer people lack – while many of the lowest paid jobs are extremely difficult and demanding. Although the wealthy pay high taxes, they use accountants to find tax loopholes (tax avoidance, which is legal) so they only pay a fraction of the tax their wealth would otherwise demand.

Wilkinson & Pickett's ***The Spirit Level* (2009)** is important for arguing that inequality is undesirable ***even if*** society as a whole is wealthy.

INEQUALITY OF GENDER

The **Feminist** Perspective takes the inequalities experienced by women as its starting point. Historically, women have been second class citizens in the UK and throughout Europe: unable to inherit property, attend university, vote or hold political office and widely seen as inferior to men in their intelligence, maturity and decision-making. This began to change in the 20th century, when women were given key rights, such as voting, education and managing their own finances.

Work & Employment

Two important pieces of legislation in the UK are the **Equal Pay Act (1970)**, which requires women be paid the same as men for doing the same work, and the **Sex Discrimination Act (1975)**, which made it unlawful to discriminate against someone in the workplace, including training, promotion, dismissal or sexual harassment because of their sex or marital status. Both are incorporated into the **Equalities Act (2010)**.

Despite this, inequalities persist, such as the **Gender Pay Gap**. This is the continuing difference between the average pay of men and women in the same occupation. In 2017, the UK Government introduced the requirement that all companies employing more than 250 people report the earnings of male and female staff. Women earn almost a fifth (17.3%) less than men (source: **ONS, 2019**). The gap is closing (it was 17.8% in 2018) but at this rate it will take decades to achieve equal pay.

You have already learned that to be in the top 0.1% of earners you need to earn £650,000 – and of the top 0.1%, only 11% are female (source: **Institute for Fiscal Studies, 2019**).

Let's be clear: employers do **not** have different pay scales for men and women (that would be illegal) – so why do women end up earning less?

There are more men in senior roles than women: Top jobs earn higher salaries for men. This is known as **vertical segregation**. Social attitudes allow men to focus on their career by working long hours while women are expected to raise families and focus on the home. In the 21st century, 'always-on' technology (like email and texts) has extended the working day to 10 or 12 hours, but senior jobs rarely offer flexible or part-time working.

Caring responsibilities are shared unequally: If they have responsibilities for childcare, women often end up in part-time jobs (and often doing work below their actual skill levels) and miss out on opportunities for training and promotion. The gender pay gap increases after childbirth and, by the time their first child is 20, women's hourly wages are about a third below men's. The assumption that part-time work is women's 'choice' suggests that women are comfortable with earning less and takes the pressure off employers to do something about it.

Women work in low-paid jobs: Poorly paid occupations are those traditionally done by women and these often involve skills that are stereotyped as 'feminine' such as caring (e.g. nurses, teachers or shop assistants). In contrast, surgeons and engineers are viewed as 'masculine' jobs and are paid more. This separation of working roles is known as **horizontal segregation**.

Feminists argue that we need to restructure the workplace around women's circumstances: place more value on feminine skills (and pay those jobs that involve them more), ensure training and promotion for part-time staff and reorganise senior roles so they can be part-time too (such as job-sharing). However, **Catherine Hakim** (**2006**, p161) argues there will always be a number of important jobs that **cannot be 'domesticated'** in this way – for example, jobs that require a lot of travel at short notice.

AO2 ILLUSTRATION: THE GLASS CEILING AT THE BBC

The **'glass ceiling'** is a phrase used by Feminists to describe the invisible barrier that prevents women from achieving senior positions in any institution. It exists because of assumptions and attitudes about gender roles as well as the way work is structured around long hours, with part-time work being under-valued.

In 2017, there was an outcry when the BBC Annual Report revealed that the DJ **Chris Evans** was the top earner, being paid £2.2 million, while the highest-paid female star was **Claudia Winkleman**, who earned just £500,000. Two thirds of those earning over £150,000 were male. A group of female presenters, including **Emily Maitlis**, **Victoria Derbyshire** and **Claire Balding**, wrote an open letter calling on the BBC to close its gender pay gap. This gap was revealed to be 9.3%, which was better than the national average of 18% at the time.

In 2018, 6 male BBC stars (including **Jeremy Vine** and **John Humphrys**) agreed to pay cuts. Chris Evans quit the BBC. **Samira Ahmed** successfully claimed £700,000 in back-wages because a male presenter (Jeremy Vine) was paid more for presenting an equivalent show: she was paid £440 per episode for presenting *Newswatch*, Vine received £3,000 per episode for *Points Of View*.

The scandal was deeply embarrassing for the BBC but has led to changes. The BBC brought in pay rises for 700 female staff and changed its practices to ensure equal representation of male and female presenters.

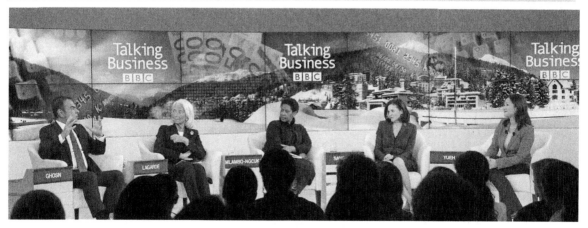

RESEARCH PROFILE: CORRELL (2017)

Shelley Correll piloted her 'Small Wins Model' to changing workplace practices so that they promote gender equality. She tested the approach over 3 years with several US tech companies. Correll focuses on **recruitment/training policies** and **unconscious bias training**.

Policies often aim to be unbiased but still disadvantage women. Correll gives the example of fire departments having a minimum height requirement, which screens out more women than men.

Unconscious bias often leads to women being passed over because their abilities are underestimated, or a role is viewed as inappropriate for a woman. **Unconscious bias training** identifies and challenges these views, but the effects tend to wear off quickly and senior workers sometimes feel threatened by criticism. Correll explains: *"Bias training can backfire, increasing bias; and formal procedures can be misused by decision makers or, worse, have gender biases built into their design."*

Correll combines the two approaches by offering bias training to employers while carrying out an audit of policies. The aim is to create objective performance checklists that eliminate bias from people using them. For example, at a mid-size tech company, managers tended to evaluate an employee's personality rather than their work; 14% of women were criticised by managers for being "too aggressive" and 8% of men for being "too soft." Correll introduced an employee score card to focus meetings on skills and accomplishments rather than judgments about personality. A year later, these figures dropped to 0% for women and 1% for mem.

Correll's approach shows how 'tweaking' working practices can have dramatic effects for women in the workplace. However, it does not address wider structural patterns of inequality, such as women working in low-paid part-time jobs.

Gender: Social Life

As with social class (p95), gender can lead to **social exclusion** due to **discrimination**, lack of **awareness of opportunities** or a **sense of unworthiness**. However, these inequalities do not always favour males. The OCR Specification expects students to consider evidence *"from a range of areas of social life"* so we will look at differences in **marriage and divorce**, **travel and leisure** and **participation in democracy**.

Marriage & Divorce

An important piece of legislation is the **Divorce Reform Act (1969)** which made it possible for couples to divorce due to the breakdown of the marriage, without having to prove 'fault' (such as evidence that their partner had cheated on them or assaulted them). In 1972, this produced a doubling of the number of UK divorces to 119,025. Over 60% of the people seeking divorce were women and this gender difference continuous and since the introduction of same sex marriages in 2013, the majority of same sex divorces are for female partnerships.

The tendency of women to seek divorce more often than men is unusual, since the petitioner pays more of the costs and men tend to have higher incomes. However, it might be that women are more proactive than men in getting out of a relationship that is no longer satisfactory, whereas men are inclined to 'bury their head in the sand.' Feminists point out that women experience violence in marriages, which explains why they are more likely to want to get out of them. The police in England & Wales receive 100 calls reporting domestic abuse every hour (source: **HMIC, 2015**) and 1.6 million women a year report being victims of domestic violence (source: **CSEW, 2019**).

Rape within marriage only became a crime in 1992, following a landmark court judgement that found a man (known as 'R') guilty of raping his wife, who was divorcing him at the time. However, a review of laws in 82 countries found ten countries that still do not recognise rape between married partners (source: **Equality Now, 2015**).

A clear difference in Perspectives exists regarding marriage and divorce. **Functionalists** view marriage positively and deplore the scale of divorces. They regard women as biologically fitted to the **expressive role** in marriage (**Parsons, 1955**) and claim women flourish best as homemakers and mothers. **Feminists** view marriage more negatively, regarding gender roles as **socially constructed** and **oppressive** towards women: marriage is a trap for women and an institution that benefits men more.

Travel & Leisure

Being male is strongly associated with risk-taking behaviour and in the past men have been more likely to smoke, binge drink or abuse drugs. In the UK, 15.9% of men smoke compared to 12.5% of women (source: **ONS, 2019**). Similarly, 29% of male adults drink alcohol a couple of times a week and 8% drink every day, compared to 23% and 4% of females (source: **Statistia, 2021**).

However, binge drinking is rising among young women, with 40.5% of 16-24 year-old women admitting to binge drinking in the previous week, compared to 34.4% of young men (source: **ONS, 2017**). Binge drinking is defined as 8 alcohol units for men (4 pints of beer or three-quarters of a bottle of wine) or six units for women. This rise has been linked to alcohol being advertised at women, with a focus on fruit-based beers and ciders which are marketed as low-calorie.

> **Research:** Link these figures with the phenomenon of **'Ladettes'** introduced in **1A: Socialisation, Culture & Identity**

Sport is another area of gender differences. 6.35 million males participate in sport for at least 150 minutes at least once a week, but only 4 million women. However, if fitness activities are considered, the figures are closer: 4.6 million males and 4.3 million females (source: **Statistia, 2021**). The difference might be in the competitiveness of sport, with women seeking out non-competitive fitness activities (gym classes, running, yoga, dance). **SportEngland's Active Lives Survey (2019)** reveals that men are more likely to be active (63%) than women (60%). This difference in physical activity impacts on physical and mental health and has an effect on **life chances**.

Gender and ethnicity **intersect** with participation in sport: all Black & Minority Ethnic groups are less likely to participant than White groups. This might be due to a lack of role models, since only 5% of coaches and only 7% of sports professionals are from BME groups (source: **SportEngland, 2019**). Culture might also be a factor; for example, 92% of South Asian women do not meet recommended levels of physical activity compared to 55% of all women.

In the past, women were also less mobile than men, travelling shorter distances by slower methods (walking and buses as opposed to cars or trains). Women are less likely to have a driving licence than men, although men are women are converging on this. Women are more likely to leave their job if it involves a long commute (source: **ONS, 2019**).

A factor often used to explain the lower mobility for women is fear of crime. For example, after the **2021 abduction and murder of Sarah Everard**, the Metropolitan Police advised women to stay at home or not go out alone, which was condemned by Feminists as a 'curfew' on women.

However, **Tilley & Houston (2016)** report that young women have overtaken men in mobility, largely because of a drop in male mobility due to increased IT use (meaning less travel for work), a rise in urban living (travel is shorter in cities) and the arrival of 'peak car' (male car use has stopped growing, but female car use is still increasing). The researchers also link this to the increasing independence and education of young women.

Participation in Democracy

In the UK, women attained the right to vote in 1918, although that was only for women over 30 who owned property. All adult women became able to vote in 1928. Part of the resistance to women voting was because of an assumption that women would be told who to vote for by their husbands or that women wouldn't be able to understand politics enough to cast a vote!

Instead, another 'gender gap' exists in voting. Throughout the 20th century, women were more likely to support the (Right wing) Conservatives and men support the (Left wing) Labour Party. Recently, this gap has reversed: in the 2019 General Election, 42% of women voted Conservative (compared to 47% of men) and 37% voted Labour (compared to only 29% of men). This might be because of the growing influence of **Feminism** (a Perspective supported by the Labour Party).

Women are more likely to identify as 'undecided' in voting polls before elections (18% compared with 10% of men) and select 'Don't Know' in political questionnaires. However, just as many women vote as men. In fact, they are slightly *more* likely to vote, but this is because the elderly vote more and women live longer than men (source: **Electoral Commission, 2019**).

At the time of writing this book, 34% of MPs are women – an all-time high, but not the 50% you would expect if representation were equal. Politics involves long hours, commuting and inflexible working patterns – all factors which disadvantage women in other occupations.

Since 1918, Labour has had the most female MPs (55% compared to the Conservatives' 31%) and the last Labour Government had the highest proportion of women in senior cabinet posts (36% between 2006-7). However, the two female Prime Ministers have both been Conservatives: **Margaret Thatcher** (p141) and **Theresa May**.

AO2 ILLUSTRATION: THE NORDIC MODEL

The **Nordic Model** is a political system found in Sweden, Norway, Finland, Denmark and Iceland. These countries have a Capitalist economy regulated by Marxist principles: high taxes (some of the highest taxes in the world) pay for free healthcare and social services and a social safety net to help people in danger of falling into poverty by offering generous benefits.

The Nordic countries are also seen as some of the most progressive places in terms of gender equality. There is generous maternity (and paternity) leave and childcare is funded by the state so that mothers can study or work. For example, in Iceland mothers and fathers both get 90 days paid leave after the birth of a baby. In Norway, 40% of the parliament must be made up of women (an example of a **quota**). Sweden ranks first in the **Global Gender Gap Index** (*c.f.* p109) and has the most generous parental leave in the world: 480 days, or 16 months of paid leave.

Can the Nordic Model be adopted by other countries? Critics point out that the Nordic countries are **culturally homogenous**, as opposed to **multicultural countries** like the UK, France and the USA. This makes it easier for the population to have a **consensus on progressive values** which is important if workers are expected to pay such high taxes. The Nordic Model doesn't have perfect results either: 36% of managers in Sweden are female and the figure is 40% in Iceland, but that's still lower than the USA where 43% of managers are women, despite the USA ranking only 51 in the Gender Gap Index.

RESEARCH PROFILE: MESSNER & COOKY (2021)

Michael Messner & Cheryl Cooky worked on a **30-year longitudinal study** (p37) involving **content analyses** (p65) of US TV coverage of men's and women's sports. The researchers analysed three two-week segments of televised sports news coverage once every 5 years on three Los Angeles TV networks and the sports highlights show on ESPN (a digital sports channel). In the latest study, the researchers also analyse social media posts.

In 2019, 95% of the TV coverage is on men's sports while 80% of the news and highlights dedicate zero time to women. Coverage of women's sports makes up 9% of online newsletter content and 10% of Twitter posts. Even the tiny amount of women's sports on TV is inflated due to coverage of the US soccer team winning the Women's World Cup in 2019. If this were deducted, women's sports would drop to 4% of TV coverage, unchanged from 10 years previously.

The researchers also carry out thematic analysis. They conclude that the sexualised or trivial representation of sports women common in the 1990s has turned into "gender-bland" reporting that is respectful but features none of the excitement found in the reporting of men's sports.

The researchers acknowledge that the latest study took place during the 2020-21 Coronavirus Pandemic, which affected sports coverage by cancelling tournaments and reducing live audiences. ESPN has since increased its investment in the women's basketball and tripled the number of games it aired across its network. It's not clear if the findings can be generalised to the UK, where **Emma Raducanu's 2021 Wimbledon victory** raised the profile of women's sport.

Life Chances

Life chances are affected by health but there is a mixed picture here. Life expectancy in the UK has increased in recent decades and, before the 2020-21 Coronavirus Pandemic, stood at 79.5 for males but 83.1 for females. This longer lifespan ought to translate into greater life chances for women. However, women experience more poor health: on average women live for 19.1 years in poor health, compared to 16.1 years for men (source: **Public Health England, 2017**). Women also experience more common mental health problems than men, with 26% of young women experiencing disorders like depression or anxiety compared to 9.1% of young men. Female suicides reached a peak in 2019, with 3.1 per 100,000 females, however this is still dwarfed by male suicide, which accounts for three quarters of deaths (source: **ONS, 2019**). The general trend in health is convergence, with males and females becoming more similar over time, which suggests their lifestyles are becoming more similar and life chances are equalising.

Education is an area where women ought to experience more life chances now than in the past. Up until the mid-1980s, boys out-performed girls in schools and universities and this was seen by some as proof that girls were less intelligent. Feminist writers instead blamed the sexism of the educational system, point out that textbooks were written from a male perspective and teachers were disinclined to push girls towards academic subjects.

Females now outperform males. Currently, more than a quarter of girls (25.3%) aged 16 received top grades of A or 7+ in England, Wales and Northern Ireland, while just 18.6% boys in Year 11 achieve the same grades; girls are 14% more likely to pass English and Maths (source: **ONS, 2019**). In higher education (i.e. universities) young women make up 56.6% of students, compared to 44.1% for young men. **Helen Wilkinson (1994)** refers to the **genderquake** of the 1990s: young women increasingly striving for a career and a high salary and becoming confident, assertive and ambitious. **Becky Francis (2006)** points out that a high proportion of working-class girls still fail in education and many women fail to achieve their full potential. Unqualified women are often limited to working in the **'4 Cs'** of cleaning, caring, catering and cash registers.

In fact, the educational performance of *both* sexes has been rising, but girls' results have improved more quickly. Are women benefiting from their educational successes? On average, a university education leads to a 20% increase in earnings but male students each gain an average of £110k over their career while female students only gain £30k (source: **Institute of Fiscal Studies, 2020**). This links to the gender inequalities that exist in the workplace (p102).

AO2 ILLUSTRATION: THE SUSSEXES

Meghan Markle, an American actress, married Prince Harry in 2018, but in 2020 the couple moved to the USA and stopped performing royal duties, although they keep the titles of **Duke and Duchess of Sussex**. The couple support charities through their **Archewell Foundation** (*"putting compassion into action"*), especially causes like gender equality. Harry speaks out on the mental health issues affecting young men and Meghan's **40x40 Initiative** arranges for 40 celebrities to use 40 minutes of their time supporting women returning to the workplace.

The couple appeared on the cover of *Time Magazine* in 2021; the pose places Meghan front and centre with Harry, perched on a wall, appearing to be the same height as her and in a supportive role. This could be interpreted as a Feminist statement about equal gender roles in marriage but was interpreted by some critics as implying the woman's superiority.

Supporters view the Sussexes as role models for equality and supporters of important causes that promote the life chances of ethnic minorities and women in particular. Critics view them as elite Capitalists with an insincere attachment to progressive trends; the 40x40 Initiative does nothing to tackle structural inequality and, though it improves the life chances of some women, can only benefit a fortunate few.

RESEARCH PROFILE: STOET & GEARY (2019)

Gijsbert Stoet & David Geary developed a new way of measuring gender inequality which measures a person's wellbeing. The **Basic Index of Gender Inequality (BIGI)** focuses on three factors: educational opportunities, healthy life expectancy and overall life satisfaction.

The researchers calculate BIGI scores for 134 countries (6.8 billion people). The BIGI scores suggest that, on average, men are *more disadvantaged* than women in 91 countries whereas women are disadvantaged in 43 countries. The most developed countries in the world come closest to achieving equality, with a slight *advantage* for women. In the least developed countries, women nearly always fall behind men – largely because of lack of education. Men's disadvantage is largely due to a shorter healthy lifespan.

The researchers argue their BIGI is a better measure than the **Global Gender Gap Index (GGGI, 2006,** *c.f.* p107**)**, since the GGGI does not take into account male disadvantages, like harsher punishments for crime, compulsory military service and dangerous workplaces. David Geary says: *"We sought to correct the bias towards women's issues within existing measures and at the same time develop a simple measure that is useful in any country in the world, regardless of their level of economic development."*

Stoet & Geary's research suggests that many of the apparent inequalities in developed countries might in fact be **differences in preferred lifestyle**. This would be supported by **Functionalists** but opposed by **Feminists**. Similarly, **Marxists** would oppose the conclusion that developed (i.e. wealthy Capitalist) countries are the most equal. These critics prefer the GGGI, which presents a more complex analysis and continues to point out gender inequality in all countries.

Research: Visit the BIGI and dip into the studies of each country at http://bigi.genderequality.info/; you can compare it with the GGGI at https://resourcewatch.org/data/explore/Gender-Gap-Index-2

The 40-Mark Essay

You could be set a 40-mark question on inequality related to gender. You could be set a question about inequality related to **work & employment**, **social life** or **life chances**, which would let you bring in class, ethnicity and age, or about a Perspective on inequality (especially on **Feminism**). Watch out for questions that ask you to address one gender in particular.

When you studied **1A: Socialisation, Culture & Identity**, you were introduced to **Faludi (1999)** who argues that a backlash occurred in the 1980s against women. Wilkinson's idea of the **genderquake** provides a context for that and the two arguments support each other (good for AO3 evaluation!). **Oakley (1974)** argues that families socialise children into gender roles, which would explain later **horizontal segregation** in work.

An important evaluation issue for gender is the distinction between **inequality** and **difference**. For example, it might be that women prefer a lifestyle more focused on home and family and regard the lower earnings as a price worth paying for quality of life: **Stoet & Geary**'s **BIGI** would support this view that different lifestyle choices are not necessarily inequalities.

According to this view, Western countries have solved most of the gender inequalities faced by women; the problem now is the inequalities faced by men who still do dangerous jobs, fall behind in education and have shorter lifespans – and are far more prone to suicide than women.

Feminists (p158) object to this, pointing out that women are overwhelmingly more at risk of violence in the home and death at the hands of a parent or partner: in England & Wales, two women a week are killed by a current or former partner (source: **ONS, 2019**). The continued existence of the **'glass ceiling'** is evidence that society is structured in a way that disadvantages women. Women who choose family over career might be happy with that choice, but it's a choice that shouldn't be forced upon them in the first place because it isn't forced upon men.

Correll's **'Small Wins Model'** is important for arguing that restructuring workplaces in a way that reduces the gender gap is not an impossible dream, but something achievable with a bit of effort and imagination. The **BBC** is a good example. The **Nordic countries** offer another example of how countries can be more equal for women while still being successful and wealthy.

However, some critics complain that 21st century Feminists have lost interest in these sorts of structural changes. **Intersectional Feminism** (p158) focuses on how different oppressed identities intersect, which means that the experiences of Black women or lesbian women or trans women are not comparable with straight White women. This has certainly raised awareness of the problems experienced in different communities, but it makes it harder to work towards meaningful changes for *all* women, because improvements usually don't benefit everybody equally – and might not benefit some people at all.

Another argument is that the focus on female inequality risks alienating men, who resent seeing themselves represented in the media as inferior to women. **Messner & Cooky** is a useful study for arguing that mainstream media is still very male-centred (the technical term is **androcentric**), whatever ideas the **Duke & Duchess of Sussex** might promote.

INEQUALITY OF ETHNICITY

In the **2011 Census**, 83% of the UK population identify as White, 8% Asian and 3% Black. However, a disproportionately high amount of people living in poverty, arrested for crimes or being turned down for jobs is non-White.

The main explanation is racism. **Individual racism** is a set of racist (prejudiced) values an individual person holds. If a racist is in a position of power, these prejudices will produce discrimination, leading to the formula:

DISCRIMINATION = PREJUDICE + POWER

In Western countries, there have been campaigns for half a century against these prejudices. Fewer people than in the past admit to these prejudices, but sociologists propose that **implicit bias** remains – a sort of hidden or unconscious prejudice that people are not aware of having.

Institutional racism – also known as **systemic racism** is when the rules, traditions and habits of a group or an institution are based on racist (prejudiced) **norms**. A non-racist individual who conforms to such a group's practices will end up functioning ***as if*** they were racist. Often, the norms are not perceived as prejudiced (they seem like common sense to members of the group). Identifying and dismantling institutional racism is a lot more difficult and controversial than challenging the bigoted views of individual racists. For example, **Judith Katz (1990)** argues that an obsession with timekeeping is a White cultural norm not shared by African cultures. Therefore, punishing Black workers or students for being late or missing deadlines is institutionally racist.

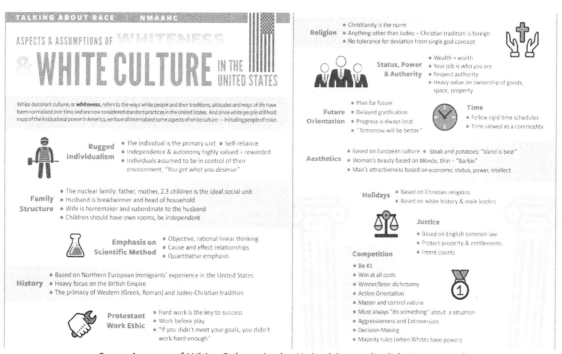

Some Aspects of White Culture in the United States (Judith Katz, 1990)

If Katz is right, should employers and schools simply abandon rules about timekeeping? Or should they keep those rules but only punish White people for breaking them? Or are the claims made by Katz (who is White) **themselves** racist, for representing Black people as unable to meet deadlines because of their race and culture?

Some would argue that, by generalising about all White people, Katz is guilty of racism **against Whites**. However, the PREJUDICE+POWER formula is important here. Racist discrimination only occurs when someone has the power to put their prejudices into effect and, in Western societies, White people are in the majority and have power, so they do not typically experience racism themselves. This immunity from discrimination is often termed **White Privilege**, which **Peggy McIntosh (1988)** defines as *"an invisible package of unearned assets."*

Research: While studying **1A: Socialisation, Culture & Identity**, you were introduced to McIntosh's essay *White Privilege: Unpacking the Invisible Knapsack* – review your notes on that

Work & Employment

Some important pieces of legislation in the UK are the **Race Relations Acts (1965, 1968, 1976, 2000)**, which forbid discrimination on grounds of race. The 1976 Act also created the **Commission for Racial Equality (CRE, 1976-2007)** which in turn became the **Equality & Human Rights Commission (EHRC)**. These government bodies promote racial equality and review government legislation and practices for discrimination.

Despite this, people from Bangladeshi and Pakistani ethnic groups are twice as likely to be in the bottom fifth of incomes than average; they have the lowest median household incomes, followed by people from Black ethnic groups.

UK median weekly household income (£)

Source: House of Commons Library (2019)

This inequality isn't just about income. Black ethnic groups in the UK also have less savings, are less likely to own homes (20% compared to 68% for White households) and experience higher unemployment (more than double that of White jobseekers).

In the past, education was a factor in this. However, 2nd generation ethnic minorities are now performing well in education. Indian, Bangladeshi and African students attain higher at GCSE grades on average than White students. Nearly 60% of 2nd generation Indian and Bangladeshi men and 50% of Indian, Bangladeshi and Black women having tertiary qualifications (college or university), compared with under 30% of White adults (source: **Institute for Fiscal Studies, 2020**).

However, education isn't always the solution, with Black male graduates being paid 17% less than White male graduates – the equivalent of £7,000 over a year. For Black women, the graduate pay gap is lower but still significant at 9%, or £3,000 over a year (source: **Runnymede Report, 2020**).

Two main factors are suggested by sociologists for this inequality of income.

- **Institutional racism:** There are implicit biases among employers that make them less likely to hire or promote workers from some ethnic groups.

- **Demographic factors**: Some ethnic minorities experience barriers of language or culture for finding work (e.g. not speaking English or having family responsibilities or religious requirements the workplace does not cater for). Some minority groups tend to live in areas of high unemployment and expensive housing (e.g. inner cities).

Many Asian immigrants arrived in the 1950s and '60s from the **Punjab** (India), **Mirpur** (Pakistan) and **Sylhet** (Bangladesh) to work in the manufacturing centres of the Midlands and the North of England, especially in the textile industry (manufacturing clothing). With the decline of these industries in the 1980s, Asian families found themselves living in areas of high unemployment.

Demographic factors also include geography. As part of **1A: Socialisation, Culture & Identity** you learned about the **'Windrush Generation'** of Caribbean immigrants who arrived in the UK in the 1950s. These immigrants often took jobs in inner city areas that did not offer jobs or opportunities for their children.

AO2 ILLUSTRATION: IMPLICIT BIAS TESTING

Implicit bias refers to prejudiced ideas a person holds without realising it. These biases reveal themselves in small ways (slight preferences, micro-aggressions) but they accumulate if they are shared by a lot of people and can be responsible for discrimination. The **Implicit Association Test (IAT)** was invented by psychologists in the USA. It is a questionnaire that claims to measure positive/negative attitudes towards different social groups.

The IAT is used today in **implicit bias testing**, which is an important part of **diversity training** in many workplaces. For example, the test asks respondents to press a button to identify good or bad words linked with Black or White faces and it measures mistakes or hesitations made when responding to Black faces. This alerts employers to the slight biases they might hold without that affect their judgment. Usually, there will then be workshops in which people are encouraged to face up to their biases and reject them.

However, the IAT has been criticised for being **invalid and unreliable** – especially for lacking **test-retest reliability** (people get different results when they re-take the test). In 2020, the UK Government scrapped implicit bias training in the civil service, claiming there was no evidence it led to any improvements in workplace behaviour.

Research: take the IAT yourself at https://implicit.harvard.edu/implicit/takeatest.html

RESEARCH PROFILE: WOOD ET AL. (2009)

Jowell & Prescott-Clarke (1970) pioneered a type of field experiment in Sociology by sending out fake job applicants to interviews. The applicants were identical in their qualifications and experience but different in ethnicity. White applicants received more job offers.

This research has been replicated in many countries in the past 50 years. **Martin Wood et al. (2009)** sent out fictional but identically qualified job applications rather than sending actors to job interviews. The researchers identified 987 job vacancies and sent three applications to each: all identical except for the name of the applicant, of which one was White-sounding and the other two from ethnic minorities (e.g. Anthony Olukayode for Black African, Latoya Williams for Black Caribbean, Cho Xiang for Chinese, Sunita Kumar for Indian, Muhammed Kahlid for Bangladeshi). The jobs were in 7 UK cities (including London, Birmingham and Glasgow) and in IT, accounting, care, sales and teaching.

The researchers had to send out 74% more applications for ethnic minority candidates than White candidates to get an offer of a job interview. All ethnic minorities suffered from this discrimination and the differences between different ethnic groups were not significant.

However, the discrimination disappeared when the jobs required filling in the employer's own form rather than submitting a CV. These forms are usually designed so that the applicant's name is hidden until the selection process is over. This strategy seems to remove the effects of **implicit bias** and Martin Wood concludes it should be used more widely.

Social Life

As with social class (p95) and gender (p104), ethnicity can lead to **social exclusion** due to **discrimination**, lack of **awareness of opportunities** or a **sense of unworthiness**. The OCR Specification expects students to consider evidence *"from a range of areas of social life"* so we will look at differences in **marriage and divorce**, **travel and leisure** and **participation in democracy**.

Marriage & Divorce

You have already learned about the **'marriage gap'** between working-class and middle-class families and this is often used (especially by the **New Right**, p141) to argue that children from single parent households have fewer life chances. A similar marriage gap exists for some ethnic groups.

For example, 18.9% of Black households are lone parent families, the highest percentage out of all ethnic groups for this type of household; the lowest percentage is found among Asian households, at 5.7%, half the rate of White households (source: **ONS, 2019**).

Roger Ballard (1982) stresses the strong family ties of British Asian families and links this to a conservative and patriarchal Asian culture that is concerned with maintaining family honour and views divorce as shameful. However, divorce rates for British Asians are rising, especially among 3rd and 4th generation immigrants.

While Asian households are associated with the **extended family** (parents and children living with or close to grandparents, cousins, etc), Black households are associated with the **beanpole family** type. This is a lone mother and child living with or receiving support from a grandmother who was in turn a lone parent. According to the stereotype, Black fathers are often absent and unsupportive. 63% of Black children in the UK live in lone parent families, compared to 6% of Indian families and 14.7% of White families (source: **CRED, 2021**).

This family arrangement is often used to explain the difficulties faced by Black children – and especially Black boys – in schools, such as high rates of exclusion. This in turn leads to fewer life chances.

Beanpole families can be explained by high rates of unemployment among Black ethnic minorities in the UK, with unemployed men unable to play the role of 'breadwinner' and support their family. This would make beanpole families the *result*, rather than the *cause*, of Black inequality. **Tracey Reynolds (2009)** argues that Black fathers are not 'absent' just because they do not live with their children; they are 'visiting' fathers who continue to support their children in many ways.

However, some sociologists argue that beanpole families are an aspect of Black culture that has been imported into the UK by Caribbean immigrants. If this were the case, it would be a **demographic factor** (p113) that might be a cause of inequality, rather than a result of it.

The main problem with household data is that it contradicts itself. British Asians have high levels of marriage and family stability, yet Pakistani and Bangladeshi households experience significant poverty while Indian households do not. Black households have the lowest level of family stability yet are in many ways better off than the more stable Pakistani/Bangladeshi households.

Travel & Leisure

We have already seen that alcohol consumption – and associated health problems – is linked to poverty. However, in the UK ethnic minorities consume *less* alcohol than the White population. This is particularly true of Bangladeshis, due to the culture of **abstinence** (avoiding alcohol) encouraged by the Islamic religion. However, Pakistani men who *do* drink consume more alcohol than people in the other ethnic minority groups. Alcohol-related deaths are higher among Indian groups than the general population but lower among Black groups (source: **Joseph Rowntree Foundation, 2010**).

However, with drugs the story changes. A NHS survey found Black people are 3½ times as likely as Asians to use drugs (source: **NHS, 2014**). Data from the **British Crime Survey (2009)** shows that Mixed Race groups are most likely to use drugs (17.6%), with White groups following (10.5%) and Black groups a distant third (5.8%). However, Mixed Race groups are also the youngest in the population, so this result might be skewed by the tendency of younger people in general to experiment with drugs. White drug use is more likely to involve Class A drugs (e.g. cocaine or ecstasy) but among ethnic minorities Class B drugs like cannabis are more typical.

This data suggests ethnic inequalities cannot be linked to alcohol or drug consumption. However, racist stereotypes persist. Over half of **police stop & search** is for drugs and there are 6 stop & searches for every 1,000 White people compared to 54 for every 1,000 Black people, making Black suspects 9 times more likely to be stopped by the police (source: **Home Office, 2020**). This experience of being disproportionately targeted by the police while traveling supports the perception of **institutional racism** in the UK.

Sport is another indicator of ethnic differences: 62% of adults of adults in England take part in 150 minutes of physical activity a week, but only 56% of Black people and 55% of Asian people reach this figure. People from these ethnic groups are also far less likely to volunteer in sport and enjoy the benefits associated with it (source: **SportEngland Active Lives Survey, 2019**). This is important because physical activity effects physical and mental health and influences **life chances** (p119).

Travel has similar patterns, with 74% of UK adults holding a **driving licence** but all ethnic minorities being less likely to drive than Whites; Black groups are least likely, with only 56% holding a driving licence (source: **NHS, 2019**).

Problems with traveling link to fewer life chances and difficulties with getting jobs. However, low rates of driving licenses might be linked to Black groups being located in large cities where private cars are inconvenient (e.g. problems parking, traffic congestion) and public transport is available.

Participation in Democracy

UK ethnic minority groups tend to be Left Wing in their voting, with Labour attracting 64% of all minority ethnic voters (source: **Ipsos Mori, 2019**). Since Left Wing politics is inspired by Marxist ideas about conflict and hegemony in society, it is not surprising that many people from minority groups would vote this way. However, 64% is a drop from 68% in 2010, which suggests ethnic minority voting patterns might be shifting, albeit slowly.

One factor behind this might be MPs in Parliament from ethnic minority backgrounds. The **2019 General Election** returned the most ethnically diverse set of MPs ever, with 1 in 10 from an ethnic minority background. The majority of these (41) were Labour, but 22 were Conservative and 2 Liberal Democrats. In 2010, the figure was 1 in 40. In 1987 there were only 4 MPs from such backgrounds.

However, before the 2019 General Election, there were concerns that 25% of Black voters were not registered to vote; this was true of 24% of Asian voters and 31% of Mixed Race voters, compared to 17% of the general population (source: **Electoral Commission, 2019**). Some critics blame this on **voter suppression**: a deliberate policy of discouraging some groups from voting. Plans to **introduce voter ID** at future elections (to cut down on voter fraud by making voters show ID at the polling station) have been criticised for adding to the problem, because ethnic minority voters are less likely to have suitable ID (*c.f.* differences in **driving licences**, p116).

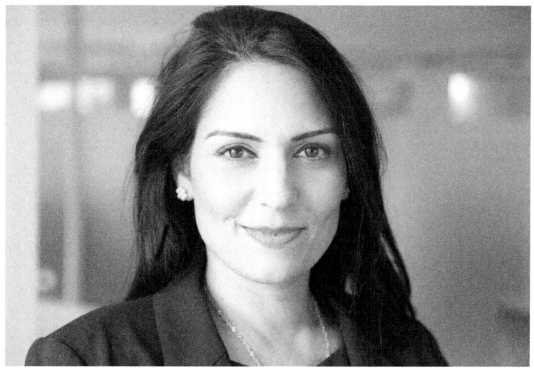

Rt Hon. Priti Patel MP

AO2 ILLUSTRATION: THE MOST DIVERSE CABINET EVER?

After the **2019 General Election**, 18% of the cabinet (the top team of MPs advising the Prime Minister) were from ethnic minority backgrounds: 6 in total, including an Asian Home Secretary (**Priti Patel**) and Chancellor of the Exchequer (**Sajid Javid**, later replaced by **Rishi Sunak**). Prime Minister **Boris Johnson** announced this to be *"the most diverse cabinet ever."* Before this there had only ever been 5 UK cabinet members from ethnic minorities.

Critics pointed out that the Conservative cabinet was still elitist in other ways: 64% of these MPs came from fee-paying schools (p84) compared to 7% of the general population. Moreover, although British Asians were well represented in the Cabinet, Black MPs were not.

The success of ethnic minority MPs in government might prompt a shift in voting patterns in future elections. However, Conservatives have an 'image problem' with ethnic minority voters. As a Right Wing political party, they are inspired by Functionalist sociological ideas and support the status quo. In particular, they are suspicious of the idea of **institutional racism** and **implicit bias testing** (p114).

The Conservatives are still tainted by the **'Rivers of Blood' speech** made in 1968 by **Enoch Powell**. Powell was a Conservative MP concerned about the level of immigration from the Caribbean and Asia, warning that immigration would lead to violence and hostility. Powell was condemned as a racist but his views were popular with 75% of the population in surveys at the time.

Research: find out more about MPs and cabinet members from ethnic minority backgrounds; research Enoch Powell's speech and reactions to it

RESEARCH PROFILE: MARTIN & BLINDER (2020)

Nicole Martin & Scott Blinder investigate *Biases at the Ballot Box* (2020), to see if ethnic minority candidates experience discrimination in UK elections.

The researchers recruited a sample of 7903 potential voters and surveyed them online. The voters had to choose between two (fictional) candidates who were described in the same way, along with their party (Labour or Conservative), ethnicity (White, Black Caribbean or Pakistani Asian) and their policies on immigration and law & order.

A Pakistani candidate received fewer votes (6 points less) than a White Candidate with the same description. However, the biggest 'voter penalty' was not for ethnicity but for supporting unpopular policies, like unrestricted immigration (14 points) – but ethnic minority candidates were **punished more severely** for supporting these policies. For example, Black Caribbean candidates were as popular as White ones overall, but not if they supported immigration or 'soft' policing of minorities. However, gender did **not** seem to **intersect** with these issues: female candidates received the same support as males and no extra penalty for unpopular policies.

Life Chances

Max Weber's concept of **life chances** proposes that people with more life chances get better jobs, experience freedom from discrimination, harassment and crime and live longer.

Recent data on life expectancy has been surprising, with many ethnic minorities living *longer* than White groups on average. White and Mixed Race women live for 83.1 years, but Black African women for 88.9 years. White and Mixed Race men live for 79.7 and 79.3 years respectively, but Black African men live for 83.8 years on average (source: **ONS, 2021** but based on data from 2011-14).

Veena Raleigh (2021) links this to the **'Healthy Migrant Effect'** with immigrant groups being less likely to drink excessively or eat unhealthily, however over time they adopt the lifestyle of the surrounding culture (which explains why African Black groups are long-lived but not Black Caribbean groups who have been in the UK for longer). However, **Raghib Ali (2021)** argues that the **2020-21 Coronavirus Pandemic** disproportionately harmed these minority groups, reversing their previous advantage.

Mental health is important for life chances but patterns are unclear. Perhaps due to the 'Healthy Migrant Effect' there is better mental health among Chinese groups than White groups and fewer suicidal thoughts among Asians than Whites. However, Black people are 4 times more likely to be detained under the Mental Health Act than White people and Black men are 3-4 times more likely to be diagnosed with a mood disorder (source: **Mental Health Foundation, 2021**).

Mental ill health could be a *result* of racism and inequality in society, especially struggling against institutional racism and implicit bias in daily interactions. However, it could also be caused by **demographic factors** (p113), such as lifestyle and geographical location (e.g. the stress of living in high crime areas in inner cities), in which case it is a possible *cause* of ethnic inequalities.

School achievement for ethnic minority groups has risen. At GCSE, 49% of White children attain Grade 5+ in English and Maths; Black Caribbean children still perform poorly (35%) but many other groups outperform White children, such as Bangladeshi (57%), Indian (70%) and Chinese (80%). At A-Level, 20% of White students attain 3 As compared to 37% of Chinese students, but only 12% of Black students, the lowest performing group (source: **DfE, 2021**).

There is some evidence that poor White children have become the group disadvantaged by school. Among children eligible for Free School Meals (FSM), only 53% of White students meet their expected targets; this is lower than most other ethnic groups and this group is the largest of all the disadvantaged groups (source: **DfE, 2021**).

This paints a confusing picture of life chances for ethnic minorities in the UK. Clearly, some minority groups do very well and there are senses in which White majority groups come off worst. Some of these findings (like superior educational achievement and life expectancy) do not correspond to previous findings about poverty and exclusion in society. Furthermore, the disadvantages experienced by Black Caribbean communities are particularly persistent, even if they are not always shared by Black African immigrants.

AO2 ILLUSTRATION: THE 2018 WINDRUSH SCANDAL

The Windrush Generation is a group of immigrants and their children who travelled from the Caribbean (in particular, Jamaica, Trinidad and Tobago) to work in Britain between 1948-1971. Many took jobs in the NHS and the transport sector in post-War Britain. The **1971 Immigration Act** gave them indefinite leave to remain in the UK.

In 2018, a scandal emerged concerning the treatment of these immigrants and their children. The Conservative Government had created a **'Hostile Environment' policy** to make it more difficult for immigrants to stay in the UK. British people from the Windrush Generation received demands that they prove their right to stay in the UK or face losing their jobs, being refused treatment on the NHS and even being deported to the Caribbean (a place many had not been to since they left as children over 50 years ago). Proving a right to stay was difficult: it involved producing some sort of documentation for every year they had lived in the UK and, to make matters worse, the Home Office had destroyed all its records of the immigrants' arriving in the UK. It appears that 83 individuals who arrived in the UK before 1973 were actually deported.

An independent inquiry was set up to investigate what went wrong. The **Windrush Lessons Learned Review (2020)** concluded that the mistreatment of this ethnic minority was *"foreseeable and avoidable"* and the tough immigration rules had been set up *"with complete disregard for the Windrush generation."* There is *"institutional ignorance and thoughtlessness towards the issue of race"* in the Home Office (the branch of government dealing with immigration).

A special taskforce was set up to make sure people receive the documentation they need. A **Windrush Compensation Scheme** was established in 2019 and is expected to pay out £200 million. For example, someone who was wrongly deported could claim £10,000.

RESEARCH PROFILE: SEWELL ET AL. (CRED, 2021)

In 2021, the **Commission on Race & Ethnic Disparities (CRED)** published a report on ethnic inequalities and differences in the UK. The chair of the Commission was **Tony Sewell**, an educationalist who had previously written on the under attainment of Black boys in UK schools.

The CRED Report concluded that **institutional racism** is not an important factor in ethnic inequality: *"the claim the country is still institutionally racist is not borne out by the evidence."* Instead, the Report argued that **demographic factors** such as class, family influence, wealth, culture and religion *"have more significant impact on life chances than the existence of racism."* The CRED Report concludes: *"We no longer see a Britain where the system is deliberately rigged against ethnic minorities."*

The CRED Report was immediately controversial. **Rohini Kahrs (2021)** called it *"a masterclass in government level gaslighting"* – 'gaslighting' is when someone tries to convince a partner that they are insane for thinking they are being abused; in the same way, the CRED Report is telling ethnic minorities that the racism they experience is all in their imagination.

Labour MP **David Lammy** called the Report: "*an insult to anybody and everybody across this country who experiences institutional racism.*" The **Lammy Review (2017)** had previously found evidence of institutional racism in the UK criminal justice system. Other reports concluding that institutionalised racism does exist in the UK include the **Public Health England (PHE) review of the outcomes of Covid (2020)**, the **Lawrence Review (2020)** and the **Windrush Lessons Learned Review (2020**, *c.f.* p120**)**.

There is some support for CRED's findings. The **EU Minorities & Discrimination Survey (*Being Black in the EU*, 2018)** surveyed 25,000 people across Europe on their experience of racial discrimination in everyday society, at work and with the police. The survey found perceptions of being racially harassed, conflict with the police and being discriminated against in looking for work are *lowest* in the UK compared to other EU countries.

Critics of the CRED Report argue it is political propaganda following the worldwide **Black Lives Matter** protests of 2020. Tony Sewell and the other commissioners were appointed because they already opposed to the idea of institutional racism and **Critical Race Theory** (p154). The CRED Report lets the Conservative Government 'off the hook' for fixing institutional racism in the UK.

However, supporters of CRED point out pro-**Marxist** biases among its critics. Labour MPs like David Lammy support Left Wing politics, inspired by Marxist ideas. Rohini Kahrs works for the Runnymede Trust, a racial equality charity. The popularity of Critical Race Theory in universities means that other sociologists might have a bias against Sewell's **Functionalist** viewpoint.

Research: find out more about the CRED Report and reactions to it in the news (and on p28); research the other reports into ethnic inequalities in the UK mentioned above

Dr Tony Sewell CBE

The 40-Mark Essay

You could be set a 40-mark question on inequality related to ethnicity or inequality related to **work & employment**, **social life** or **life chances**, which would let you bring in ethnicity, or about a Perspective on inequality which you could focus on ethnic inequalities.

When you studied **1A: Socialisation, Culture & Identity**, you were introduced to the **Windrush Generation** and the idea of ethnic Identity studied by **Gilroy (1993)**.

An important evaluation issue for ethnicity is the distinction between **inequality** and **difference**. This expresses itself in two competing explanations: **racist discrimination** and **demographic factors** (p113). These two explanations ought to be complementary, but there is a tendency for them to be opposed to each other.

Racist discrimination is the explanation preferred by the Conflict Perspectives (**Marxism** and **Feminism**), especially concepts like **institutional racism**, **implicit racist bias** and **White Privilege**. These arguments are sharpened by **Critical Race Theory** (CRT, p154) which sees racism as universal among White people, with greater bias against persons with darker skin.

There's no shortage of evidence for institutional racism, including governmental reports like the **Lammy Review** (2017, p121), statistical disparities in exam results, employment and imprisonment for ethnic minorities and scandals like the **2018 Windrush Scandal** which shows how the government itself treats ethnic minorities in a thoughtless and/or hostile way. The disproportionate impact of the **2020-21 Coronavirus Pandemic** on ethnic minorities is also seen as evidence for institutional racism in health services.

However, there are contradictions in the evidence, such as the rising exam success of Bangladeshi students but the persistent low achievement of Black Caribbean boys and the different outcomes for Black African immigrants from Black Caribbeans. These differences are not easily explained by institutional racism alone.

The Consensus Perspective (**Functionalists**) prefers to concentrate on demographic factors, effectively viewing ethnic inequality as a sub-category of class inequality (because many ethnic minorities are disproportionately working class in background). This has the advantage of explaining the high attainment of Chinese and Indian minorities who tend to be more middle class in background. This Perspective identifies the family structure in Black Caribbean communities as the source of their distinctive problems. **Tony Sewell** argues that 50% of Black boys grow up without a father and form their Identities through gang culture, leading them away from educational success and into crime. However, this risks ignoring racism entirely and tends towards blaming Black communities for their problems rather than acknowledging how society is structured against them.

These debates come to a head in the controversy surrounding the **2021 CRED Report**. This illustrates how **choice of Perspective** influences sociological research, either from the Government appointing people with Functionalist views to conduct the Report or the opponents of CRED being influenced by their own Marxist (and CRT) Perspectives in condemning it.

INEQUALITY OF AGE

In 1901, the UK population had a high proportion of children (32% aged under 15) and a small elderly population (only 5% aged 65+). In 2018, the proportions of people in these two age groups had become equal (18% for each). This shows the UK has an ageing population: people are living longer and having fewer children. The number of people aged 65+ will increase by more than 40% over the next 20 years and the number of households where the oldest person is 85+ is increasing faster than any other age group (source: **ONS, 2020**).

There is a danger of viewing the elderly as a homogenous group because they have very different experiences. **Jane Pilcher (1995)** argues we should divide old age into three periods: **65-74** for the **young-old** who often continue working and earning. **75-84** for the **middle-aged-old** who withdraw from work and public roles and **85+** for the **old-old** who are particularly likely to be social excluded and experience disability.

As society has more and more elderly people in it and proportionally fewer young people, you would expect this to affect their relative influence. The second half of the 20th century was dominated by the 'Baby Boom' in Western societies, with large numbers of young people promoting changes in culture, from rock'n'roll music to the sexual revolution. In future, it looks as though the elderly will have more influence on society than the young.

Work & Employment

An important fact is that the young have not started work and the elderly retire from work. That puts both of these groups at a disadvantage because they cannot easily earn money. There are 14 million people in poverty in the UK – including 4 million children and 2 million pensioners (source: **Joseph Rowntree Foundation, 2018**).

The **Age Dependency Ratio (ADR)** is the number of people of working age in relation to the number of people of non-working age (including children under 15 and over-65s). The graph below shows how the ratio is increasing (and stood at 57% in 2020).

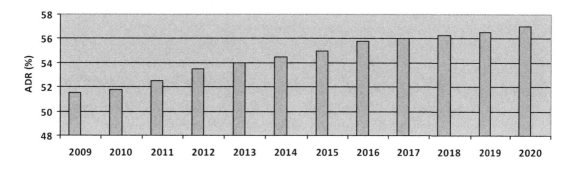

Age-Dependency Ratio for the UK (source: World Bank)

If the ADR continues to increase, a shrinking number of working age people will bear a larger and larger burden of supporting the retired population, which includes paying the State Pension but also their health care and accommodation in care homes.

However, the ADR assumes that all those aged 65+ are economically inactive, but increasingly people who have reached the **State Pension Age (SPA**, currently 66) continue to work and earn.

Age-related poverty intersects with **ethnicity**, because although 16% of those aged 65+ live in relative poverty, the figure is only 14% for White people, but 33% for Black people and 29% for Asians (source: **Department for Work & Pensions, 2018**).

The poverty of the elderly is particularly troubling because, unlike younger people, the elderly cannot try to improve their financial position by getting a better job or a promotion. They are dependent on the State Pension which is a fixed amount and does not vary to take into account their particular circumstances.

However, this is not the full picture. On average older people in Great Britain have higher levels of wealth than younger age groups – largely because of rising property prices. To be in the top 0.1% of UK earners you need to earn £650,000 – and of the top 0.1%, 40% are aged 45-54. The next second wealthiest group are the over-65s (source: **Institute for Fiscal Studies, 2019**).

The over 65s were the only age group in the UK that did not see their overall wealth drop as a result of the **2008 Global Financial Crisis** that closed many businesses and produced a wage-freeze for younger workers.

Sarah Milne (1999) coined the phrase **'Grey Power'** to mean the influence wielded by the (well-off) elderly because of their financial independence and spending habits.

The term **'the Grey Pound'** refers to the spending power of elderly people, who no longer have to support children and might have paid off their mortgages and other loans. Spending by those aged 65+ increased by 75% between 2001-2018 while spending dropped by 16% among those aged 50 and under (source: **International Longevity Centre UK, 2018**).

Meanwhile, young people are half as likely to own a house as they were at the start of the 21st century. This intersects with **class inequalities**, because for 25-34-year-olds, only 30% of those with parents in lower-skilled jobs (e.g. delivery drivers or sales assistants) own their own home, compared to 43% with parents in higher-skilled jobs (e.g. lawyers and teachers, source: **IFS, 2019**).

Young people were hit hard by the **2020-21 Coronavirus Pandemic**, with 16-24-year-olds accounting for two-thirds of all job losses (source: **ONS, 2021**). There was also a surge in **'Neets'** (16-24 year-olds Not in Education, Employment or Training). Young people often lack the work experience and the confidence to get back into the jobs market. They often find themselves working for **Zero Hour Contracts (ZHCs)** that don't guarantee a fixed amount of work and wages from one week to the next: 9.1% of 16-24-year-olds work on ZHCs compared to 1.7% of 35-49-year-old workers (source: **Statistia, 2021**).

AO2 ILLUSTRATION: THE PENSION TRIPLE LOCK

In the UK, the basic state pension can be claimed at the age of 66. It is currently (in 2021) £137.60 per week. In the past, there have been times when inflation (the rise in the price of goods in the shops) has made the pension worth less. In 2010, the UK Government introduced a **'triple-lock' on pensions**. This was a guarantee that pensions would increase every year to stay in line with **inflation**, or the **average increase in wages**, or **2.5%** - whichever came to the most. This guarantees that, whatever happens to the economy, the elderly won't be left behind.

The triple-lock is one reason why the elderly have become a relatively wealthy group during a time of low wages following the **2008 Global Financial Crisis**. However, some critics argue that this protection of the elderly comes at the expense of the young (who have to pay for pensions through their taxes). The basic state pension is not **'means tested'** which means it is paid to everyone, regardless of how rich they are or whatever pensions they claim from their job or private pension plan.

In 2021, the triple-lock was temporarily suspended, because people returning to work after the **2020-21 Coronavirus Pandemic** meant average wages in the UK went up by 8% and this would mean pensions would have to increase by 8%, which would be very expensive for taxpayers.

Research: find out more about pensions and the winter fuel allowance; look into the pros and cons of means-testing

RESEARCH PROFILE: JONES ET AL. (2010)

Iain Jones, Miranda Leontowitsch & Paul Higgs carried out semi-structured interviews with 20 UK men and women from upper management jobs who had taken early retirement as a matter of choice. The aim was to explore the subjective meaning that retirement and old age had for them.

Jones et al. use the Interactionist theory of **Ulrich Beck (2004)** because they describe their participants as **'quasi-subjects'** – people whose individuality is negotiated as part of an institution that shapes them. This means that, by studying the individuals, you learn about the institution of retirement because the individuals are never entirely free to make anything they like of their life, but neither are they entirely shaped by the institution, so their views and motives have to be investigated too (a classic **Social Action** position, p165). They also use the Marxist ideas of **Pierre Bourdieu (1984)** because they explore the participants' **'habitus'** – their lifestyle that reveals but also creates their **cultural capital**.

This sort of research investigates the meanings associated with retirement and three themes emerged: (1) the respondents saw themselves making a **conscious choice** to take early retirement that wouldn't be available to other people their age; (2) they had a **positive view of retirement** as a time of creativity and renewal where they could pursue new and exciting projects; (3) they were aware that **earlier generations** (their parents) did not have this economic freedom and also that **later generations** (their children) might not have it either.

Social Life

Old age is linked to **social exclusion**, which is when people are unable to participate fully in society because of their background. This can be due to **economic deprivation** but it also to **discrimination**, lack of **awareness of opportunities** or a **sense of unworthiness**. The OCR Specification expects students to consider evidence *"from a range of areas of social life"* so we will look at **marriage and divorce**, **travel and leisure** and **participation in democracy**.

Marriage & Divorce

Marriage is declining and divorces has increased, especially among the elderly. These **'silver splicers'** or **'silver separators'** are increasingly ending the marriages that they were in during their working lives and starting new ones in retirement. Between 2004-2014, the elderly population (aged 65+) increased by 20%, but marriages among this population increased by 46% (source: **ONS, 2020**). These figures intersect with gender, because of men's tendency to marry younger women: 56% of men aged 65+ marrying in 2014 married a woman under 65; only 22% of women aged 65+ married a man under 65.

This is happening partly because people are living longer: in 2004 a man retiring at 65 could expect to live a further 17 years and a woman 20 years; by 2014 this had increased to 19 and 22 years. Other factors include older people continuing to work and earn and also using the Internet (including online dating).

Meanwhile, the age at which people *first* marry has been getting later. In 1972, this was 27 for males and 25 for females, but in 2017 it was 38 and 36. This suggests younger people are delaying marriage. This is partly due to the social acceptability of **cohabitation** (an unmarried couple living together, perhaps with the intention of marrying later if the relationship is successful) but also financial pressures, job uncertainty and the difficulty of buying a home.

Another factor behind the young putting off marriage is the cost of weddings themselves. The average wedding costed £20,000 in 2009, but £30,000 in 2019 (source: **Statistia, 2021**).

Despite all this romantic activity, old age is a time of loneliness. According to **Age UK (2018)**, over half (59%) of those aged 85+ and 38% of those aged 75-84 live alone; half a million older people go 5-6 days a week without seeing or speaking to anyone at all and 40% of all older people say the television is their main company.

However, this needs to be seen in the context of UK society experiencing an **'epidemic of loneliness'** with 45% of adults feel occasionally, sometimes or often lonely in England (source: **ONS, 2018**). A survey by **Action for Children (2017)** found that 43% of 17-25-year-olds experience problems with loneliness; 24% of parents surveyed said they were always or often lonely.

Women report feeling lonely more frequently than men overall, but a greater number of older men (50+) report moderate to high levels of social isolation: 14% compared to 11% of women.

Travel & Leisure

The 'Baby Boomers' now entering old age show the largest rise in alcohol consumption (source: **Royal College of Psychiatrists, 2018**). Between 1990-2017, alcohol rose from 14th to 6th risk factor for disability for people aged 50-69 and from 61st to 18th for those aged 70+.

Meanwhile, binge drinking continues to fall among young adults. The number of 16-24-year-olds who do not drink alcohol at all rose from 10% in 2001 to 25% in 2016. In the same period, abstinence (not drinking alcohol) among those aged 65+ actually decreased by 5% (source: **ONS, 2017**). The drop in drinking among the young is partly due to the popularity of 'dry' months like Dry January ; it is also driven by the rise in numbers of ethnic minorities like British Muslims who have are less likely to drink alcohol and have a young population.

Alcohol misuse impacts on health (physical and mental) and therefore is a factor in inequality. This is on top of the declining health the elderly experience anyway.

Men aged 65 can expect to live about half the remainder of their life without disability (10 years out of 19); women can expect 10 disability-free years too, but since they live longer (21 years after age 65) the prospect is worse. More than half of people aged 65+ have 2+ chronic health conditions. **SportEngland's Active Lives Survey (2019)** shows that 42% of people aged 55+ are inactive compared to 29% of the adult population. This difference in physical activity impacts on physical and mental health and has an impact on **life chances**.

These problems intersect with class, with richer people experiencing less disability. For example, a person aged 71 in the top 20% of wealth has an average walking speed of 0.91 metres/second compared to 0.75 for someone in the poorest 20% (source: **Ageing Better, 2019**).

When it comes to holidays, all age groups are equally likely to travel but those aged 55+ were most likely to go on more than three holidays during the year (source: **Statistia, 2020**). Over a 20 year period (1998-2018) the number of over-65s traveling abroad for holidays has gone up by 35% which is more than the increase in the total number of elderly over that period (which is 30%). This is a good indication that older people are wealthier and healthier than they used to be and also possess more **cultural capital** (*c.f.* **Bourdieu**'s theory in **1A: Socialisation, Culture & Identity**).

Participation in Democracy

There is a saying attributed to the British Prime Minister **Benjamin Disraeli (1804-81)**: *"A man who is not a Liberal at sixteen has no heart; a man who is not a Conservative at sixty has no head."* In other words, it is normal for young people to be Left Wing in their politics (and Marxist in their sociological ideas) but people grow more Right Wing (and Functionalist) as they get older.

In the **2019 UK General Election**, 54% of 18-24-year-olds voted Labour. With every ten years of age, the chance of voting Conservative increases by 9 percentage points. The tipping point, at which a voter is more likely to vote Conservative than Labour, is 39 (source: **YouGov, 2019**).

Turnout is another factor, with people becoming more likely to cast a vote as they get older. This mans that Left Wing parties suffer because their supporters are the least likely to vote, whereas Right Wing parties have much more reliable older voters.

There are serious implications for this. The **Grey Vote** is used to explain the **2014 Scottish Independence Referendum** (with older people less likely to vote for Scottish independence) and the **2016 EU Referendum** (with older people more likely to vote for Brexit). Politicians often hope that the older generation will 'die off' and allow a different result on a future vote, but it is probable that as the young voters age their views on these matters change too.

Another implication of the Grey Vote is that politicians are more influenced by the growing number of reliable elderly voters than the smaller numbers of unreliable young voters. This means policies and laws tend to be passed that suit the old rather than the young. For example, the **Triple Lock on Pensions** (p125) and, during the **2020-21 Coronavirus Pandemic**, the priority given to protecting the health and livelihoods of the elderly rather than the young. Critics complain that policies about **climate change** have a huge effect on the young (who will grow up in a warming world) but are largely decided by the elderly (who vote for cheap energy prices to heat their homes).

In terms of political representation, older people dominate Parliament. Most MPs are aged 50-59 (source: House of Commons Library, 2020). The average age drops slightly at each election, when younger MPs replace older ones. At the time of writing (2021), **Nadia Whittome** is the youngest MP and currently the "Baby of the House" – she was 23 when elected in 2019.

All over the world, the elderly are in power. **Donald Trump** was 70 when he became US President in 2017 – America's oldest President until **Joe Biden**, who was 78 when he became President in 2021. However, young world leaders include **Jacinda Ardern** (New Zealand Prime Minister, 37 in 2017) and **Sebastian Kurz** (Austrian Chancellor, 31 in 2018).

Jeremy Corbyn speaks to the Glastonbury crowd, 2017 (image: Alex J Donohue)

AO2 ILLUSTRATION: THE 2017 'YOUTHQUAKE' ELECTION

In 2017, a snap General Election was called: the Conservative Government lost its majority and the Labour Party enjoyed unexpected success. This was attributed to the popularity of the Labour leader **Jeremy Corbyn** among younger voters – especially **'Millennials'** born in the late-1980s and '90s. Polls suggested that 18-24-year-olds were more likely to vote (between 12 and 16 percentage points) and when Corbyn appeared at the Glastonbury Festival, he was greeted by young crowds chanting *"Ooh-ooh Jeremy Corbyn"* (to the tune of the 2003 song *Seven Nation Army* by the White Stripes). The Oxford English Dictionary declared 'Youthquake' (the political awakening of younger voters) to be its 'Word of the Year.'

However, the **British Election Study (2017)** found no evidence that the 2017 election turnout among the young actually increased relative to other age groups. It is difficult to measure election turnout, because ballots (election votes) are anonymous and the people who don't vote are also the people least likely to answer polls about their voting intentions.

RESEARCH PROFILE: GENTLEMAN (2009)

Amelia Gentleman is a journalist and author who spent 4 days observing routines for 26 elderly residents in a care home (Raglan House) in Ipswich. *"More of us will end our lives in these institutions,"* Gentleman says. She conducted **overt observations** (p61) and **unstructured interviews** (p59) with the residents and the staff. Her findings were published in *The Guardian*.

Gentleman observes that many of the residents do not leave their rooms and, if they gather in the day room, they do not talk to each other. She calls the atmosphere of *"torpid, joyless inertia … very dispiriting."*

If residents have savings, it must be used to pay for their care and only once it is all gone does the NHS cover their costs. One woman has sold her flat, where she lived for years with her husband before he died.

A nurse who has arrived as a refugee from Iraq finds the institution of the care home strange: *"In Iraq, as part of our culture we look after our grandmothers and grandfathers at home until they pass away."* Gentleman praises the cheerfulness and dedication of the staff and the bright surroundings but writes: *"the home's unspoken function: a place where elderly people are left by their families to die."*

Gentleman's research considers how the meaning of old age is **negotiated**, with the elderly residents coming to terms with their situation in different ways but shaped by a wider culture that is not prepared to care for the old and the dying at home.

Research: read the full article at https://www.theguardian.com/society/2009/jul/14/older-people-care-home

Life Chances

Max Weber's concept of **life chances** proposes that people with more life chances get better jobs, experience freedom from discrimination, harassment and crime and live longer. We have already considered how life expectancy intersects with class, gender and ethnicity.

Older people, with fewer years left to live, could be seen as having fewer life chances than the young. On the other hand, freedom from financial and family responsibilities gives some of them more chances to change their lives; this would explain the rise in **'silver splicers'** (p126) and older people taking foreign holidays. Many older people are not so liberated. Nearly a quarter of those aged 45-64 are carers (this is likely to be an underestimate) and 5% provide more than 35 hours of care a week. 8 out of 10 unpaid carers feel lonely or socially isolated (source: **Carers UK, 2017**).

Another problem is **age discrimination** or **ageism**. This can include losing a job, being refused credit or insurance, receiving a lower quality of service in a shop or restaurant, and being refused membership to a club or trade association because of your age.

Swift & Steeden (2020) produced the report *Doddery But Dear* which found that older workers are seen as less competent, less able to learn and more expensive than younger workers; stereotypes of the elderly are negative, focused on death and physical decline, with ageing seen as a process of increasing ill health. **Martin Green** (**Care England, 2018**) describes the UK as *"completely and institutionally ageist."* The media drives negative attitudes, representing ageing as a crisis or a burden. Green identified phrases used like 'grey tsunami,' 'demographic cliff' and "demographic timebomb' as well as older people depicted as 'villains' who unfairly consume too much of society's resources.

AO2 ILLUSTRATION: CAPTAIN SIR TOM MOORE

'Captain Tom' became a household name in the UK during the **2020-21 Coronavirus Pandemic**. The 99-year-old former-soldier set up a *JustGiving* web page to raise £1,000 for the NHS by walking 100 laps of his garden before his 100th birthday. He walked 10 laps per day – a significant challenge since he needed a walking frame. The event went viral online and ended up raising £32,796,475 with donations from 1½ million individuals.

Tom Moore used *Twitter* to communicate with fans, then appeared on BBC radio and TV. He performed on a number one single of the song *You'll Never Walk Alone* sung by the musical star Michael Ball. He was given a Pride of Britain Award, appointed an honorary Colonel, was knighted by the Queen and awarded a gold *Blue Peter* badge.

Moore died in 2021, aged 100. His accomplishments in his long life are worth celebrating. However, it should be remembered he enjoyed significant privileges: he had already been a British army officer and a successful business manager; he lived with his daughter in a £1.2 million house in the Bedfordshire village of Marston Mortaine. In other words, Moore had **life chances** that were not available to all 99-year-olds. In particular, despite his disability, he was not abandoned by his family in one of the care homes described by **Gentleman** (**2009**, p129).

RESEARCH PROFILE: MOORE & CONN (1985)

Patricia Moore [not related to Captain Tom] **& Charles Conn** wrote *Disguised: A True Story* **(1985)** about 27-year-old Moore's experiences of going through life disguised as a 85-year-old woman (referred to by the authors as 'Old Pat'). Moore carried out a **covert participant observation** (p61); she put on makeup to make her look wrinkly, wore glasses that blurred her vision, clipped on a brace and wrapped bandages around her body so she was hunched over, plugged her ears so she couldn't hear well, and wore uneven shoes so she was forced to walk with a stick. Moore could only adopt this disguise for 12 hours at a time, once every 4 or 5 days, because of the damage it did to her skin and posture.

Over a 3-year period between 1979-82, Moore played 'Old Pat' in three different ways: as a **wealthy widow**, as a **comfortable granny** and as **destitute bag lady** (which explores how class intersects with gender and age). She visited 114 US cities in 14 States, as well as 2 Canadian Provinces. At one point she was robbed, beaten and left for dead by a street gang in Harlem, New York. Everywhere, she found she was treated differently – for example, people would shout, assuming she was deaf, and push in front of her in queues – and also found she viewed herself differently because of this treatment.

"What it all added up to was that people feared I would be trouble so they tried to have as little to do with me as possible. And the amazing thing is I began almost to believe it myself … I think perhaps the worst thing about age may be the overwhelming sense that everything around you is letting you know that you are not terribly important any more."

Moore's experiences illustrate the **self-fulfilling prophecy (SFP)** that occurs because of **labelling**. She used the empathetic understanding (*'verstehen'* p166) this experience gave her to design appliances to make life easier for the elderly.

Patricia Moore as a 27-year-old designer and as 85-year-old 'Old Pat'

The 40-Mark Essay

You could be set a 40-mark question on inequality related to age or inequality related to **work & employment**, **social life** or **life chances**, which would let you bring in age, or about a Perspective on inequality which you could focus on age inequalities.

When you studied **1A: Socialisation, Culture & Identity**, you were introduced to the **Baby Boomers** and the idea of the **social construction of childhood** by **Aries** and **Laslett**.

Watch out for questions that specifically address old age or youth rather than 'age' in general. If the question is about 'age' generally and you have studied **1B: Youth Subcultures**, you will be able to refer to some of that material too. Age inequalities also feature in the future topic **3A: Globalisation & the Digital Social World**.

It is easy to argue that the elderly suffer significant inequalities: they are likely to experience poverty through lack of earnings, their physical and mental health can decline and they can experience ageist discrimination and negative stereotyping. All of this can lead to social exclusion. The experiences of old people in care homes (described by **Gentleman**) and **Pat Moore**'s story of disguising herself as 'Old Pat' help support this point.

However, it's important to argue that in many ways the elderly are more privileged than the young. Many older people have **economic** and **social capital** (such as owning a mortgage-free house) and this is seen in the rise of **'silver splicers'** who divorce and re-marry as well as the boom in holidays for the elderly. The interviews conducted by **Jones et al.** show how retirement can be a positive thing.

Meanwhile, younger people are priced out of the housing market, work insecure **Zero Hour Contracts (ZHCs)** and most pay for the care of the elderly through their tax and National Insurance contributions.

You can illustrate and evaluate these ideas by pointing out the 'Cult of Youth' in Western society that represents youth as attractive and desirable, with people paying a lot of money for cosmetics and treatments that preserve the appearance of youth. In non-Western cultures, old age is valued as a time of wisdom and respect but in Western society the elderly are viewed as a burden or a threat.

However, it's important to point out that the conflict between the interests of the old and the young is not **'zero sum'** – in other words, not all benefits for one group automatically come at the expense of the other. Although the proportion of elderly people is increasing, the UK population as a whole is growing. Immigration brings in groups of young adults who tend to have larger families once they settle, which corrects the **Age Dependency Ratio**.

It's important to consider the **intersection** of age with other social categories, perhaps especially **class**. The young and the old are not homogenous groups and their experiences vary based on their wealth and status as well as factors like gender and ethnicity.

EXAM PRACTICE: PATTERNS & TRENDS IN INEQUALITY

The OCR exam has two questions in **Paper 2 Section B**:

5.   Outline ways in which ethnicity is a significant source of inequality in British society today. **[20 marks: 12 AO1 + 8 AO2]**

This is one of those 'describe & illustrate' questions, but with no Source A or Source B to lean on. There is no need to evaluate.

*Make **three** sociological points about ethnic inequalities and differences. For example, you could argue that ethnic minorities are more likely to experience poverty, that Black Caribbean boys underachieve on average at school and that immigrant groups are underrepresented in politics.*

It's a good idea to refer to particular statistics (like 20% home ownership in Black ethnic groups compared to 68% of Whites) and you should definitely use some sociological terminology (like institutional racism and implicit bias). Then offer examples of discrimination and make sure each example has an explanation linked to ethnicity. For example, "Black Caribbean boys are one of the lowest-attaining groups at GCSE and A-Level and this could be due to institutional racism in schools that do not support their learning in the same way as other students."

*Don't get drawn into a debate about whether or not institutional racism exists or whether White people are in some ways more disadvantaged than other ethnic groups: there are **no** marks for AO3 evaluation with this question.*

6.   'In Britain today, it is the young rather than the elderly who suffer significant disadvantages.' Discuss. **[20 marks: 16 AO1 + 8 AO2 + 16 AO3]**

This is a long essay with a requirement for developed evaluation. You should spend 50 minutes and write 1000 words.

*Write **four** points. Each point should introduce a sociological idea with some illustration from the real world. Each point should finish off with a developed evaluation (see **Chapter 7** for this).*

For example, you could write about poverty in old age, lack of opportunities for young people to buy their homes, ageist discrimination, young people not being represented in politics and the epidemic of loneliness among the young.

Each point should be backed up with research or statistics and then illustrated with some real-world example (AO2). This doesn't have to be very precise. For example, you could point out that recent US Presidents have been very old men and British MPs tend to be in their 50s.

*Each point needs to lead into some developed discussion; see **Chapter 7** for this. Keep your focus on the debate about whether the young or the old have it worse and whether this is a genuine inequality of just a difference in interests and lifestyles. For example, the young are less likely to vote, but is this because they are shut out of politics or simply because they have other interests and priorities? Make sure you answer the question: are the young suffering more inequality than the old?*

CHAPTER SIX – EXPLAINING INEQUALITY

Crime and deviance can be explained by a number of "*theories*" that match the Perspectives you have learned about earlier in the course. However, new Perspectives are introduced: the **New Right** (p141) and **Weberianism** (p165).

CONSENSUS PERSPECTIVE: FUNCTIONALISM

Functionalism is a **structuralist** Perspective that looks at inequality and difference across society as a whole. This means Functionalists are often prepared to excuse some inequalities as unfortunate but necessary side-effects of some greater good, such as freedom or the need to offer people incentives to be successful. Inequality is in fact **functional** if it produces positive outcomes. For example, a fear of falling into poverty might motivate people to work harder.

Functionalism is also unusual among sociological theories for the role it allows to **nature** in the **Nature-Nurture Debate** (*c.f.* **1A: Socialisation, Culture & Identity**). Functionalists insist we are to some extent shaped by our biological characteristics and so social structures are either **functional or dysfunctional** depending on whether they are compatible with or in conflict with our biological characteristics. Because we are not all the same biologically, Functionalists accept some inequalities are the inevitable expression of **biological differences**: some people are just naturally smarter, healthier or more hard-working than others.

There are limits to inequality, even for Functionalists. It is important for societies to experience **social solidarity** – the sense of having something in common and shared values. Without social solidarity, individuals suffer from **anomie**, which results in mental ill health, drug abuse as a coping mechanism, crime and ultimately suicide. Too much inequality in society causes anomie and is therefore **dysfunctional**.

Functionalists argue there is a 'sweet spot' where inequality exists but is **functional**. Society has a tendency to move towards this **state of balance (homeostasis)** and ORGANIC FUNCTIONALISTS use the metaphor of society being like an organism which can cope with infection or injury. Sometimes the imbalance becomes too great and the **agencies of social control** are needed to restore **social order**. This is why Functionalists have a reputation for supporting authoritarian policies like heavy policing and tough prison sentences and wanting to control immigration.

AO2 ILLUSTRATION: THE NUCLEAR FAMILY

The **nuclear family** is the small family unit consisting of a married couple and their biological children. It contrasts with the **extended family**, in which the couple lives with their parents and grandparents, their brothers and sisters, their cousins, uncles, aunts and in-laws.

Functionalists regard the nuclear family as the ideal form of family for modern life – it is **functional** whereas other types of family are **dysfunctional**.

Talcott Parsons argues that in pre-industrial societies the extended family is functional, because it is best for farming and looking after the young, the sick and the elderly. In industrialised societies, the nuclear family has evolved because families need to be mobile (moving from one job to the next). The state has taken over many family functions, such as education and healthcare, but two *"essential and irreducible functions"* remain: **primary socialisation** of children and the **stabilisation of adult personalities** (de-stressing after a day's work).

There are often claims that the nuclear family is 'under threat' (*c.f.* the **New Right**, p141). Functionalists also believe that adopting the nuclear family structure is vital for immigrants to **assimilate** (p138) into UK society. Critics of the nuclear family point out that it makes workers very isolated and unable to stand up to their employers and is particularly isolating for women.

Nuclear Family (image: Donald Lee Pardue)

Functionalism & Class Inequalities

Functionalists understand social class through the concept of **Meritocracy**. This is a social arrangement where individuals are rewarded for their talent and hard work. Functionalists accept that not everyone is equally talented (because of biological differences or just luck) so they will always deserve different rewards, with some people getting more than others.

In **1A: Socialisation, Culture & Identity**, you were introduced to the theory of **social stratification** by **Davis & Moore (1945)**. They argue that some social roles are **functionally unique** (only a few talented people can do them) but others are highly **dependent on others** (needing experts and managers to guide them). Jobs that aren't functionally unique but are highly dependent (e.g. a cleaner in a large office block) aren't highly paid, but jobs that are functionally unique and independent of others (e.g. the manager of a big Trans National Corporation who makes all her own decisions) deserve the highest wages.

For Functionalists, the working classes do the work that is not functionally unique but is highly dependent on others. People who can work independently and possess hard-to-master skills will work their way up to the middle or upper classes. This is called **social mobility**.

RESEARCH PROFILE: TUMIN (1953)

Melvin Tumin (1919-1994) criticises Davis & Moore in *Some Principles of Stratification: A Critical Analysis* **(1953)**. Tumin claims it isn't possible to determine the functional importance of most jobs. Tumin argues that the unskilled workmen in a factory are as important to the factory as the skilled engineers who also work in that factory. On the other hand, Tumin proposes that it's not clear what difference it makes if the manager of a big company isn't particularly good at her job.

Similarly, Tumin argues that it isn't clear that the **highest-paid people have rare talents**. A lot of other people might have exactly the same talents – or better ones! – but they never get the chance to show it in a high-paid job.

Davis & Moore argue that the long period of training needed to get the qualifications needed for top jobs is a **sacrifice** (e.g. losing out on earnings and getting into debt as a student), but Tumin questions this, pointing out that students enjoy great **freedom and stimulation** and quickly **repay their debts** and **recoup lost earnings** with their higher salaries.

Tumin also argues that there are other motivations beside monetary reward, such as the **desire to benefit society**. Davis & Moore's social stratification leads to a **resentful and divided society** of haves and have-nots rather than everyone working together for the benefit of the whole.

Functionalism & Gender Inequalities

Functionalists understand gender as a product of **biological sex**. Children need to be **socialised** into appropriate gender roles and those roles need to be **stabilised** by adult (secondary and tertiary) socialisation.

In **1A: Socialisation, Culture & Identity**, you were introduced to **Talcott Parsons'** theory that fathers are the **instrumental role leaders** and mothers the **expressive role leaders** in a family. Put simply, fathers teach children discipline to be successful in the world outside home and mothers teach the emotional skills to form close relationships with others.

Parsons believes daughters naturally imitate their mothers and sons their fathers. This leads to a **division of labour**, with **males as breadwinners** and **females as homemakers**.

Functionalists don't insist that *everyone* follows these traditional gender roles, but they propose that individuals are more fulfilled, and society is more functional when most people do. This leads to inequalities, especially for women, but Functionalists insist these are really innate differences and that, in any event, individual families and society as a whole benefit from men and women playing these traditional roles.

These Functionalist ideas were proposed in 1950s America when a working adult's wage could support a family. In 21st century America and the UK, this is no longer true; in most families both parents need to bring in a wage to support the family. So even if the gendered division of labour is ideal, it's only possible now for wealthier families.

RESEARCH PROFILE: ANSLEY (1972)

Fran Ansley is a Feminist who criticises Talcott Parson's view of women, especially the idea of the family functioning to stabilise adult personalities. Parsons argues that the function of the wife is to be an **'emotional safety-valve'** to absorb the husband's frustrations (created by working in the Capitalist system). By acting as an emotional safety valve, the wife helps keep society stable. This is known as the **'Warm Bath' Theory**, with the man returning to the family being like stepping into a warm bath (comforting and refreshing).

Ansley interprets the situation differently: "*When wives play their traditional role as* **takers of shit***, they often absorb their husband's legitimate anger and frustration at their own powerlessness and oppression.*"

This **'takers of shit'** explanation focuses on conflict in society rather than consensus as Parsons' does. Ansley argues that gender roles are not 'different but equal' (as Functionalists claim) but rather 'different and *unequal* – and benefiting Capitalism.'

A Warm Bath (image: Kaptain Kobold)

Functionalism & Ethnic Inequalities

Although Functionalists believe in biological differences, they do not focus on biology to explain ethnic inequalities – instead they focus on **culture**. The idea is that immigrants arrive in an industrially developed country with low skills for the sort of work required there and cultural practices that hold them back (such as not speaking the language).

The **host-immigrant model** suggests that, over time, immigrants must they **assimilate** into the **host culture** in three stages:

1. **Accommodation:** the immigrants adjust to the host society in minimal ways, such as finding jobs and learning the customs of co-workers and neighbours
2. **Integration:** immigrants and hosts begin socialising together outside of work
3. **Assimilation:** immigrants adopt the norms and values of the host community and are fully accepted

This view completely ignores the possibility of **racial discrimination**, which might lock immigrants out of high-wage, high-status jobs regardless of their skills, and **institutional racism** which would make it impossible for some groups to assimilate no matter how hard they try.

This model is the opposite of a truly **multicultural society** because the immigrants are expected to sacrifice their cultural distinctiveness and adopt the culture of the hosts. It ignores the phenomenon of **cultural defence** and **hybrid cultures** and assumes that **cultural homogeneity** is an entirely good thing.

RESEARCH PROFILE: PATTERSON (1965)

Sheila Patterson studied post-War Britain in the 1950s and '60s, especially the experience of the Windrush Generation of immigrants from the Caribbean. She views these immigrants as disrupting a stable, homogeneous society, resulting in a culture clash between the norms and values of the immigrants and the host community. Patterson argues that the hosts were not racist, just unsure of how to behave towards the newcomers.

Patterson identifies 3 causes of ethnic inequality: (**1**) the hosts **fear the cultural differences** of the 'strangers;' (**2**) the hosts **resent having to compete** with immigrants for jobs and housing; and (**3**) the immigrants **fail to assimilate** into the host culture.

Patterson takes an **optimistic view** (like most Functionalists) that ethnic inequality will fade away in time, but immigrant groups have only themselves to blame if they do not assimilate and must accept an inevitable hostility from the host community until they do.

Marxists reject Patterson's ideas, arguing that Capitalism itself structures society to keep immigrants in an inferior position so that they can do the unpleasant low-paid jobs. **Critical Race Theory** (CRT, p154) argues that White hosts have an **unconscious bias** against dark-skinned immigrants and do not intend them to assimilate and become equals.

Functionalism & Age Inequalities

Functionalists claim that inequalities experienced at different ages are really differences, with a biological basis, that need to be embraced – or else endured for the greater good of society. **Talcott Parsons** argues that youth is a **'bridge'** connecting childhood to adulthood. **Shmuel Eisenstadt (1956)** was a student of Parsons and argues that youth is a time of 'storm and stress' as young people break away from the authority and comfort provided by their parents and work out their own role in society; youth culture is a time of experimentation and testing of boundaries, but this is for the good of individuals and of society in the long run.

In **1A: Socialisation, Culture & Identity** you were introduced to the **Disengagement Theory** proposed by **Henry & Cummings (1961)** to explain the role of the elderly. As people's abilities deteriorate with age, they need to disengage from their social responsibilities and give up their power and status and come to terms with their inevitable death. This allows a new generation to take their place, which is good for society to progress.

These theories view ageing as an inevitable process which, if managed correctly, maintains **social solidarity** and allows for social progress in a non-disruptive way. Even apparently disruptive events – such as the wild behaviour of adolescents or the retirement of a capable leader – are in fact for the greater good in the long run.

RESEARCH PROFILE: HAVIGHURST (1961)

Robert J. Havighurst criticises Disengagement Theory for being too pessimistic about ageing. He argues that withdrawing from social roles—work, marriage, raising a family—means that older people risk suffering a personal crisis and demoralisation. Instead, he proposes **Activity Theory**.

Activity Theory states that people are happiest when they stay active and maintain social interactions. Meaningful activities help the elderly to replace lost roles after retirement and resist social exclusion. Examples including continuing to work part time or volunteering, going on foreign holidays, engaging in charity work and fundraising, helping with community projects and political campaigning. It could also include starting new romantic relationships (like the **'silver splicers,'** p126). The theory assumes there is a link between this sort of activity and life satisfaction.

Critics of Activity Theory claim it ignores **class inequalities** (p99) that prevent older people engaging in meaningful activities.

The research by **Jones et al.** (p125) is not from a Functionalist Perspective but it illustrates some aspects of Activity Theory because the respondents experienced retirement as a positive time of renewal and creativity. However, they were all wealthy middle-class people whose well-paid jobs enabled them to take early retirement, rather than ordinary people who have to work right up to the **State Pension Age (SPA)** and this illustrates the main criticism of Activity Theory too.

The 40-Mark Essay

You could be set a 40-mark question on Functionalist explanations for inequality. Often, this question will take the form of inviting you to discuss a concept that Functionalists have distinctive views on, such as **meritocracy**, **social mobility** or **multiculturalism**. You could also bring Functionalism into an essay on inequalities of class, gender, ethnicity or age, especially as a developed evaluation (see **Chapter 7** for more on this).

Functionalist arguments dominated post-War Sociology of the 1950s and '60s, especially in America. However, by the end of the 1960s, Functionalism had fallen out of favour and sociologists were exploring **Conflict Theories** as a better way of explaining the rapid social changes going on. This tells us that Functionalism works best as an explanation of life in stable and homogenous societies but is much less persuasive when it comes to explaining life in rapidly changing and diverse societies – such as the UK in the 21st century.

Nonetheless, Functionalism has an enormous 'common sense' appeal. It takes social institutions and problems at face value, and it suggests that life isn't perfect, and never will be, so a certain amount of inequality and dissatisfaction is inevitable. It finds value in traditional institutions (which people are often sentimental about), it recommends gradual change rather than sudden breaks with the past and it offers an optimistic picture of progress over time.

This is in contrast to the Conflict Perspectives, which argue that things are never what they seem, that society is currently in crisis but that some sort of ideal society is achievable if only we can make a decisive break with the past.

Young people often find Functionalism dull and complacent, but to older people it is a reassuring outlook. After all, Western societies are surprisingly stable and successful, with power changing hands without violence, riots being the exception rather than the norm and most people feeling safe and trusting in the police to protect them.

Nevertheless, there are many problems with the Functionalist worldview. It is often accused of representing the outlook of comfortable middle-class people and ignoring the much more difficult and dangerous life on the streets of big cities.

Functionalism tends to represent inequalities as inevitable, ignoring the possibility that they are caused by fixable flaws in our institutions, or else it views them as as the fault of the disadvantaged groups themselves, for failing to conform to social norms. This ignores the extent to which inequality is structural – a bias built into our social institutions that will continue to discriminate against some groups no matter *how* they behave.

Nonetheless, it is probably the case that some inequalities *are* in fact inevitable and that sometimes disadvantaged people *do* bring trouble upon themselves by reacting unhelpfully to the problems they face – such as children who struggle at school reacting by truanting, which makes the problem worse. The **Social Action (Weberian) Perspective** explores the relationship between oppressive social structures and individual choices (p165).

CONSENSUS PERSPECTIVE: THE NEW RIGHT

Functionalism fell out of favour with sociologists at the end of the 1960s but Functionalist ideas continued to circulate. In the 1980s, these ideas returned as the **New Right.** However, the New Right departs from Functionalism in one crucial way: it claims that the **value consensus** in society has collapsed, and emergency measures are needed to restore it. The New Right diagnoses the core institution for value consensus as the **nuclear family** (p134) and claims that the biggest threat to this is the **Welfare State**. The Welfare State is the political arrangement that collects taxes from the rich and redistributes it in the form of benefit payments to the poor.

These criticisms derive from the work of writers like **Milton Friedman (1962)** and **Friedrich Hayek (1944)** who argue that the state (meaning all the powers of government) needs to be shrunk so that businesses and families can manage themselves without interference.

AO2 ILLUSTRATION: NEOLIBERALISM & THATCHERISM

The ideas of 'shrinking the state' and de-regulating businesses (removing restrictions from them) have become central to a political philosophy known today as **neoliberalism**. Neoliberalism also supports free trade, which tends to benefit powerful **Trans National Corporations (TNCs).**

In the 1980s, these neoliberal ideas were taken up by two influential leaders: the Conservative Prime Minister **Margaret Thatcher** in the UK and the Republican President **Ronald Regan** in the USA. Their influence was so great that political philosophies were named after them: **Thatcherism** in the UK and **Reaganomics** in the USA. Both **cut taxes** and **deregulated businesses**, allowing companies (and wealthy people) to make more money. They **restricted benefits** to encourage the unemployed to seek work. They urged personal freedom, arguing that people should take responsibility for their lives and not expect to be looked after by the 'nanny state.'

The New Right & Class Inequalities

Charles Murray wrote *Losing Ground* **(1984)** which is the key statement of New Right thinking. Murray traces the rise of crime in the USA since the 1960s and finds it does not match trends in unemployment; however, it **does** match the trend for children born outside of marriage. Murray argues that boys born to unmarried mothers grow up to be *"essentially barbarians."* A key assumption is that males are only civilised by marriage and without the pressure to marry (which the Welfare State removes) they turn to drugs and crime. This is how **the Underclass** is created.

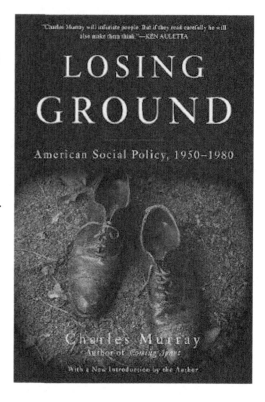

Murray blames this state of affairs on the Welfare State; he argues it **rewards worklessness** and **undermines the nuclear family** (since couples are not forced to stay together if the state pays for their children). The lone parent family (especially the single mother) cannot effectively **socialise** children, who grow up 'feral': the girls get pregnant without marrying, repeating the cycle, while the boys search for a father-figure and join gangs. Murray argues that this is the lifestyle of the Underclass.

Murray identifies a **'benefits trap'** that means unemployed people end up worse off if they take a job, creating an incentive to stay unemployed and leading to **generational unemployment**, where families have parents and grandparents who do not work and claim benefits. Murray's solution is to cut back benefits, forcing health adults to find work and take responsibility for their families. This is exactly the approach adopted by **Margaret Thatcher** and **Ronald Reagan** (p141). It is based on the idea that trying to help the poor through benefits actually makes their situation worse and in order to deal with poverty you need to 'be cruel to be kind.'

Critics (e.g. **Dean & Taylor-Gooby, 1992**) claim there is **no evidence** for the existence of the Underclass that Murray describes. They suggest that the poorest families have little in common with each other except a motivation to find work. Moreover, even fathers who do not live with their children can continue to play a big part in their upbringing. Murray's solution is particularly contested, since shrinking the state removes support for poor families which worsens their situation rather than improving it.

Deborah Chambers (2001) argues that lone parent families and their 'feral' children is just a **moral panic** used by Conservative Governments to blame someone for problems in society.

Research: find out about moral panics in the media and spread by governments

RESEARCH PROFILE: DENNIS & ERDOS (1992)

Norman Dennis & George Erdos are **Marxist** thinkers – pretty much the opposite of the New Right, but they came to some similar conclusions in *Families Without Fatherhood* (1992).

They argue that the inner-city riots in the UK and USA in the 1980s and early '90s could not be linked entirely to poverty, because there was far more hardship for the poor in the 1930s and '50s but much less unrest. They propose that increasing numbers of **lone parent families** are a factor and that this is linked to a wider problem of **moral collapse** in the poorest communities.

Dennis & Erdos argue that, until the 1960s, people made a moral distinction between a mother raising children alone because she had been widowed and one who had never been married. From the 1970s on, social workers and politicians felt they could not make moral judgments about people's sex lives so there was no **stigma** attached any more to having children outside of marriage. They cite a longitudinal study of 1000 children in Newcastle who had a greater chance of poor health, low IQ and a criminal record if they were fatherless or 'poorly fathered.'

Even though they diagnose the same problems as the New Right, Dennis & Erdos propose very different solutions from Charles Murray. They suggest the state should intervene to help disadvantaged families. However, Dennis & Erdos describe themselves as *"ethical socialists"* and argue that benefits should favour the 'deserving poor' who are unlucky rather than the 'undeserving poor' who are lazy or irresponsible.

Furthermore, Dennis & Erdos blame the **neoliberal values** of Conservative Governments (p141) for adding to the problem of broken families: the 'free market' mentality that there should be no regulation on the behaviour of the rich has encouraged poor young men to believe that they can behave irresponsibly as well.

Dennis & Erdos' views were very influential in the New Labour Government that came into power in 1997 with a mission to help the poor *without* undermining the family.

The New Right & Gender Inequalities

The New Right follows the **Functionalist** understanding of gender (p136) as binary (masculine and feminine) and based on biological characteristics, with males as breadwinners and females as homemakers and child-raisers. **Talcott Parsons** recognised back in the 1950s that the nuclear family was losing its functions to the state, especially in educating its children and caring for its sick. However, he thought that *"essential and irreducible"* functions would remain. The New Right argues that these functions are now under threat too.

Specifically, young mothers are encouraged to become 'wives of the state' once they become pregnant: they can claim free housing and benefits to pay for the children, so they don't need the father's presence in their life as a breadwinner. They ability to **socialise children** suffers and without these responsibilities adults do not benefit from the **stabilisation of personality**.

As well as the Welfare State, the New Right blames **Feminism** for this state of affairs. Feminism is usually hostile to the nuclear family, regarding it as an arrangement that subordinates and even enslaves women (p137). More generally, Feminism encourages women to believe that they don't need men and that men have nothing valuable to offer them or their children, especially when the Welfare State is paying the bills.

The New Right acknowledges that middle class mothers have the skills and resources to function as lone parents. However, the burden of lone parenthood falls heaviest on the poorest people, leading to the creation of an **Underclass** where children look for their missing father figures in inappropriate places: young men in gangs, young women in irresponsible lovers who impregnate them then leave. Raising children by different fathers all by themselves means women are unable to further their education or find rewarding careers.

Critics argue that this is a distorted picture of what is going on in poor families and that fathers who do not live with their children still have a role in their upbringing.

RESEARCH PROFILE: WENTE (2014)

Margaret Wente is a Canadian journalist who asks, ***Do we still need Feminism?*** She reports a social media campaign that began on Tumblr with the hashtag **#WomenAgainstFeminism**. Young women post selfies with handwritten signs such as: "*I don't need feminism because* [fill in reason here]." The reasons include: "*My self-worth is not directly tied to the size of my victim complex!*" "*I love being an engineer, but I'd rather just be Mom*" and "*I like men looking at me when I look good.*"

Wente reports surveys that find fewer than half of younger women support feminism. This is backed up in the UK by a survey that finds fewer than 1 in 5 young women identify as a Feminist (source: **Fawcett Society, 2019**).

Wente argues this is because the moderate and reasonable demands of **2nd Wave Feminism** have been achieved. In its place, she detects "*a hard core of misandry* [man-hating] *and victim-culture in modern feminism that is deeply disturbing.*" Wente identifies rape culture as a "*myth*" and dismisses the popular claim that 1 in 5 female students will be sexually assaulted by the time they get their degree as "*utterly fictitious.*"

Wente is not a speaker for the New Right. She supports the equal rights achieved by 2nd Wave Feminists and believes Feminism is needed to help girls and women in cultures that do not yet enjoy those rights. However, some of Wente's views are shared, not just by the New Right, but by Far Right extremists who accuse Feminists of being **'Feminazis'** who hate men. Moreover, the antifeminist movement in America is linked to the campaign to remove women's right to abortion, which is a major achievement of 2nd Wave Feminism.

Research: research the current debates on America between feminists and the Christian Right about abortion rights

The New Right & Ethnic Inequalities

The New Right doesn't have much to say about ethnic inequality, except to point out that some ethnic minorities exist in the growing Underclass and for the same reason as White families: lone parent mothers on benefits, absent and irresponsible fathers, children growing up without discipline or good role models.

Charles Murray wrote another controversial book in the 1990s: *The Bell Curve* (**1994**, co-authored with **Richard Herrnstein**). Murray & Herrnstein analyse differences in IQ and how they relate to achievement. In one infamous chapter, they consider the racial basis of IQ and claim that, on average, Black people in the USA score lower on IQ than other ethnic groups.

Murray & Herrnstein's data has been hotly contested. Murray stands accused of being a racist for even making the claim. The argument that some ethnic groups are biologically inferior is known as **scientific racism** and it has a long history, including links to **eugenics** (the movement to restrict the birth rate of inferior groups) and of course Nazi ideology. Murray & Herrnstein aren't Nazis or eugenicists, but critics fear their book gives support to people who are.

Murray & Herrnstein's views are a stark example of **viewing inequalities as a biological differences**. This leads to a typical New Right conclusion that benefits are wasted on trying to fix a difference that exists in nature and is not a result of discrimination or social structures.

RESEARCH PROFILE: SEWELL (1997)

Tony Sewell has been introduced as the chair of the **2021 CRED Report** into racism in the UK (p120). He is not a speaker for the New Right, but in *Black Masculinities & Schooling* (**1997**), his analysis of the problems in the Black community is similar to the New Right diagnosis.

Sewell argues that there is a **subculture of hyper-masculinity** among young Black males. A high proportion of Black Caribbean boys are raised in lone mother households with an absent father: 57% of Black Caribbean families compared to only 25% of White families when Sewell published his findings. Without a father to act as a role model and provide discipline, these boys are more vulnerable to peer pressure and get drawn into gang culture which uses violence to gain respect. This subculture provides peer support which makes up for their rejection by their fathers. It also compensates them for the racism and injustice they feel from wider society. The subculture emphasis displays of wealth ('bling') such as the latest street fashions. Crime is preferred to 'hard work' as a quick and easy ('smart') route to success.

Sewell does not accept that disadvantage is an excuse for failure but otherwise his solution is very different from that of the New Right. He argues Black boys need **strict schooling** that demands **high expectations** and offers **positive opportunities** that middle class students get through their social and cultural capital.

Research: find out about Sewell's 'Generating Genius' programme to turn around Black boys

The New Right & Age Inequalities

The New Right does not have much to say about the elderly. The New Right perspective on youth is that a youth subculture has emerged among the Underclass, characterised by **educational failure**, **offending**, **sexual irresponsibility** and **worklessness**. The New Right view is that they could turn their lives around if they were motivated to, but the availability of benefits means that they do not choose to.

The New Right places the blame for this with politicians who have expanded the Welfare State in a misguided attempt to help the poor and **Marxist** and **Feminist** thinkers who have encouraged this out of a desire to dismantle the nuclear family because of its connection to traditional values. However, **Conflict Perspectives** see the lone parent family structure as irrelevant: it's the unfairness of Capitalism that puts young people in this situation, not their absent fathers.

Shrinking the state has implications for the elderly. **Thatcherism** (p141) promoted the concept of 'care in the community' which moved people out of hospitals and care homes to be looked after by their families. If you read **Gentleman's account of life in a care home** (p129) you might agree with this policy; however, **Marxists** condemn it as a way for the state to save money by forcing families to look after old people who are a burden on Capitalism now they cannot work.

RESEARCH PROFILE: O'NEILL (2002)

Rebecca O'Neill produced a report for the Right Wing think tank CIVITAS (p41), entitled *Experiments In Living: The Fatherless Family* (2002). The report brings together the findings of research into the effects of fatherlessness on young children growing up. She argues that, since the 1960s, politicians and feminists have been organising a gigantic social 'experiment' to see if alternatives to the traditional nuclear family can be successful. She concludes they are *not* successful and instead the families taking part in this 'experiment in living' have experienced *"poverty, emotional heartache, ill health, lost opportunities, and a lack of stability."*

O'Neill argues that, despite the declining number of marriages, the two-parent nuclear family is still the ideal and that most people wish to get married. However, during the 1990s, 55% of divorces involved a child under age 16 and 25% of children whose parents divorced in 2000 were under age five. O'Neill argues this has damaged a generation of children.

Teenagers living without their biological fathers are more likely to smoke, drink alcohol and take drugs but also more likely to become teenage parents or break the law. Adults who grew up without their biological fathers are more likely to attain poor qualifications, work in low-paid jobs, be unemployed and be homeless. They are more likely to get divorced themselves, leading to a '**Cycle of Fatherlessness.**'

However, unlike the New Right, O'Neill draws short of blaming this entirely on the Welfare State. She points out that increasing numbers of lone parent families and welfare dependency could be *"mutually reinforcing"* rather than one causing the other.

The 40-Mark Essay

You could be set a 40-mark question on New Right explanations for inequality. Often, this question will take the form of inviting you to discuss a concept that the New Right has distinctive views on, such as **absent fathers** or **benefits dependency**. You could also bring the New Right into an essay on inequalities of class, gender, ethnicity or age, especially as a developed evaluation of Marxism or Feminism (see **Chapter 7** for more on this).

The presence of the New Right on this Specification is a bit odd. The New Right isn't really a complete theoretical Perspective the way **Marxism** or **Functionalism** are. It only really has sociological ideas about one phenomenon (**lone parent families on benefits**), it only really has one significant scholar (**Charles Murray**) and it only really applies to the political situation of the 1980s and '90s (although it has had a longer impact on educational policy in the UK).

The New Right is really on this course to be a bit of a punchbag (set up its arguments and then knock them down when you evaluate) but it can also be used to offer critical evaluations of Marxism and Feminism by showing up the unforeseen side-effects of some of their attacks on the family or their solutions to poverty.

New Right thinkers often claim to be **Functionalists** (or Neo-Functionalists) but the New Right differs from Functionalism in two important ways.

First, Functionalism argues that the nuclear family has evolved because it is **the most functional family structure**. If it ceases to be functional, it must fade away and be replaced by other more functional arrangements. However, the New Right insists that **the nuclear family is 'under threat'** and needs to be saved. From a strictly Functionalist viewpoint, the nuclear family can only be threatened by something that is in fact *better* – in which case, good riddance to the nuclear family because its replacement will be superior.

Secondly, Functionalism insists there is a **value consensus** that everyone in society shares. The New Right insists there has been a **moral collapse** among poor communities, where getting pregnant outside of marriage and fathering children on different women but not taking responsibility for them is seen as a perfectly normal thing to do. This is a clear departure from the way Functionalists view social problems.

There are some strengths to the New Right outlook. Divorce is widespread among the elite in society (such as movie stars, many politicians and the Royal Family) but when the poor try to imitate this lifestyle they suffer because they do not have the wealth to cope with the difficulties it creates. **Dennis & Erdos** come from a Marxist Perspective, but they agree that middle class sociologists have encouraged the working classes to abandon traditional notions of marriage, family and duty without considering the problems this leads to. It also resembles **Jock Young**'s diagnosis of the **'bulimic society'** you were introduced to in **1A: Socialisation, Culture & Identity**.

The New Right solution is to try to drag society back to the way it was in the past (as they imagine it) in some 'golden age' when everyone was more self-reliant and disciplined and unselfish. However, even if you think this sounds desirable, it is probably completely impractical.

CONFLICT PERSPECTIVE: MARXISM

Marxism is another **structuralist** Perspective that looks at inequality and difference across society as a whole. However, unlike **Functionalists**, Marxists don't make excuses for inequality or justify it as inevitable. They don't accept that it is in any way functional or related to people's innate biological differences.

Instead, Marxists explain that inequality is a non-accidental product of **Capitalism**. It is part of the **structure of a Capitalist society** and it's a result of the greed of the ruling class and their willingness to oppress and exploit the working classes.

Karl Marx proposes that society consists of an economic **base** (valuable land, raw materials, natural resources) and a **superstructure** built from it. The superstructure consists of the social institutions we see around us: government, schools, hospitals, jobs, families. The ruling class control the base; as Marx would say, they own the 'means of production.' The base dictates the superstructure. Therefore, the ruling class dominates the entire fabric of society, including our culture and how we feel about things. Marx refers to this as RULING CLASS IDEOLOGY.

Ruling class ideology has two effects: it **hides** inequality and, when it cannot hide it, it **justifies** inequality. Inequality is hidden when we don't notice it: it's out of sight, not reported in the news, not discussed in conversation, kept off the streets; it is 'swept under the carpet.' If inequality is actually noticed, it is justified by being described as normal, natural, inevitable or even well-deserved. Most Functionalist explanations of inequality (p134) can be dismissed as *ideological* by Marxists.

Most Marxists do not accept that there are significant biological differences between people that could justify social inequality. Attempts to prove the existence of these differences (e.g. by IQ testing) are criticised as ideological.

Here to protect you – or oppress you? (image: Thomas Hawk)

Since the ruling class are a tiny minority, any system to keep them in power and the vast majority of working-class people oppressed will be very unstable. Marx diagnoses Capitalism as continually in crisis but staving off a full-scale revolution by the working classes through ideological appeals, scapegoating minorities, short term compensations and, ultimately, the coercive power of the police and the military. **Louis Althusser** refers to this as the **Ideological State Apparatus (ISA)** and the **Repressive State Apparatus (RSA)**.

Marxists hope that the working classes will achieve **class consciousness** – they will see through the ruling class ideology that keeps them in a subdued state of **false consciousness**. To do this, Marxists believe in the importance of **consciousness raising**: making people aware of how oppressed they are. This is particularly important for **Neo-Marxists** (*see below*).

AO2 ILLUSTRATION: POLITICAL CORRECTNESS

'Political correctness' (PC) means avoiding language that insults or excludes people who are already experiencing discrimination.

The debate about political correctness emerged in the late 1980s. Marxists and feminists urged politicians and publishers to replace language that had discriminatory effects. For example, replacing 'chairman' with 'chairperson' or just 'chair' and avoiding phrases that used 'black' in a negative sense, like giving someone a 'black mark.' PC language involves replacing terms like 'cripple' with more neutral terms like 'disability' and disapproving of comic stereotypes of homosexuality and ethnic groups that were hurtful for those minorities (and introducing the positive of the term 'gay').

More recently, political correctness has involved using people's **preferred pronouns**. For example, in 2019 the pop star **Sam Smith** came out as non-binary gender and asked fans and journalists to use the pronouns **'they/them'** when referring to them.

It's easy to criticise political correctness for its fussiness and the confusion it can cause. For example, a recruitment agency once advertised for *'reliable and hard-working'* applicants for a cleaning job but was told by the Jobcentre that the advert wasn't allowed because these words *"may discriminate against the unreliable"* (source: **BBC, 2010**). Stories like this give rise to the complaint of *'political correctness gone mad!'*

Most of the time PC language is a straightforward policy of avoiding hurt and being sensitive to people's feelings. For example, the PC term 'actor' is used for men and women now, rather than 'actress' which suggests female actors do a less serious sort of job.

Political correctness is a Marxist cause, especially a **Neo-Marxist** one, since its focus is on **consciousness-raising** and challenging assumptions about power and identity. **Functionalists** tend to oppose political correctness, because it is an attempt to police language rather than letting it evolve naturally. However, Functionalists also police language themselves (for example, they are often concerned about obscene language on TV and other media).

Neo-Marxism

Neo means 'new' and **Neo-Marxism** emerged in the 1970s as a new development in Marxist thought. **Antonio Gramsci (1891-1937)** observed that the ruling class was no longer a literal class of aristocrats and factory owners, but had become a **Hegemony**, a confederation of influential people with a vested interest in keeping Capitalism going. Gramsci pointed out that Hegemony **'manufactures consent'** through education and the media. This insight marks a move away from a literal revolution to overthrow Capitalism to what Gramsci called *"the long march through the institutions"* which means changing people's ideas – especially the people in charge of education, religion, government and the media – through **consciousness-raising**.

This Neo-Marxist view sees inequality as resulting from some groups having **privileges** while other groups are **marginalised** (pushed to the edges, disadvantaged). People in privileged (or **hegemonic**) groups try to maintain their privileges and this seems to them to be a normal and natural thing to do. Part of the mission for Neo-Marxists is making people see how their privileges cause other people to be marginalised.

This leads to the Neo-Marxist instruction that people should **'check their privileges'** (i.e. think about how unearned your privileges are and the power imbalance between you and people who don't have your privileges).

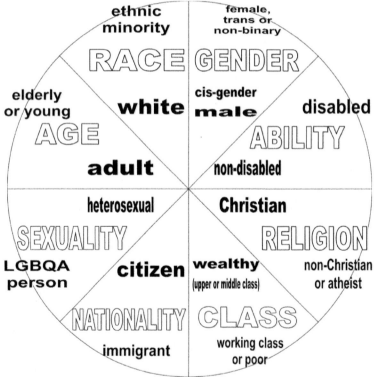

Wheel of Privilege: the closer to the centre, the greater your privilege, but the closer to the edges (or margins) the more marginalised you are

The idea of **privileges-versus-marginalisation** takes in many more types of inequality than just the four types covered in this Specification – for example, there is also immigrant status, religion, disability and sexuality. For Neo-Marxists to extend their activism to these marginalised groups could be seen as a big improvement on traditional Marxist ideas which focus largely on economics and class (however, *see below* for a counter argument).

Important features of Neo-Marxism today are the concepts of allyship and equity.

Allyship is the idea that people who experience one type of marginalisation should be allies with people who experience another type. For example, working class people should be allies to ethnic minorities, the elderly and women rather than seeing themselves as being in competition with them.

Equity is an alternative to the ordinary idea of equality. **Equality** is where everyone gets the same opportunities and it's an important part of the **Functionalist** idea of **Meritocracy** (p135). Equity is where everyone gets equivalent outcomes, usually because special assistance is given to disadvantaged groups. One popular way of ensuring equity is to use **quotas** to make sure that a certain number of people from disadvantaged backgrounds are given important jobs or places on courses. For example, in the **Nordic Model** (p107), there are quotas to ensure a certain number of women in parliament. Equity can involve **positive action** or **positive discrimination** (p88).

These ideas are controversial. Allyship assumes that groups don't *have* to be in competition, but sometimes they are. For example, working class White people and people from ethnic minorities might be chasing the same jobs. Equity can be seen as unfair, because it means giving one group special help that another group doesn't get. For example, if a quota makes sure that women (possibly White and middle-class women) get positions in parliament, then men (possibly working class or Black men) can't get those positions, even if they are better qualified.

Marxism & Class Inequalities

Traditional Marxists are **materialists** who believe that society's inequalities all stem from the fact that a tiny minority of people (the **ruling class** or *bourgeoisie*) control the **means of production** (the raw resources, land and machinery needed to create wealth) and the vast majority of people (the **working class** or *proletariat*) are forced to work for them, **selling their labour** in return for wages.

This simple analysis explains a lot but it means that Marxists in the past focused on class inequalities at the expense of other types of inequality. As materialists, many Marxists argue that ethnic, gender and age inequalities are just side-effects of the economic inequality they see at the heart of Capitalism. If the economic inequalities can be abolished, the other types of inequality will disappear too.

Neo-Marxism tends to argue that the other types of inequality are separate and distinct. **Intersectionality** (p158) draws attention to how different types of inequality intersect and intensify. For example, being working class, female and Black means that a person experiences multiple types of discrimination that combine together to create intense marginalisation.

This debate within Marxism has important consequences. For example, in the **2019 General Election**, the poor results for the Labour Party in some working-class constituencies were explained by some critics as a backlash from working-class voters who felt betrayed that the Labour Party supported other groups more than them. Whether or not this is true, it illustrates a danger for Marxists in moving beyond class as their main focus.

Research: research the results of the **2019 General Election**, especially the **'Red Wall'** constituencies and different explanations of why Labour lost seats in them

RESEARCH PROFILE: BRAVERMAN (1974)

Henry Braverman wrote a Marxist classic in *Labour & Monopoly Capital: The Degradation of Work in the Twentieth Century* (1974). Braverman updates the traditional (materialist) Marxist view by studying how working conditions changed in the late 20th century.

Throughout the 20th century, Functionalist writers noticed the **automatisation of labour**, with machines taking over the difficult and dangerous tasks in factories. They concluded this would benefit workers, leading to more leisure time and more stimulating jobs. Braverman disagrees. He argues that mass production **alienates** and **de-skills** the worker.

Deskilling is a mechanism through which the owners of the means of production increase profits by **reducing their labour costs**. For example, in car factories and warehouses robots replace human workers. Computerisation intensifies this trend: barcodes on shop products and and Internet banking means supermarkets and banks don't need workers competent in arithmetic; self-service checkouts mean human workers are barely needed at all.

Braverman argues that it's not just the working classes who have been deskilled. Middle class workers have seen their jobs broken up into simpler tasks that can be completed by less-skilled workers. **Frey & Osborne (2013)** predict professions like lawyers, doctors and accountants will be next as computer apps create online self-help services or allow people to diagnose themselves.

Deskilled workers have **less status and control** over their working conditions. They are **easier to fire and replace**. This leads to **proletarianization**: the process where formerly middle-class workers find themselves in the same powerless position as the working class.

Braverman's ideas can be evaluated by Neo-Marxism or used to criticise Neo-Marxism by show that a focus on class and working conditions is growing more important, not less.

Marxism & Gender Inequalities

Karl Marx gave little attention to the experiences of women, but his friend and collaborator **Friedrich Engels** explains the subordinate position of women as resulting from Capitalism. Engels suggests that long ago men and women were more equal, but Capitalism introduced inequalities. The **exploitative relationship** between the bourgeoisie and the proletariat is mirrored in the family, with men exploiting women by making them labour for them. Men also want to pass on private property to their children; this leads to the **emergence of the nuclear family** as an arrangement that controls the sexual behaviour of women and helps men be certain that children are their own legitimate offspring. This is a different theory of the nuclear family from that proposed by **Functionalists** (p134).

From a **Neo-Marxist Perspective**, this economic view of gender inequalities fails to account for differing **privileges**. For example, some women (White, middle class women, for example) have far more privileges than some men (working class men from ethnic minority backgrounds, homosexual men, trans men, etc.).

Feminists accuse Marxists of offering a **male-centred (androcentric) view** of gender inequalities, with women's status being defined by their husband's place in the Capitalist economy.

RESEARCH PROFILE: ZARETSKY (1976)

Eli Zaretsky wrote *Capitalism, The Family & Personal Life* **(1976)** in response to the analysis of gender roles by **Talcott Parsons**.

Zaretsky argues that the family performs a psychological function to nurture and support its members, adults as well as children. This is similar to **Parsons' warm bath theory** (p137). However, Zaretsky claims that, rather than helping individuals, the family cushions the psychological damage caused by Capitalism.

Ordinarily, the alienation experienced at work would drive the working class to a revolution. Zaretsky says that the family prevents this. He agrees that the family helps relieve the stress of the working day and prepare a worker for the next day of labour, but he sees this as a negative thing. If it wasn't for family life comforting workers, they would see more clearly how they are being exploited! The happiness of the family is therefore **false consciousness** – a sort of illusory or substitute happiness that distracts people from achieving equality.

Women work for the Capitalist system for free, as housewives, feeding the male workers, cleaning their houses and having children to provide the next generation of exploited workers.

Zaretsky's ideas are out-of-date now that so many women are earners alongside men or even the main earner of the family. **Delphy & Leonard (1992)** argue that **the Patriarchy** benefits from family life, rather than Capitalism. They build on earlier research by Ann Oakley, who claims that working women had a dual burden of paid work and unpaid domestic work, whereas time at home for men is leisure time.

Marxism & Ethnic Inequalities

Oliver Cox (1970) argues that 'race' itself is a **social construct** that is used to justify exploitation. Cox (who grew up in Trinidad, a former British colony) gives the example of **colonialism**: the supposed racial superiority of white Europeans was used to justify exploiting other races for the economic benefit of their empires. Cox argues that **racism is dependent on Capitalism**.

Cox's ideas developed into **Critical Race Theory (CRT)** – a term coined by **Kimberlé Crenshaw**, (who also proposed **Intersectionality**, making her one of the most influential thinkers in the Conflict Perspective alive today). CRT proposes that **racism is institutionalised** in majority-White societies (like Europe and North America) and all White people have **implicit racial bias** (p114).

These are the main claims of CRT:

- Racism is often **invisible** and promoted by a **system that discriminates against people of colour (POC)**
- Calling out examples of racism, even trivial ones (**microaggressions**), is an important strategy for exposing and defeating racism
- **Liberalism** — the culture of individual rights and tolerance — actually supports **a system that privileges a White elite**
- **Stories of lived experience** from POC are a powerful tool for challenging the system
- **'Colourblindness'** is a myth that denies the legitimacy of POC's lived experience of racism
- **Gradual progress is doomed to fail** because advances for minorities are only granted when it suits the dominant group (Whites) and are withdrawn when they are not

CRT criticises the liberal solutions to ethnic inequality (e.g. laws against discrimination) as being inadequate, because after 50 years of civil rights racism is still with us. The powerful institutions (education, law, government, etc.) always work in favour of White people. Instead, White people are challenged to **acknowledge their White privilege**, **become Allies** to POC and **listen with empathy** to their lived experiences.

> **Research:** review your notes from **1A: Socialisation, Culture & Identity** on **Peggy McIntosh**'s essay *White Privilege: Unpacking the Invisible Knapsack* **(1989)**

Some CRT supporters further claim that **skin tone** is the basis of racism. This is termed **colourism**: discriminating against people with darker skin tones. If true, this could explain things like the educational under attainment of some Black boys and the economic success of ethnic groups like Chinese and Indian minorities in the UK (p119). **Ronald Hall (2018)** argues that **Critical Skin Theory (CST)** should replace Critical Race Theory in order to understand and combat institutional racism.

To its supporters, CRT is a technique for exploring the deep causes of ethnic inequality and it has grown particularly relevant since the **2020 murder of George Floyd**, a Black American, by a White police officer. To its critics, CRT is a conspiracy theory that stirs up resentments over injustices in the past (like slavery) and undermines attempts to improve race relations in the 21st century.

Say No To Racism! (image by Daviniodus)

RESEARCH PROFILE: BONILLA-SILVA (2013)

Eduardo Bonilla-Silva is a leading CRT scholar and author of ***Racism Without Racists* (2013)** – the title is a good summary of the idea of institutional racism. Bonilla-Silva argues that the liberal ideal of aiming for a 'colourblind' society actually ***supports*** racism in four ways.

(1) 'Abstract liberalism' promotes individualism and choice, but this is used by Whites to justify inequalities as being down to lifestyle choices by ethnic minorities; **(2)** a **'frame of naturalisation'** presents continuing inequalities as natural and inevitable **differences**; **(3)** the **'frame of cultural racism'** uses negative stereotypes of ethnic minorities, such as Black people being lazy or aggressive; **(4)** the **'minimisation of racism frame'** promotes the idea that successful civil rights campaigns and the success of a few unrepresentative celebrities from ethnic minorities have achieved equal rights (in theory but not in practice).

Bonilla-Silva criticises the traditional Marxist idea that **'class matters more than race.'** He refers to as the **'invisible weight of Whiteness'** – a theme of White Supremacy running through society's institutions that is not acknowledged by anyone but which is immensely burdensome for ethnic minorities. The 'weight of Whiteness' includes things like White concepts of beauty, White language possessing cultural capital and White fashions being seen as respectable.

Emma Dabiri (*Don't Touch My Hair*, 2019) complains that Black and Mixed-Race children are excluded from school in the UK for having Afro-textured hairstyles (fades, locs, braids, natural afros). Dabiri explains that Black people need to reclaim the *"deep spiritual and cultural significance of African hairstyling"* and demands that the **Equality Act (2010)** be amended to make Afro-textured hair a protected characteristic.

Marxism & Age Inequalities

Marxism views the elderly as a **'reserve army of labour.'** Because Capitalism is unstable, it goes through 'booms and busts.' During the economic booms employers need to recruit a lot of extra workers but during the bust periods they need to sack them. The elderly are useful in this regard: they can be hired but then fired and they are unlikely to agitate for better conditions because they will simply be grateful for the work and the extra income it brings in.

According to this view, Capitalism needs to keep the elderly in a dependent and desperate state, which explains age inequality. The elderly and the young are both **reserve armies of labour**, which is why they are the workers most like to be offered – and have no choice but to accept – **Zero Hour Contracts (ZHCs)** that offer them no security.

The elderly provide benefits to Capitalism in the same way as housewives: they help **support the workers' families**, for example by offering free childcare, enabling younger adults to work and removing employers of the responsibility to provide creches or pay higher wages to cover childcare costs.

Notice that Marxists here treat something as exploitative that **Functionalists** regard as beneficial. For Functionalists, it is beneficial for society if the elderly **'disengage' from work** (p139) and involving grandparents in childcare helps socialise children by passing on norms and values from the past, creating social solidarity. Young people might gain valuable skills from the flexible work that ZHCs provide without having to commit themselves to a fixed number of hours each week.

The study by **Jones et al.** (p125) shows that some elderly people experience retirement as a time of renewal and creativity, not exploitation. However, Marxists point out that this might be **false consciousness** or a result of the privileges of middle-class workers.

RESEARCH PROFILE: PHILLIPSON (1982)

Chris Phillipson suggests that the logic of capitalism is about exploiting workers and consumers for profit, and this is fundamentally incompatible with the needs of the elderly. The elderly are neglected by the capitalist system because they no longer have the spending power which is so attractive to capitalists. However, they are a drain on resources, because they require care and support through pensions. Meanwhile, Capitalism wants to replace them with younger workers who are more productive but also easier to control. Phillipson argues that the elderly are **institutionally marginalised**: they are forced to retire and take a cut in income and a drop in status. **Negative stereotypes** about the elderly as incompetent, troublesome or incapable of learning new skills often justify this discrimination against them.

Phillipson agrees that the elderly are also a reserve army of labour and suggests that this role is growing with the expansion of the retail sector (e.g. trolley collectors in supermarket car parks). However, his arguments ignore the **relative prosperity of the elderly** since the **2008 Global Financial Crisis (GFC)** and the growing influence of the **'Grey Pound'** (p124).

The 40-Mark Essay

You could be set a 40-mark question on Marxist explanations for inequality or a concept that Marxism has distinctive views on, such as **exploitation, ideology** or **Capitalism**. You could also bring Marxism into an essay on inequalities of class, gender, ethnicity or age, especially as a developed evaluation of Functionalism or the New Right (see **Chapter 7** for more on this).

Marxism is a very popular Perspective, especially among sociologists, but it is currently going through a theoretical conflict. Traditional Marxists cling to a **materialist** framework, viewing economics as the driving force in social behaviour; they prefer to analyse inequality in terms of class and working patterns and assume that other types of inequality are really side-effects of Capitalism. They take a **macro approach**, looking at society as a whole rather than the experiences of individuals. They take a **structuralist approach**, which sees people as shaped by (in this case, corrupt and exploitative) institutions with little choice or free will.

Many **Feminists** criticise the view that women's experiences are best understood as a by-product of men's working patterns. The **Social Action (Weberian) Perspective** argues for the importance of understanding individuals and small groups, the significance of choice and the degree to which people negotiate their own relationships with Capitalism.

The biggest critique of traditional Marxism comes from **Neo-Marxism**, especially from **Intersectionality** (p158) and **Critical Race Theory** (**CRT**). These theories see economic disadvantage as just *one* type of oppression but there are other ways to be **marginalised**, such as sexuality, disability and immigrant-status. CRT sees racism as an oppressive force throughout society that distorts all relationships and institutions. According to this view, the White working-class males that are the focus on traditional Marxism are a relatively **privileged** group.

This has created an ongoing debate about *whose side Marxism is on* and whether it's even possible (through **Allyship**, p151) to be on the side of *all* marginalised groups. By encouraging a focus on victimhood, Neo-Marxists might be making it harder to achieve equality. Some Neo-Marxists don't even want equality as an ideal – they aim for **equity** instead.

Neo-Marxism also moves away from the materialist focus on economics to analyse **language** as the expression of power. This supports **political correctness** (**PC**, p149) and has produced '**Cancel Culture**' – a trend emerging from universities and Internet forums of silencing people who express hurtful ideas. Critics attack this for being **illiberal** (meaning, opposed to freedom of speech and tolerance for different views). However, thinkers like Bonilla-Silva explicitly reject the liberal approach to racism as a failed project. Freedom of speech often means that privileged (or **hegemonic**) groups continue to dominate the discussion.

For traditional Marxists, this focus on language is a distraction, because renaming things doesn't change material reality. Only a **revolution that takes control of the means of production away from the ruling class** can do that. Consciousness-raising can only go so far. This debate is further explored in **3A: Globalisation & the Digital Social World**.

CONFLICT PERSPECTIVE: FEMINISM

Feminism is largely concerned with one type of inequality: the subordination of women to men in a **Patriarchal** society. As explained in **1A: Socialisation, Culture & Identity**, there have been four 'Waves' of Feminist thought and activism:

- **1st Wave Feminism** (19th century and early 20th century) and **2nd Wave Feminism** (1960s and '70s) were **materialist** philosophies, rather like traditional Marxism. They concerned themselves with economic equality (such as women inheriting property and managing money), legal rights (such as the right to vote) and the status of women's bodies (such as access to contraception and abortion and protection from domestic violence).

2nd Wave Feminism is considered to begin with the publication of **Betty Friedan**'s *The Feminine Mystique* **(1963)** which begins with a discussion of *"the problem with no name"* – the widespread unhappiness of women living suburban lives in 1950s and '60s America.

- **3rd Wave Feminism** (1990s) and **4th Wave Feminism** (2012 onwards) resemble **Neo-Marxism** (p150) in criticising this materialist philosophy. 3rd Wave Feminism is dominated by two scholars:

Kimberlé Crenshaw is an American lawyer and Feminist who coined the term **'Critical Race Theory'** (p154) and developed the concept of **Intersectionality**. Intersectionality is a key concept in 3rd Wave Feminism: people have intersecting Identities, some of which enjoy **privileges** and others are **marginalised** (*c.f.* p150). Being a woman is a marginalised Identity but so, for example, is being Black. Crenshaw argues that Black women suffer from **the intersection of sexism and racism**. This argument has been used to displace (largely middle class, middle-aged and heterosexual) White women from being the leading voices of the women's movement.

Kimberlé Crenshaw (image by boellstiftung)

Intersectionality has been criticised for directing concern away from the subordination of women to other causes. It risks creating a **competition over victimhood**. For example, are disabled Black women more or less marginalised than able-bodied and White women who are working class and lesbians? The idea of **Allyship** (p151) is used to solve this problem, with groups acting as allies for each other rather than being in competition.

Judith Butler is also American and developed the concept of '**Gender Performativity**.' Butler takes the idea that gender is a social construct but goes further with this, arguing that gender is a **performance**. She rejects as **binary view** of masculine/feminine and uses drag subculture as an example of how these concepts can be **problematised** (made to look less convincing).

A longstanding concept in Sociology is that gender is social constructed but **sex itself is binary and biological**: male and female. Butler questions this binary and argues that sex is also socially constructed. According to Butler, **sex is assigned at birth**, given to us by medical experts and the performance of it is enforced by family and wider society.

Research: Butler uses the example of **David Reimer** to illustrate her point about sex being assigned; review your notes from **1A: Socialisation, Culture & Identity** on **John Colapinto**'s case study of David Reimer's (*As Nature Made Him: The Boy Who Was Raised As A Girl*, **2004**).

Gender Performativity supports the interpretation of Trans individuals as fully members of the sex they identify with. Materialist Feminism criticises this, viewing women as a biologically defined group which excludes people who are born male. Judith Butler and her supporters argue that there is no 'right' or 'essential' way to be female.

AO2 ILLUSTRATION: TERF WARS

The conflict between different branches of Feminism has spilled out into a wider debate about the definition of 'woman.' 3rd and 4th Wave Feminists tend to be Allies of Trans people generally and support the statement that '*Trans women are women.*' 2nd Wave Feminism often rejects this definition; these critics term themselves **Gender Critical Feminists** but their opponents refer to them as **TERFs (Trans-Excluding Radical Feminists)**.

The debate is made more heated by the inclusion of Trans Identity as a protected characteristic in the **Equalities Act (2010)**, which makes attacks on Trans Identity a form of **hate speech** and possibly a criminal offence.

The Media now routinely run stories illustrating this controversy. For example, in the Tokyo Olympics in 2021, **Laura Hubbard** competed for New Zealand in the women's weightlifting event. Critics complained that a male-bodied athlete taking part was unfair for the other competitors, although in the event Hubbard was knocked out of the competition at an early stage.

Research: Students might like to examine some of the news stories about Trans rights and Gender Critical Feminists/TERFs – but beware of getting drawn into hostile online discussions

Feminism & Class Inequalities

Social class is a preoccupation of Functionalist and Marxist sociologists, because of their **structuralist approach** that views individuals through the lens of work and economic position. Although **1st and 2nd Wave Feminists** tended to share that structuralist approach, Feminism has always been closer to the **Social Action Perspective** (p165) in terms of focusing on **micro-scale interactions**, individual experiences and qualitative data.

This has led Feminists to criticise some of the methods used to study class and place women in social classes. In **1A: Socialisation, Culture & Identity**, you were introduced to ways of measuring social class, such as the **Registrar General's Scale**. These measures assign class based on the job of the main earner in the family, traditionally a man. Feminists criticise the idea that a woman's social class is defined entirely by her husband.

For example, one of the most famous studies into social mobility was the Oxford Mobility Study **(OMS)** which investigated a sample of 10,000 people to see if the children had improved on the social class of their parents. The study used the **Hope-Goldthorpe Scale** to measure social class – a very similar scale to the Registrar General's Scale. However, the OMS only looked at men, only investigated the difference in class between sons and their fathers and the Hope-Goldthorpe Scale only looks at the husband's job to work out the social class of a family household.

Research: research the results of the OMS and other, more recent studies into social mobility, such as the **2016 Report** by the **Social Mobility Commission**.

RESEARCH PROFILE: ARBER, DALE & GILBERT (1986)

Sara Arber and her colleagues responded to the shortcomings in the Oxford Mobility Study by setting up the **Surrey Scale** that would measure social class in a way that is fair to women. Women are marrying later and divorce rates mean that women are more likely today to have to depend on their own skills and qualifications than on a male partner.

In the Surrey Scale, women are classed based on their own jobs, not their husband. The 7-point scale places **secretarial/clerical** (4) above **supervisors/self-employed manual** (5) which enhances the status of women's office-based jobs. It also splits the second-lowest category (6) into **sales/personal services** (6a, including jobs like hairdressing and beauticians) and **skilled manual** (6b, including many jobs dominated by men).

The Surrey Scale isn't perfect. Women often work part-time or take time out of paid work for pregnancy and childcare, making it unreliable to measure their class by their paid work. There is an argument that the best indicator of a household's social class is the job that provides the family's main income, even if that means ignoring one partner's job in favour of the other's.

Feminism & Gender Inequalities

Feminism explains gender inequalities as resulting from the subordination of women by men under a system of male privilege called **Patriarchy**. Despite huge changes to the law and to social norms that have taken place during the 20th century – much of it due to effective campaigning by 1st and 2nd Wave Feminists – there is still **a glass ceiling** for women who seek promotion and a **gender pay gap** (p102). Women are still a long way from being equally represented in politics (p104) and are disproportionately victims of domestic violence and sexual assault.

A common explanation for this is that women are socialised into different expectations and behaviours. In **1A: Socialisation, Culture & Identity**, you studied the work of **Anne Oakley** who explains how the family raises children in different gender roles. However, a ground-breaking study by **Sue Sharpe (1994)** shows that London schoolgirls in the 1990s are more assertive and confident than they had been in the early 1970s. Their ambitions changed from *'love, marriage, husbands & children'* to *'job, career & being able to support themselves.'* Yet despite this progress, inequalities remain stubbornly in place.

RESEARCH PROFILE: HAKIM (2006)

Catherine Hakim is a British sociologist who challenges Feminist assumptions about gender inequalities. She proposes **Preference Theory**, which argues that these inequalities are really **differences in preferred lifestyle** between the sexes.

Hakim claims there are three **work-lifestyle preferences**: **(1) work-centred**, includes most men but only 20% of women and involves committing to long hours and sacrificing personal relationships; **(2) adaptive**, accounts for 60% of women and involves combining work and family, even if that means taking part-time or lower-status jobs to achieve this balance; **(3) home-centred**, which is 20% of women but very few men and avoids paid work after starting a family unless the family is in financial difficulties. Hakim argues that Preference Theory explains why countries with family-friendly policies often end up with higher gender inequality: she criticises the **Nordic Model** (p107) and points out that Sweden has a bigger **glass ceiling** than the USA, where more women are senior managers.

As well as conducting surveys in the UK and Spain, Hakim makes use of **Anthony Giddens'** interactionist concept of **'Reflexivity'** to explain how women adapt their lifestyle/aspirations to changes in their circumstances. She criticises relying entirely on macro-level data and cites **case studies** of top female managers: she claims such women are typically childless or have a single child, whereas male colleagues have larger families (and a home-centred wife).

Preference Theory links to **Functionalism**, suggesting that men earn more than women because, on average, they are prepared to work harder and sacrifice family time. It links to **Weberianism** by focusing on how women choose the adaptive work-lifestyle for their own reasons. Hakim has been criticised for ignoring **structural factors** that force women into part-time or low-paid jobs as well as the **patriarchal ideology** that shapes women's preferences from an early age.

Feminism & Ethnic Inequalities

There has been a long tradition arguing the Black women experience a distinctive and intense form of marginalisation and have special insights into both racism and Patriarchy as a result. For example, **Sojourner Truth (1797-1883)** was both a 1st Wave Feminist and a campaigner against slavery in America; her 1851 speech at the Ohio Women's Rights Convention was titled ***Ain't I A Woman?*** and inspired the 1981 book by **bell hooks** (*below*). The speech complained about the way Black women were side-lined in the campaign for women's rights and the end of slavery

There was also a lot of activism by Black Feminists in the 1930s-50s, such as **Zora Neale Hurston** and **Rosa Parks**, but they tend to be ignored in favour of the 'Waves' of Feminism which match White women's activism. Since then, Black Feminism has moved into the mainstream of the women's movement, in large part due to **Kimberlé Crenshaw (1989)** developing **Intersectionality** and **Critical Race Theory**, which calls on White Feminists to listen to the lived experience of Black women and become their **Allies** (p151).

Some Feminists argue that there is too much focus on the American history of slavery and segregation in Black Feminism, which is not entirely relevant to the experience of racism in the UK. **Lola Young (2000)** complains that an American like **bell hooks** is more likely to be cited in Feminist scholarship than Black British Feminists. Islamic Feminists like **Leila Ahmed (2011)** have a different view on the effect of colonialism, arguing that Islam offers a different model of equality and female empowerment from the liberal and individualistic model pursued by White Feminists. For example, Ahmed controversially defends Muslim veiling as a way for women to escape being **sexually objectified** in terms of their bodies and therefore resist Patriarchy.

RESEARCH PROFILE: hooks (1984)

The Black Feminist author **bell hooks** (her pen name, which is always written lower case) triggered a change within feminism with her first book, *Ain't I A Woman?* (1981). The book traces the marginalisation of Black American women back to slavery and argues they suffered the worst conditions of any group. She argues that stereotypes about Black female immorality meant they were not welcome to speak at anti-slavery events.

hooks argues that these negative stereotypes continue right down to the present day, with Black women being excluded from full participation in the civil rights movement of the 1960s and '70s. This idea that current racism is a product of historic and structural racism going back centuries is one of the key ideas of Critical Race Theory in the 1990s. Black women were excluded from the Feminist movement, which was largely supported by White and middle/upper class women.

However, hooks has been criticised for her methodology. Her book includes no bibliography or footnotes, making it hard for other scholars to check or criticise the sources she uses. hooks defends this by saying she wanted to write in a non-academic manner, to make her ideas accessible to all readers. **Nicole Abraham (1999)** criticises this approach, arguing it is wrong to assume the average reader is too lazy or unsophisticated to care about sources.

Feminism & Age Inequalities

Feminists are particularly concerned with age inequalities because of the way ageing impacts women. In a **patriarchal society**, women are judged in terms of **physical beauty and fertility**. **Cosmeticisation** means seeking expensive treatments to slow or conceal the signs of ageing.

Naomi Wolf (1990) identifies beauty as a **social construct** that oppresses women and terms it 'the Beauty Myth.' She links it to eating disorders among women and sees it as a patriarchal reaction against Feminism, to punish women physically and psychologically. **Mary Daly (1978)** links this idea to global practices like **Female Genital Mutilation (FGM)** and argues there are no equivalents practices to mutilate young men before they become adults.

RESEARCH PROFILE: SONTAG (1972)

Susan Sontag is a film maker as well as a writer. In *The Double Standard of Aging* **(1978)** she argues women are pressured with respect to age, with very high psychological costs for them.

Susan Sontag, 1979 (image by Lynn Gilbert)

There is only one ideal for female beauty: *the girl*. Women must invest resources to maintain the appearance of youth: *"the single standard of beauty for women dictates that they must go on having clear skin. Every wrinkle, every line, every grey hair, is a defeat."*

There are two ideals for male beauty: *the boy* and *the man*. Men gain respect as they age but for women ageing brings a loss in status and self-esteem. This is the '**double standard:** one rule for men but another for women.

Sontag argues that society demands that Feminine accomplishments are **passive**: to *look* a certain way, rather than to *do* certain things. These accomplishments decline with age. The masculine ideal is active, associated with *doing things*, which increases with age.

The double standard is seen in attitudes towards marriages between older women and younger men, which produce scandal and outrage, but older men marrying younger women are treated sympathetically. Sontag claims *"rules of taste enforce structures of power"* which means these attitudes to ageing contribute to the systematic subordination of women. She claims society's norms keep women *"in a life-long minority"* (i.e. in a childlike state, never becoming true adults).

Research: Sontag's essay is well worth reading in its entirety: find it at https://archive.org/details/pdfy-Y6o4iGliJNpAyGcb/mode/2up

The 40-Mark Essay

You could be set a 40-mark question on Feminist explanations for inequality or concepts such as **women's rights, the family** or **Patriarchy**. You could also bring Feminism into an essay on inequalities of class, gender (especially!), ethnicity or age, especially as a developed evaluation of Functionalism or the New Right (see **Chapter 7** for more on this).

Feminism is a Perspective that has arguably brought about more social change than any other, especially 1st and 2nd Wave Feminism, which changed the legal status of women in many countries. By the 1980s, it seemed as though many aims of the women's movement had been achieved, but some perceived a backlash against Feminism (*c.f.* Faludi's book **Backlash** in **1A: Socialisation, Culture & Identity**) linked to the **New Right's dominance in politics** (p141).

Other Feminists feel that true equality for women is still out of reach – for example, the **gender gap** persists (p102) as does violence against women – and that such equality as had been achieved is enjoyed by privileged women but not marginalised ones. This led to the emergence of 3rd Wave Feminism and **Intersectionality** (p158), with its focus on **Black Feminism** and on Feminism being an Ally for other marginalised groups.

This has created a debate similar to the one dividing Marxism about *whose side Feminism is on* and whether it's even possible to be on the side of *all* marginalised groups. By **focusing on victimhood**, 3rd Wave Feminists might be ignoring – and perhaps putting at risk – the advances that have been made already.

Feminism is critiqued by Functionalists, who argue there are innate and biologically-based differences between males and females that will always be expressed in social arrangements, even if all discrimination ends. This informs Hakim's **Preference Theory** (p161). The Feminist response is that *all* these supposed differences are socially constructed inequalities. This leads to **Butler**'s argument that there is **no such thing as the essentially female** and that sex and gender are entirely **performative**. Not everyone is happy with this conclusion, which risks making the definition of 'woman' entirely subjective.

An even more forceful critique comes from the **New Right**, who accuse Feminism of liberating women by dismantling the nuclear family, with disastrous consequences for the poor. The study by **Dennis & Erdos** (p143) shows that even **Marxists** can agree with this criticism.

The **Weberian** Perspective has a different critique, which focuses on autonomy. Feminism is about empowering women, yet it often ends up representing women as victims of forces beyond their control – a common problem with **structuralist** perspectives. For example, **Wolf** blames **cosmeticisation** for trapping women through the **'Beauty Myth'** but it could be argued that people use cosmetics willingly and purposively to take control of the ageing process in their own way. Weberians focus on how women negotiate their position in society, sometimes leveraging beauty to acquire status. This is similar to Hakim's **Preference Theory**, since she claims women are choosing adaptive work-lifestyles for their own subjective reasons.

SOCIAL ACTION PERSPECTIVE: WEBERIANISM

The Social Action Perspective rejects the sort of **structuralist** explanations presented so far, like the idea that inequalities exist entirely because of social forces beyond anyone's control or that membership of a marginalised group automatically makes you a victim. Rather than studying things on a **macro scale**, this perspective looks at the **micro scale** of individuals and small groups.

> **Research:** Review your notes from **1A: Socialisation, Culture & Identity**, where you were introduced to **Interactionism** and in particular **Labelling Theory** as an explanation of individual and small group behaviour, and **2A: Measuring Inequality**, where you learned about **ethnography** (p62) as a way of studying small groups.

Max Weber (1864-1920) is one of the 'Big Three' founders of Sociology, along with Emile Durkheim and Karl Marx. Weber's ideas have been described as a lifelong *'debate with the ghost of Karl Marx.'* Marx died when Weber was still a teenager, but Weber agreed with many of Marx's ideas about economics and the importance of social class. However, he disagreed with Marx's **determinism** – the belief that there is no freewill and people are entirely shaped by their economic position in society – and Marx's **positivism** – the use of strictly scientific methodology.

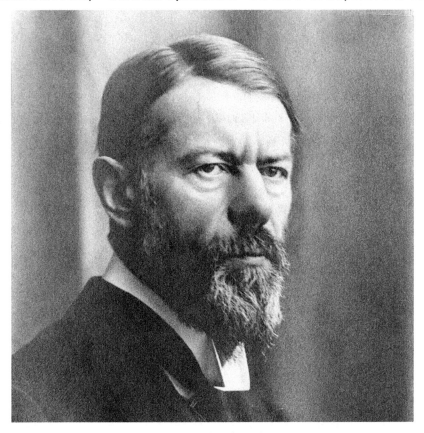

Max Weber (1919)

Weber proposes three factors explaining social behaviour: **class**, **status** and **party**. These combine to create **life chances** which are important for understanding inequality (*c.f.* pp99, 108, 119, 130).

Class is just like Marx's understanding of social class, however Weber understood class to be **relative** rather than absolute: it doesn't matter how rich or poor you are, but rather how much richer or poorer you are compared to everyone else.

Status is position in society earned through talents, skills or valued attributes. For example, some people can leverage their physical beauty, acting skills, sporting ability or artistic flair to rise up in society despite coming from a poor background. This is similar to the Functionalist view of **Meritocracy** (p135) but Weber recognises that not every talent is equally valued in society. Marxists recognise that Capitalism allows some poor people to 'rise through the ranks' (e.g. working class footballers) but this is just to offer false hope to the rest, encouraging them to be content with their position – it is **ruling class ideology**.

Party is membership of a group of likeminded people who combine forces to accomplish things collectively that they could not do individually. A great example is **trade unions** (p89). Sometimes religion can be a Party. This is similar to the Functionalist belief in **gradualism**, which is the idea that oppressed or marginalised people might be able to make gradual reforms to society this way. Many Marxists (and **Critical Race Theory**, p154) reject gradualism, arguing that the ruling class will only allow reforms when it suits them and will take those reforms away the moment it stops suiting them. They argue **revolutionary change** is the only way to reform society.

Weber also proposes the idea of **social closure**, which is when privileged groups arrange things so that they don't have to share their privileges with anyone else. This might be done through discouraging outsiders from marrying into their set or introducing arbitrary restrictions to stop other people joining their well-paid professions – a good example is the insistence on elite schooling for top jobs exposed by **Rivera** (p85) or the **meritocratic paradox** identified by **Hecht et al** (p95). It is similar to the **Neo-Marxist** idea of **hegemonic privilege** (p150).

Weber's focus on relativism and freewill means that society could be changed by powerful ideas rather than just redistributing economic power. Weber gives an example in his famous book *The Protestant Work Ethic & the Spirit of Capitalism* (**1905**). He argues that Capitalism came about because of **Calvinist Christianity**. Calvinists believed in hard work and self-denial, so their businesses made big profits which they didn't spend on themselves; neither did they donate the money to the Church, since their faith rejected religious works. Instead, they invested profits back into their businesses, leading to even more profit which is the central idea of Capitalism.

Since ideas are drivers of social change as well as materialist factors like money and resources, Weber argues it is as important to understand people's motives as it is to understand their economic position. He uses the term '*verstehen*' (understanding) to refer to this empathy that helps a sociologist interpret social behaviour in sophisticated way; see p16 for more on this.

*Why does Weber only make an appearance here instead of earlier in the course – or later? Most of Weber's ideas have either been developed further by **Interactionists** or else adapted by **Neo-Marxists**. But he's too important to leave out of the course altogether, so here he is!*

AO2 ILLUSTRATION: MARCUS RASHFORD (cont'd)

A profile of footballer **Marcus Rashford** in **1A: Socialisation, Culture & Identity** illustrated **Intersecting Identities**.

Rashford was born and grew up in Manchester. His grandmother was from Saint Kitts in the Caribbean. Rashford's mother, Melanie Maynard, was a **lone parent** who worked multiple jobs and skipped meals herself to make sure Rashford and his siblings ate. Rashford started playing football at age 5, was **spotted by talent scouts** and admitted to Manchester United's training academy. He often needed help getting to the academy since his working mother could not drive him there. When he was 11, he became the youngest ever player to be selected for the Manchester United Schoolboy Scholars (usually reserved for age 12+).

Rashford set up a campaign to give homeless people essential items over Christmas. He and his mother visited homeless shelters to hand out boxes. In 2020, Rashford influenced the UK Government to change its policy by continuing free school meals for children during the summer holidays. Rashford set up the **Child Food Poverty Task Force** and was later awarded the **MBE** honour for his charity work.

From a **Functionalist** viewpoint, anyone could achieve Rashford's success and his charity work (and the MBE awarded for it) is evidence of social solidarity. **Marxists** point out that many working class and Black boys with Rashford's talents do *not* get such opportunities and his success only confirms the illusion of Meritocracy in society. **Weberians** acknowledge that Rashford's **Class** (and race) counted against him but argue he leveraged his talents to acquire **Status**, thanks also to supportive **Parties** like Manchester United.

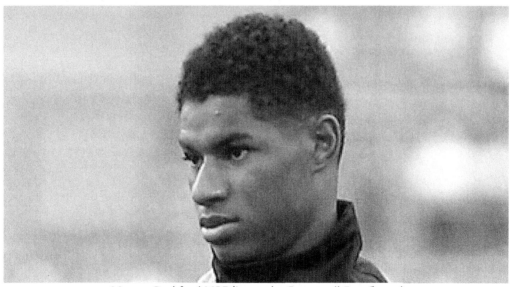

Marcus Rashford MBE (image by Дмитрий Голубович)

Weberianism & Class Inequalities

Weberianism questions the Marxist/Functionalist assumption that class is the defining feature of inequality or **social stratification** (p136). Weber introduces **Status** and **Party** as complicating factors. He also suggests that there are really four, rather than two, social classes:

- **The propertied upper class:** wealthy landowners and business bosses
- **The white-collar workers:** the educated middle classes who don't own property and still have to work for a wage
- **The petty bourgeoisie:** owners of small businesses, like shopkeepers or café owners or the self-employed
- **The manual working class:** Marx's proletariat who lack the skills or qualifications to improve their position

This sophisticated approach to social class inspires the various scales you have learned about, such as the **Registrar General's Scale** in **1A: Socialisation, Culture & Identity** or the **Hope-Goldthorpe Scale** (p160). These scales follow Weber's idea that the difference between classes comes from their **market situation** – how in-demand their skills are and how hard it is to qualify to do them. The idea that people can slide up or down the scale is in contrast to the Marxist view that people are defined by a fixed social class.

'Party' is an important factor in the 21st century, when a lot of protest and reform is focused on things like the environment, nationality, religious affiliation and sexuality. Weber is an important sociologist for arguing that class is not the only – and perhaps not even the most important – factor that determines inequality and difference in society.

RESEARCH PROFILE: STALLINGS (2002)

Robert A Stallings uses Weberian methods and concepts to critique an earlier classic study, **Henry Moore**'s *Tornadoes Over Texas* **(1958)**. Moore studied tornadoes which destroyed much of the Texas towns of Waco and San Angelino. His analysis helped found the discipline of Disaster Studies and offers a **Functionalist analysis** of various agencies (government, businesses, charities, the public) coming together for the general good and restoring the *status quo*.

Stallings re-examines Moore's data but comes to very different conclusions. Stallings analyses the disaster in terms of class, status and party. He sees in Waco and San Angelino a conflict between the **propertied upper class** and the **petty bourgeoisie** anxious to modernise after the War. Local government was in the pocket of the elite and blocked a lot of rescue work in order to protect property; the poorest sections of the community (manual workers and ethnic minorities) were the losers. The communities were rebuilt to achieve **social closure** for dominant groups.

The advantage of a Weberian perspective for this is that it views society as being 'in flux' with different groups always jostling for position – a disaster simply shows in stark relief what is in fact going on all the time.

Weberianism & Gender Inequalities

Weber's ideas of Status and Party link to the role of women in society, especially to **vertical segregation** (p169) where the top levels of any job are dominated by men. This is known as the 'glass ceiling' and the tendency of men to rise up the promotional structure faster than women is known as the '**glass elevator**.' This might be because there is more **Status** attached to being male and because males are members of Parties that assist them in advancing in their careers.

Weber's concept of **social closure** is also relevant, because in the past women have been excluded from certain careers or from the **Parties** that assist in giving access to those careers. For example, for a long time women could not go to university. More recently, organisations like golf clubs functioned as unofficial places for men to exchange career news, make valuable contacts and strike deals – but women (and many ethnic minorities) were barred from them. Feminists would agree that men reserve the elite positions in society and exclude women and they have campaigned for women to be admitted to male-only clubs for precisely this reason.

However, Weber's ideas are not so helpful in explaining **horizontal segregation** (where women do different sorts of jobs from men) or why women have lower status than men in the first place.

RESEARCH PROFILE: BARRON & NORRIS (1976)

Barron & Norris wrote *Sexual Divisions & the Dual Labour Market* **(1976)** in which they argue that the labour market can be divided into two sectors: (**1**) **primary employment** in which pay and job security is high and there is a promotional ladder, and (**2**) **secondary employment** involving unskilled/semi-skilled work, low pay and poor job security (no promotion structure and high turnover of workers).

Barron & Norris argue point out that men are employed in both sectors, but mainly in the primary sector. Women are mainly employed in the secondary sector.

There are reasons for this "***gendering of the workplace***." Women choose low-paid secondary sector jobs because they have a dual role as earner but also as homemaker and carer. This limits their market situation compared to men who do not have a dual role. In particular, men are more able to commit to a long-term career in the primary sector because they do not have to plan for pregnancy or childcare. This is linked to Weber's idea of **Status**: women's role as housewife/mother does not carry status in society and women are forced to seek low-status jobs in the secondary sector.

Barron & Norris also note that women are less likely to belong to a **Party** like an organised trade union, making them easier to get rid of.

However, **Hakim's Preference Theory** (p161) looks at the same differences, also from a Weberian perspective of status and choice, but draws different conclusions; Hakim argues that primary sector work does not carry Status *for women*, but homemaking/motherhood *does*, so they prefer work that offers *their* notion of Status.

Weberianism & Ethnic Inequalities

Weberian theory suggests that Whiteness confers **Status** in a White-dominated society and often agrees with **Neo-Marxism** that this is a legacy of colonialism and slavery. **Social closure** means that **Parties** that offer White people help in improving their **market situation** are often closed to ethnic minorities, or at least more difficult for them to access.

Barron & Norris (**1976**, p169) extend their **Dual Labour Market theory** to explain ethnic inequality. They point out that ethnic minorities are disproportionately confined to the **secondary employment sector** (low pay, low security, poor promotion prospects) whereas White workers dominate the **primary employment sector**. They attribute this to the cultural Status of Whiteness: employers discriminate against ethnic minority job applicants (*c.f.* the job application study by **Wood et al**, p114). They also argue that trade unions tend to be White-dominated and are less interested in protecting the rights of ethnic minorities in the workforce.

However, Barron & Norris' study is from the 1970s. In the UK in the 21st century, there is a greater representation of ethnic minorities in the primary sector and in the **trade union movement** (*c.f.* p89). This fits with a Weberian view that changing attitudes can lead to an improved **market situation** for minorities. It is in contrast to **Critical Race Theory** which argues there can be no gradual progress for minorities from liberal reforms (p154) or to **Marxism** which views the success of some marginalised people as '**tokenism**' – a token gesture to persuade oppressed people that success t is possible for all of them when in fact it is not.

RESEARCH PROFILE: REX & TOMLINSON (1979)

John Rex & Sally Tomlinson wrote *Colonial Immigrants in a British* City (1979) – the title tells you that they are linking the experiences of Black British people in the 20th century to Britain's colonial past, as **Critical Race Theory** does today (p154). However, Rex & Tomlinson bring a Weberian critique to their study of the **Handsworth** district in Birmingham in the 1970s.

Rex & Tomlinson argue that Black British people are trapped in an **Underclass** beneath the White working class. However, they are not using this word in the same way that **Murray** does (*c.f.* the **New Right**, p141). By 'Underclass,' they mean a group of people who are **socially excluded in a systematic way**: cut off from acquiring Status or joining Parties that would improve their Class. Rex & Tomlinson identify how ethnic minorities experience disadvantages regarding employment, housing and education. These disadvantages are worsened by racist hostility directed at them by White society – and Rex & Tomlinson link these racist attitudes to Britain's history as a colonising empire.

Rex & Tomlinson's conclusion stands in contrast to the **2021 CRED Report** (p120) which argues that Britain's Black population is no longer defined by the colonial past. Race relations may have changed since the 1970s – and Weberianism supports the idea that powerful ideas like anti-racism can change society – but **Critical Race Theory** (p154) argues that ethnic inequalities *cannot* be understood without reference to colonialism and slavery.

Weberianism & Age Inequalities

Weber's ideas can be used to explain age inequality: the very young and the elderly lack **Status** and, because they are not in full-time employment, they are cut off from powerful **Parties** that could represent them. **Social closure** means that, once older people retire, those still in work try to cut their former co-workers off from status (e.g. by discouraging them from returning to the workplace, which is seen as 'interfering').

This still allows some older people to experience retirement positively, if they already have high social **Class**; the study by **Jones et al** (p125) is a good example of Weber-inspired research.

The shift in the Status of the elderly, with the rise of **Grey Power** (p124) and the significance of the **Grey Pound** in consumer culture fits in with Weber's idea that groups in society are in flux and always shifting their **market situation**.

Some sociologists argue that ageing is more complex than this. **James J Dowd (1986)** describes the elderly as "*immigrants in time*" and "*strangers in their own land.*" Dowd suggests that ageing is about being **trapped in an identity rooted in the past**. In effect, the elderly have a different culture from the young, who are 'at home' in the present. If this is the case, then a loss of Status is inevitable as the elderly become equivalent to 'immigrants' (*c.f.* the **Wheel of Privilege**, p150).

RESEARCH PROFILE: TURNER (1989)

Bryan Turner wrote *Ageing, Status Politics and Sociological Theory* (1989) in which he criticises **Marxist** views that age inequality is entirely due to experiencing economic disadvantages from leaving the workforce (p156). Turner links it to **Status** and explains why.

Turner argues that ageing takes away **control of social resources** (not just economic ones) that can be exchanged for Status. For example, there is **cultural capital** and **social capital**. However, as people age, their cultural capital becomes out of date (the films, books, music and artists that they know are no longer fashionable) and their social capital shrinks as their friends and acquaintances die.

Turner illustrates this through the **reciprocity-maturation curve**. Reciprocity is about giving something back when people give to you; if you can't do this, you are in the position of a **dependent** who is always receiving but can never 'return the favour.' Turner argues reciprocity is low for children and the young (they have little to offer), peaks in middle age when people have the most control of resources but then declines again in old age.

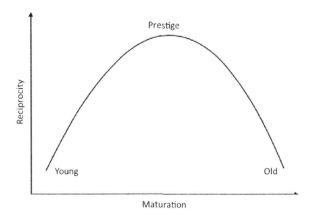

The 40-Mark Essay

You could be set a 40-mark question on Weberian explanations for inequality. Often, this question will take the form of inviting you to discuss a concept that Weberianism has distinctive views on, such as **empathic understanding**, **status** or **freewill**. You could also bring Weberianism into an essay on inequalities of class, gender, ethnicity or age, especially as a developed evaluation of Marxism (see **Chapter 7** for more on this).

Weberianism isn't a particularly popular Perspective. Most Social Action theorists pursue Interactionist research on small groups, employing ideas like **Labelling Theory** and methods like **ethnography** (p62), but these approaches are limited in explaining inequality on a society-wide scale. For that, you need **structuralist** insights into systematic disadvantages.

Weber's insights about factors other than just Class being important for explaining inequality have been adopted by **Neo-Marxists** (see, for example, the **Wheel of Privilege** on p150). The idea of social closure is similar to Gramsci's idea of **hegemonic groups protecting their privileges** (p150). **Critical Race Theorists** argue along with Weberians that social attitudes and beliefs create inequality and racist attitudes stem from the colonialist history of White societies.

The distinctive feature of Weber's thought is its **openness to flux or change**: groups are always shifting in their **market situation**, which is why they try to use **social closure** to 'shore up' their position and make their privileges permanent, but this is doomed to failure in the end. An important reason for this is the **influence of beliefs and values** on social Status. Traditional 'materialist' Marxists see all beliefs and values as coming from economic position, but Weber thinks ideas are more than just justifications for the status quo: they can actually change things.

One implication of this is that sustained and successful campaigns to change public opinion (e.g. on women's rights or anti-racism) can make a genuine difference to the status of disadvantaged groups. Some Marxists and Feminists would deny this, arguing that only revolutionary change can improve things because the benefits of gradual reform will always be snatched away by the ruling elites when it suits them.

Another implication is that bigoted or hate-filled ideas can change public opinion for the **worse**, increasing the problems for disadvantaged groups. For example, viewpoints like White Supremacy impact negatively on the status of minorities if they aren't challenged.

Marxism and Feminism could be accused of contradicting themselves when they accept that things can be made **worse** for disadvantaged groups by the spread of negative ideas but deny they can be made **better** by the spread of positive ideas. Weberianism argues that **both** trends are possible.

On the other hand, Weberianism can be criticised for downplaying the importance of poverty and class and exaggerating the possibility of positive change for disadvantaged groups. Weberians risk 'falling between two stools' – if **'conflict Weberians'** emphasise social closure and the power of elite groups, they end up just like Neo-Marxists; if **'consensus Weberians'** downplay this in favour of gradual social change, they end up very similar to Functionalists.

EXAM PRACTICE: EXPLAINING INEQUALITY

The OCR exam has two questions in **Paper 2 Section B**:

5. Outline ways in which a person's age may restrict their social life in modern Britain. **[20 marks: 12 AO1 + 8 AO2]**

This is one of those 'describe & illustrate' questions, but with no Source A or Source B to lean on. There is no need to evaluate.

*Make **three** sociological points about age inequalities and differences. For example, you could argue that older people are more likely to be socially excluded due to divorce, loneliness and disability.*

It's a good idea to refer to particular statistics (like over half of people over 65 have 2+ chronic health conditions) and you should definitely use some sociological terminology (like social exclusion, silver separators, life chances). Then offer examples of restrictions and make sure each example has an explanation linked to age. For example, "Elderly people are likely to end up in the sort of care home studied by Gentleman, where their younger relatives do not visit and they don't speak to anyone."

*Don't get drawn into a debate about whether or not old people are getting better or worse or whether old people are worse off than young people: there are **no** marks for AO3 evaluation with this question.*

6. Assess the view that working class people have been harmed rather than helped by government policies to reduce inequality. **[20 marks: 16 AO1 + 8 AO2 + 16 AO3]**

This is a long essay with a requirement for developed evaluation. You should spend 50 minutes and write 1000 words. The idea of well-meaning government policies harming the working classes links this question to the New Right's explanation of inequalities.

*Write **four** points. Each point should introduce a sociological idea with some illustration from the real world. Each point should finish off with a developed evaluation (see **Chapter 7** for this).*

*For example, you could write about the Underclass, lone parent families, young men joining gangs, the benefits trap and the solution of shrinking the state. Alternatively, some ideas from **Chapter 5** can be discussion points, such as the 'marriage gap' emerging from easy divorces or the failure of Grammar Schools to benefit the working class.*

Each point should be backed up with research or statistics and then illustrated with some real-world example (AO2). Charles Murray should certainly feature in your answer, but Dennis & Erdos have valuable ideas too as well as different solutions.

*Each point needs to lead into some developed discussion; see **Chapter 7** for this. Keep your focus on the debate about whether benefits have created an Underclass. For example, Rex & Tomlinson identify a Black Underclass below the White one but due to racism, not benefits.*

CHAPTER SEVEN – EVALUATION

In **Paper 2 Section B**, question 5 assesses **AO3**/evaluation and requires a developed evaluation; this needs to address theoretical and/or methodological issues. It needs to go deeper than a 'brief evaluation' and look at an issue from alternative perspectives or work through the implications of a viewpoint.

As well as the evaluative points you can find in the preceding chapters, here are some evaluative positions candidates can adopt:

Brief Evaluations

These points are simple ones that are hard to turn into developed points, so you might miss out on the higher AO3 band marks. Still, better to write something than nothing at all.

"Not all people…" / Over-generalising

Structuralist Perspectives (like **Functionalism** or traditional **Marxism** and **Feminism**) are particularly prone to sweeping generalisations. They often claim that everyone is motivated by the same thing or experiences the same oppression or wants the same outcomes. For example, Functionalists claim everyone shares the same basic values in society and Feminists claim all women are in some way oppressed.

To evaluate these ideas, point out that not all people fit into this mould. Not all working class people remain stuck in poverty, not all women let themselves be held back by sexism.

If you are writing about empirical research, point out that its sample group doesn't resemble everyone. Not all retired people come from top management jobs like the ones that **Jones et al** studied (p125).

It's important not to be formulaic. Say *why* not all people are like this: give an example of one of the exceptions. Not all women are held back by sexism, because some have successful careers *because of their superior qualification*. Not all retired people are like **Jones et al**'s sample *because they can't afford to take early retirement before the State Pension Age (SPA)*.

"It's out-of-date…" / Time-locked

You will probably have noticed that an awful lot of sociological research comes from the 1950s, '60s and '70s. Those were important decades when a lot of ground-breaking Sociology was done. But do theories and samples from the 1970s tell us anything about the UK in the 21st century?

To evaluate these studies, point out that so much has changed. **Mass employment in factories** has ended, **equal rights for women** has arrived (at least, in principle), the UK has **become a multicultural society**, the **Internet** has transformed the way we communicate and find out about the world (this last point makes studies from the 1980s and early '90s out-of-date too).

Once again, it's important not to be formulaic. Say **why** one of these changes matters for this particular study: give an example of one of the exceptions. **Rex & Tomlinson**'s study of the Black Underclass (p170) is out of date because *the Equalities Act (2010) makes a lot of discrimination illegal now*. Sontag's idea of the double standard in ageing is out-of-date *because in the 21st century, lots of men feel a pressure to remain young-looking too*.

"Things are changing" / Social progress

Sociologists tend to assume that everything is fixed and nothing is going to change (indeed, it's foundational for some versions of Marxism) but there are popular and successful campaigns to challenge inequality and create a more fair society.

To evaluate these ideas, point out that people are aware of these inequalities and doing something about them. It would be formulaic just to say "things are changing because of campaigns" and leave it at that. Say **why** these campaigns are working. For example, Black History Month raises awareness of non-White cultures *which challenges racist stereotypes about ethnic minorities have less important history*.

Developing Evaluations

These points have a complexity that makes them suitable for turning into developed points, so you can qualify for higher AO3 band marks.

"It's a macro-perspective" / Interactionist critique

Structuralist Perspectives make sweeping generalisations because they study society as a whole and focus on important institutions rather than individual people. The **Social Action (Interactionist)** Perspective criticises this, saying it is better to look at society 'from the bottom up' (a **micro Perspective**).

To evaluate these ideas, point out that an Interactionist or Weberian approach might be better. Rather than studying the Underclass as a trend in society, take a micro approach and study individual members of the Underclass.

Avoid being formulaic. Say **why** the micro approach would be better: give an example of one of the benefits. Take a micro approach to studying the Underclass, *because they will tell you why they are unemployed, which may or may not have anything to do with a benefits trap*.

Development

If you bring in Interactionism as the solution to the problem, give examples of studies that employ this micro approach (like **Gentleman** studying an old people's care home, p129) or explain how research incorporates aspects of the micro approach (like the way Weberianism recognises that individuals like Marcus Rashford can gain Status by leveraging their talents).

Alternatively, criticise your own improvement: discuss the drawbacks of using the micro approach (the Underclass people might lie to the interviewer; after all, they are supposed to have no sense of right and wrong according to **Murray**, p142).

"This is similar to…" / Comparisons

Sometimes, different sociologists or different Perspectives end up saying similar things, although usually for different reasons Marxists and Feminists both agree there is propaganda and brainwashing (**ideology**) in the news. Marxists and Functionalists both agree that modern Capitalism is stressful and difficult for the poor.

To evaluate these ideas, point out the similarity between the sociology you are writing about and another Perspective or research study. If you have explained that the New Right think that there is a depraved Underclass, explain that some Marxists agree that working class families have been harmed by divorce and absent fathers.

As usual, don't be formulaic. Say *why* the two approaches are so similar *or* say why they are also different: give an example. The New Right and Marxists agree on lone parents because they both think that children need fathers, *although the New Right think the solution is to cut benefits,* but *Marxists recommend increasing the help for disadvantaged families*.

Development

If you think two Perspectives are similar, don't stop there. You could give examples of studies from each perspective, like **Murray**'s study of lone families on benefits compared to **Dennis & Erdos**' study of working-class children without fathers (p143).

Alternatively, criticise the very similarity you suggested: discuss the how differences between the two approaches are more important than similarities (Marxists recognise that working class people are being exploited by Capitalism, whereas the New Right want to shrink the state and de-regulate capitalist businesses).

"Inequalities might be Differences …" / Interpretations

Most people accept that everyone is different, so even in a perfectly fair world some people would be more talented, more hard-working, more ambitious or just more sensible than others – and the untalented, lazy or foolish people would come out worse. We don't accuse the Olympics of inequality because most people can't run 100m in 10 seconds.

In order to avoid being formulaic, say **why** an apparent inequality might actually be a difference. There might be fewer women in top paying management jobs **because women have different preferences from men and don't want to commit to a career that involves working long hours away from their families.**

Development

If you think a difference might be at work, give examples of studies which back up this position, such as **Hakim**'s preference theory (p161) which explains vertical segregation (the 'glass ceiling') as being due to lifestyle preferences.

Alternatively, criticise the idea you suggested: discuss the flaws with focusing too much on difference (such as the way it can ignore bias and systematic unfairness or end up 'victim blaming' by suggesting that it is disadvantaged people's own fault for their problems).

"A Left/Right Winger would say …" / Political critique

Research into inequality has a practical application: politicians use these ideas to pass laws and to launch or abolish social policies. Some of these are successful, others backfire. It's a good idea to praise sociological research if it leads to effective social policies or criticise it if it doesn't.

In order to avoid being formulaic, say **why** the research has practical benefits or drawbacks: give an example. Research into families on benefits help working class communities, **because they dispel negative stereotypes about the Underclass and encourage governments to spend tax money on generous benefits.**

Development

If you think a political implication is good or bad, don't stop there. You could give examples of studies which back up this political position, such as **Dennis & Erdos**' recommendations that influenced the New Labour Government in the UK (p143).

Alternatively, criticise the political idea you suggested: discuss the flaws with focusing too much on inequality (such as the way it can encourage a victim mentality that stops people from solving their own problems and expecting the state to do it for them).

"A weakness of this Perspective is …" / Standard theoretical critiques

Functionalism

Functionalism ignores diversity: Functionalism assumes we are all the same and want the same things, but the things it says we all want tend to be the sort of things that the white middle classes want. Functionalism doesn't take seriously the idea that ethnic minorities, the working class or women might have different goals and values.

Functionalism ignores social injustice: Functionalism assumes that society is harmonious and **meritocratic,** but it turns a blind eye to a lot of inequality, corruption and barriers to social mobility. It defends Capitalism as the best system we have discovered for making people healthy and wealthy while ignoring the huge human and environmental cost of Capitalism worldwide. It is also prepared to accept a lot of crime for the sake of consensus.

Functionalism celebrates Western superiority: Functionalists believe in the **'March of Progress'** and claim that the sort of liberal democratic nations you find in Europe, North America and Australia are the most advanced. Other societies ought to imitate them and immigrants ought to assimilate (according to **Patterson's host-immigrant model**, p138). This ignores many flaws in Western societies (e.g. Capitalism, patriarchy, institutional racism).

Functionalism overrates the biological: Functionalists believe society reflects unchangeable biological needs or 'human nature.' Critics argue there is no such thing as 'human nature' and that everything is **socially constructed**. 'Human nature' is often used to excuse certain inequalities (such as the subordinate position of women or the marginalisation of the elderly).

Development

If you offer a theoretical weakness, don't stop there. You could give examples of studies that illustrate that weakness (like **Talcott Parsons**' theory that suggests that women naturally have a role of homemaker and mother and damage their children if they don't accept it). Alternatively, follow through the implications of this weakness (what would happen if Right Wing politicians acted on Functionalist ideas) or bring in other Perspectives that have something to say about this weakness (like Marxists characterising Functionalist ideas as serving Capitalism).

Alternatively, evaluate the weakness you suggested by arguing that it *isn't really a weakness*: like Patterson's idea that once ethnic minorities assimilate to the host culture, the hosts will automatically stop treating them with racist hostility, but there hasn't been long enough for this to happen yet.

Make a point of discussing how **Meritocracy** justifies inequality by proposing that everyone has ended up where they deserve to be – or they can change where they end up by putting in more study and effort. It is easy to offer a Conflict Theory or Weberian criticism on this, based on discrimination or social closure.

The New Right

The New Right lacks empirical support: Most of the support for the New Right comes from news stories about working class deviance – but those stories might be exaggerated. Hard evidence for the existence of an **underclass** is not plentiful and there's even less evidence for a whole group of people (rather than a few individuals) who reject society's values, don't want to work, don't want to live in families and embrace crime as a lifestyle (**Dean & Taylor-Gooby** is a good study to cite, p142).

The New Right demonises the vulnerable: The New Right is accused of 'punching down' – targeting the group in society that most needs help and making them out to be monstrous and calling for any sort of help (in the form of benefits) to be taken away. **Marxists** find it fairly easy to characterise the New Right as a **hegemonic attack on the poor**. However, Marxists can be characterised as glamorising delinquents and criminals as noble underdogs and ignoring the damage they do in society.

The New Right exaggerates deviancy: The New Right presents the underclass as a growing problem that threatens the whole of society. Even **Functionalists** criticise this approach as alarmist. Functionalists believe that deviancy is necessary and ultimately benefits society. However, the New Right emerged partly because both Functionalists and Marxists seemed to be making excuses for crime rather than doing anything practical to put a stop to it.

Development

If you offer a theoretical weakness, don't stop there. You could give examples of studies that illustrate that weakness (like **Murray**'s warning that single mothers are raising feral boys and promiscuous girls illustrates the New Right demonising the vulnerable). Alternatively, follow through the implications of this weakness (what would happen if politicians acted on Murray's suggestions) or bring in other Perspectives that have something to say about this weakness (like Marxists characterising the attack as serving hegemonic power).

Alternatively, criticise the weakness you suggested by arguing that it isn't really a weakness: Murray thinks the real enemies of the poor are the people who keep them in a benefits trap that appears kind but is actually dehumanising – you would be doing the underclass a favour by getting them off benefits and into family arrangements.

Make a point of discussing how **shrinking the state** is an important part of New Right thinking – but without benefits and social care, would people be even more exploited by ruthless Capitalist businesses, with families suffering even more? How can we be sure stronger families would rise up once the support of the state is withdrawn?

Marxism

Marxism ignores progress: In the last 200 years, Capitalist societies have abolished slavery, set up human rights, created a welfare state and free education and healthcare for all. Marxists often talk as if this hasn't happened or as if it happened *in spite of* Capitalism. This pessimistic view of the past and the future perhaps exaggerates social injustice as much as Functionalism downplays it.

Marxism is a conspiracy theory: It's standard for Marxists to argue that society is controlled by a sinister group of billionaires who brainwash everyone through **ideology**. This underestimates the independence of many journalists and politicians well as the ability of ordinary people to think for themselves and work out what's true.

Marxists assume class is homogenous: *Homogenous* means 'all the same' and traditional Marxists think that all working-class people share the same relationship to labour and power. However, **Neo-Marxists** are more aware of **intersecting Identities** and how behaviour is shaped by particular circumstances.

Marxism offers no solutions: You don't have to be a Marxist to spot the Capitalism has flaws – Functionalists would admit *that*! Marxists argue that Capitalism is intrinsically rotten and destructive, and it needs to be replaced rather than reformed. But replaced with what? Marxism can be accused of criticising Capitalism without offering a coherent alternative. After all, how can we be sure that whatever replaces Capitalism would be less unequal rather than more unequal?

Development

If you offer a theoretical weakness, develop it. You could give examples of studies that illustrate that weakness (like **Braverman** suggesting automatisation is deskilling the workforce without suggesting how businesses could adapt *without* bringing in robots and computers). Alternatively, follow through the implications of this weakness (what would happen if Left Wing politicians acted on Marxist suggestions) or bring in other Perspectives that have something to say about this weakness (like the New Right characterising Marxism as trapping the working class by making them dependent on benefits).

Alternatively, criticise the weakness you suggested by arguing that it isn't really a weakness: Marxism might sometimes look like a conspiracy theory but the big newspapers, Right Wing politicians and business owners could all be 'on the same side' without deliberately conspiring so long as they share vested interests.

Make a point of discussing how Neo-Marxism improves on the standard Marxist position in various ways – but at the cost of abandoning certain important Marxist ideas.

Feminism

Feminism ignores biology: Feminists insist that gender is **socially constructed,** and it certainly is up to a point. However, Psychology reveals lots of biological differences in brain structure, hormones and genes between the sexes and it's unlikely that *none* of this makes *any* difference to social behaviour. But if Gender Identity is even partly based on unchangeable sexual differences, then some of the situations women are in might not be *entirely* due to Patriarchy.

Feminism ignores progress: In the last century women have won the vote, the right to be educated at university and manage their own affairs. In Britain, the **Sexual Discrimination Act (1975)** outlawed sexual discrimination. Feminism can be accused of downplaying this progress and exaggerating the scale of injustice. However, the gender pay gap still exist and the top jobs in business and politics have nothing like 50% representation of women.

Feminists assume gender is homogenous: As with Marxists and social class, traditional Feminists are accused of treating all women as if they experienced the same oppression – which in practice means assuming that the difficulties of White women are typical for all women. Young women (and especially young Black women) might have different experiences.

Feminists ignore the oppression of men: Feminists sometimes seem to assume that Masculinity is homogenous, and all men are complicit in the Patriarchy, but men are much more likely than women to die by violence, to be homeless and to work in dangerous conditions. Many young men are also victims of oppression and die in dangerous jobs, through violence or suicide.

Development

If you offer a theoretical weakness, develop it. You could give examples of studies that illustrate that weakness (like Hakim arguing that women choose not to sacrifice their quality of life in elite professions that demand long hours). Alternatively, follow through the implications of this weakness (what would happen if Left Wing politicians acted on Feminist suggestions, such as the quotas for women in top jobs) or bring in other Perspectives that have something to say about this weakness (like Marxists agreeing that Capitalism oppresses men and women in different ways).

Alternatively, criticise the weakness you suggested by arguing that it isn't really a weakness: Feminism might ignore progress but the gender pay gap is stubborn and the glass ceiling still exists so maybe the progress has been exaggerated.

You could discuss how 3rd and 4th Wave Feminism improves on the standard Feminist position in various ways – but at the cost of abandoning certain important Feminist ideas.

Weberianism

Weberianism cannot be objective: The Weberian research focus on *Verstehen* means it can be insightful but this insight is also very **subjective** – just a matter of opinion – whereas Sociology claims to be a social *science* that explores facts in an **objective** way.

Weberianism is an incomplete explanation: Weberianism is a good *description* of how inequality works but it might be an incomplete *explanation* because it doesn't explain where inequality ultimately comes from. Just why, exactly, do some groups suffer from low Status or get excluded from powerful Parties? Marxism can explain this through the ruling class controlling of the means of production and Functionalists can relate it to biological differences and the idea of some lifestyles being a functional 'fit' but Weberianism does not offer this sort of explanation.

Weberianism is too optimistic: Weberianism, like Functionalism, supports a **gradualist** view of social progress, with disadvantaged groups slowly improving their market situation and good ideas (hopefully) replacing bad ones. This ignores the idea that the very structure of society itself might be unchangeably biased in favour of certain groups: the wealthy, White people or men. These elites will not surrender their Status unless forced to.

Weberianism is contradictory: Weberianism believes in freewill and the possibility of Social Action – people changing society – but it also believes in social closure as powerful groups try to keep other groups in a subordinate position. Ultimately, one of these has to be false for the other to be true.

Development

If you offer a theoretical weakness, develop them with examples of studies that illustrate that weakness (like **Jones et al**'s study failing to explain why these retirees had the freedom to enjoy their old age while other old people do not). Alternatively, follow through the implications of this weakness (what would happen if politicians acted on Weberian suggestions, such as Rex & Tomlinson's identification of a Black Underclass) or bring in other Perspectives that have something to say about this weakness (like Neo-Marxism claiming to offer an explanation of where unequal Status comes from in the first place).

Alternatively, criticise the weakness you suggested by arguing that it isn't really a weakness: Weberianism might lack objectivity but the point about *verstehen* is that it gives insight into what 'makes people tick' rather than focusing on statistics or mass trends.

You could discuss how Neo-Marxism (and Critical Race Theory) improve on the standard Weberian position in various ways – but perhaps at the cost of abandoning the idea that disadvantaged groups can be helped through gradually reforming the law and positive messages.

EXAM PRACTICE: SECTION B

The OCR exam has two questions in **Paper 2 Section B**:

   5. Outline the evidence for women experiencing inequality in the workplace. **[20 marks: 12 AO1 + 8 AO2]**

This is one of those 'describe & illustrate' questions, but with no Source A or Source B to lean on. There is no need to evaluate.

*Make **three** sociological points about gender inequalities and differences. For example, you could argue that there is a gender pay gap, that women experience a glass ceiling and that women are forced to take on childcare responsibilities at home.*

It's a good idea to refer to particular statistics (like women earning a fifth less than men) and you should definitely use some sociological terminology (like vertical and horizontal segregation). Then offer examples and make sure each example has an explanation linked to women. For example, "At the BBC Claudia Winkleman is paid less than a quarter of what Jeremy Vine earns, showing the gender pay gap."

*Don't get drawn into a debate about whether or not the gender pay gap really exists or whether women prefer less well-paid but more family-friendly jobs: there are **no** marks for AO3 evaluation with this question.*

   6. 'Racism is institutionalised in British society.' Discuss. **[20 marks: 16 AO1 + 8 AO2 + 16 AO3]**

This is a long essay with a requirement for developed evaluation. You should spend 50 minutes and write 1000 words. The idea of institutionalised racism links this question to the Marxist (especially Neo-Marxist) explanation of inequalities.

*Write **four** points. Each point should introduce a sociological idea with some illustration from the real world. Each point should finish off with a developed evaluation (see **Chapter 7** for this).*

*For example, you could write about White Privilege, the Race Relations Act, demographic factors, the Windrush Scandal and the study by Wood et al. Alternatively, some ideas from **Chapter 6** can be discussion points, such as Critical Race Theory, the Wheel of Privilege and Bonilla-Silva's discussion of racism.*

Each point should be backed up with research or statistics and then illustrated with some real-world example (AO2). Household incomes, exam results and political representation could all feature.

*Each point needs to lead into some developed discussion; see **Chapter 7** for this. Keep your focus on the debate about whether racism is institutionalised or a product of demographic factors. The 2021 CRED Report into racism in the UK is a great discussion point.*

KEY RESEARCH

The 34 studies here cover all the topics that arise in this Section of the exam and many will prove useful in later sections too. Start learning them. For each study, I include the key terms, a Perspective (if relevant) and the particular topics it is linked to.

Ansley (1972): criticises Parsons' 'Warm Bath' theory, **Feminism**; p137

Arber, Dale & Gilbert (1986): *The Surrey Scale*, measure social class without sexist bias; **Feminism/Weberian**, p160

Barron & Norris (2013): *Sexual Divisions & the Dual Labour Market*, primary vs secondary employment sectors, gendering the workplace; **Weberian**, p169

Bonilla-Silva (2013): *Racism Without Racists*, invisible weight of Whiteness, institutional racism, Critical Race Theory; **Marxism**, p155

Brandt (1980): *The Brandt Report*, Global North v Global South; patterns of inequality, p83

Braverman (1974): *Labour & Monopoly Capital*, automatization & deskilling; **Marxism**, p152

Correll (2017): Small Wins Model, unconscious bias training; **Feminism**, p104

Dennis & Erdos (1992): *Families Without Fatherhood*, working class lone parent families face disadvantage; **Marxism**, p143

Gentleman (2009): overt observations & unstructured interviews in a care home; **Weberian**; p129

Hakim (2006): Preference Theory, work-lifestyle preferences; **Feminism/Weberian**; p161

Havighurst (1961): Activity Theory; **Functionalism**; p139

Hecht et al. (2020): *Elites Pulling Away*, social mobility, meritocratic paradox, social closure, longitudinal study, secondary data; **Weberian**; p95

hooks (1984): *Ain't I A Woman?*, Black Feminism; **Feminism**; p162

Jones et al. (2010): early retirement as positive change, semi-structured interviews, habitus; **Weberian**; p125

Martin & Blinder (2020): Biases At The Ballot Box, ethnic minority candidates get fewer votes; **Weberian**, p118

Messner & Cooky (2021): content analysis of women's sport on TV, longitudinal study; **Feminism**, p107

Moore & Conn (2014): *Disguised*, covert participant observation disguised as 'Old Pat;' **Weberian**; p131

O'Neill (2002): *Experiments In Living: The Fatherless Family*, harmful effects of lone parenting, **Functionalism**; p146

Patterson (1965): host-immigrant model, assimilation; **Functionalism**; p138

Phillipson (1982): elderly are institutionally marginalised; **Marxism**; p156

Prieto-Arranz & Casey (2014): *Pedigree*, content analysis of *Benidorm*, social class & leisure; **Weberian**; p98

Rex & Tomlinson (1979): *Colonial Immigrants In A British City*, social exclusion, Black Underclass in 1970s Handsworth, **Weberian**; p170

Rivera (2015): *Pedigree*, Old Boys Network, double filters in EPS jobs; patterns of inequality, **Weberian**; p85

Sewell (1997): *Black Masculinities & Schooling*, Black subculture of hyper-masculinity, **Functionalism**; p145

Sewell et al (2021): *CRED Report*, no evidence of institutional racism, **Functionalism**; p120

Sontag (2019): *The Double Standard of Ageing*, feminine accomplishments are passive, women subordinated by focus on youthful beauty, **Feminism**; p163

Stallings (2002): critiques *Tornadoes Over Texas* to show social closure after a disaster, **Weberian**; p168

Stoet & Geary (2019): *Basic Index of Gender Inequality*, contrast with GGGI, **Functionalism**; p109

Tumin (1953): criticises **Davis & Moore**'s idea of stratification; **Marxism**; p136

Turner (1989): *Ageing, Status Politics & Sociological Theory*, criticises Marxist view of ageing, reciprocity-maturation curve; **Weberian**; p171

Wente (2014): *Do We Still Need Feminism?*, attacks 3rd Wave Feminism, **Feminism**; p144

Wilkinson & Pickett (2009): *The Spirit Level*, negative effects of inequality on life chances, **Marxism**; p100

Wood et al. (2009): institutional racism & job applications, implicit bias, field experiment, **Weberian**; p114

Zaretsky (1976): *Capitalism, The Family & Personal Life*, attacks Parsons' 'Warm Bath' theory, family supports Capitalism; **Marxism**; p153

FURTHER RESEARCH

These studies are less central to any argument. Some of them just reference a useful piece of terminology. Others offer criticism of a Key Study or are the original research that a Key Study is criticising.

Abraham (1999): criticises **bell hooks** for not citing sources, p162

Ahmed (2011): Islamic feminist, interprets wearing veil as resistance to colonialism, p162

Ali (2021): Coronavirus pandemic disproportionately harmed ethnic minorities, p119

Ballard (1982): honour in British Asian family ties, p115

Chambers (2001): Underclass are just a moral panic; p142

Cox (1970): race is a social construct created by colonialism; p154

Crenshaw (1989): developed Intersectionality & Critical Race Theory; p158

Dabiri (2019): *Don't Touch My Hair*, discrimination against Afro-textured hairstyles; p155

Daly (1978): global discrimination against women focused on appearance; p163

Davis & Moore (1945): Functionalist idea of stratification and meritocracy, p136

Dean & Taylor-Gooby (1992): no evidence for Underclass; p142

Delphy & Leonard (1992): family supports Patriarchy; p153

Dowd (1986): elderly as *"immigrants in time"* and *"strangers in their own land,"* p171

Eisenstadt (1965): supports **Parsons**, youth testing boundaries; p139

Francis (2006): criticises idea of genderquake, p108

Frey & Osborne (2013): extend ideas of Braverman to elite professions, p152

Friedan (1963): *The Feminine Mystique*, started 2nd Wave Feminism, p158

Hall (2018): colourism, Critical Skin Theory, p154

Jarvie (2006): popular sports by social class, p96

Kahrs (2021): attacks **CRED Report** as 'gaslighting' ethnic minorities, p120

Katz (1990): institutionalised racism and White focus on timekeeping, p111

Mack & Lansley (1985): *Poor Britain*, perceived poverty, p94

Magowan (2016): hierarchy of accents, p92

McIntosh (1988): White Privilege, p112

Milne (1995): 'Grey Power,' p124

Murray (1984): *Losing Ground*, presents New Right view of the Underclass; p142

Murray & Herrnstein (1994): *The Bell Curve*, argues for differences not inequalities, infamous chapter on race and IQ, p145

Pilcher (1995): three periods of old age, p123

Raleigh (2021): the Healthy Migrant Effect, p119

Reynolds (2009): Black fathers absent but still supportive, p115

Sharpe (1994): found changing aspirations in London schoolgirls, p161

Snowden (2010): Criticises Wilkinson & Pickett for 'cherry picking' data, p100

Swift & Steeden (2020): *Doddery But Dear*, age discrimination, p130

Tilley & Houston (2016): young women more mobile than men, p106

Webb (2013): working-class stealth democrats, p97

Weber (1905): *The Protestant Work Ethic & The Spirit Of Capitalism*, religious ideas led to creation of Capitalism, p166

Wilkinson (1994): genderquake in 1990s, p108

Wolf (1990): *The Beauty Myth*, beauty is a social construct to control women, p163

Young (2000): British Black Feminism based too much on American experiences, p162

GLOSSARY

Benefits trap: the **New Right** idea that the **Welfare State** makes it not worthwhile for poor people to work and encourages a lifestyle of irresponsibility and broken families

Capitalism: an economic system that promotes the private ownership of property, the pursuit of profit and the concentration of wealth in the hands of a minority of people; the opposite is Communism, which abolishes private property to make everyone economically equal

Case study: a research tool focusing on a single person, a small group or a single incident; makes use of **methodological pluralism**.

Cohort: the **sample** that takes part in a **longitudinal study**.

Colonialism: originally, the way European Empires imposed their culture on colonised peoples; currently, the lasting influence of that in cultural attitudes that give status to Whiteness and subordinate non-White ethnicities

Consciousness-raising: making people aware of inequality and injustice in their daily life and institutions; important for exposing **ruling class ideology**, **institutional racism** and **Patriarchy**

Content analysis: a research tool for studying a cultural artifact, which might be a media text or a communication of some sort (e.g. a TV show or a set of letters), for what it reveals about the society that produced it

Critical Race Theory: theory proposed by Crenshaw (1989) and others, that White society is **institutionally racist** due to its colonial history

Cultural Capital: an understanding of high culture that gives you access to the privileges of the wealthy elite, according to **Bourdieu (1984)**

Culture: the set of norms and values passed on by one generation to the next, including a version of history and traditional institutions that make up a way of life; cultures vary from one society to another and change (slowly) over time

Deviance: Behaviour that goes against **norms** and **values**

Disengagement Theory: theory proposed by Henry & Cummings (1941) that it is desirable for older people to disengage from work and other social responsibilities

Empathy: having sympathy with and sharing in the emotional states of other people.

Ethnography: a methodological approach taken by **Interpretivists** that involves spending time inside a culture you are studying so as to get a deeper understanding of its members.

Feminism: a sociological Perspective that identified conflict between the sexes; believes in a Patriarchy which subordinates women and maintains male power through coercion and violence

Functionalism: a sociological Perspective that promotes consensus around shared values; believes in a biological basis for human social behaviour and the inevitability of deviance

Gatekeeping: controlling whether or not researchers can have access to a population they want to study.

Gender: the norms and values linked to biological sex; males are often expected to behave in a masculine way and females in a feminine way

Generalisability: how a study's findings can be applied to wider society or a **sample**'s behaviour attributed to the target population

Genderquake: Term used by Wilkinson (1994) to describe the social changes that led to young women overtaking men in academic success and career ambition

Glass ceiling: the barrier to women looking to be promoted into management jobs; also known as vertical segregation

Globalisation: a process going on that makes different parts of the world more interconnected through travel, global **Capitalism** and the **Mass Media**

Global Financial Crisis (GFC): a banking crisis in 2008 that affected the economies of many countries, especially Western countries; the crisis led to a decade of restricted spending, low wages and unemployment for many people; some groups did better than others during the GFC, creating new inequalities or intensifying old ones

Gradualism: the idea that social change can happen slowly, through reforms to the law and campaigns to raise awareness; supported by **Functionalism** and **Weberianism** but rejected by **Marxism** and some **Feminists**

Grey Pound: the economic influence of older people due to their spending habits and relative wealth

Grey Power: the political influence of older people due to their consistent voting habits and growing numbers, according to Milne (1999)

Habitus: your lifestyle and attitudes (including things like dress, accent and values) which place you in a particular social class, according to **Bourdieu (1984)**

Hegemony: the dominance of one group and their culture in society; hegemonic culture is the version of culture that commands the most respect; according to **Neo-Marxists** hegemonic culture manufactures consent

Ideology: a set of ideas and values that influence how people interpret society; ideology is usually promoted by the **hegemonic** culture hides and justifies things which go against that culture; for example, a racist ideology might make people ignore racism or (if they can't ignore it) view racism as justified

Institutional Racism: a form of systemic bias that makes people within an institution carry out racist practices even though they may not consciously harbour racist views

Interactionism: a sociological Perspective that adopts a micro (small scale) approach; believes in understand individual motives and perceptions

Interpretivism: a methodological Perspective that aims for **empathy** and **rapport** with participants in order to have understanding (**verstehen**) of the meaning of their social world.

Intersectionality: A 21st century approach to Sociology which focuses on how different identities combine to create privilege or oppression

Interview: a self-report tool consisting of questions asked out loud that respondents answer by speaking

Implicit bias: discriminatory attitudes that a person is not aware of holding, because they are unconscious or part of a wider culture; an important part of **institutional racism** and **Patriarchy**

Left Wing: a political tendency to value progress, equality and justice highly

Life chances: a **Weberian** concept that groups have different opportunities to increase their status, based on their wealth, education, health and social capital

Longitudinal: research which takes place over days, weeks or years and measures trends over time.

Market situation: a **Weberian** idea that people are not all able to convert their skills, effort or qualifications into high status, because factors like discrimination, lack of opportunity or lack if social capital might be against them

Marxism: a sociological Perspective that identifies conflict between social classes; believes in a **ruling class** exploiting a **working class**, both through violet force and **ruling class ideology**

Meritocracy: A system that rewards talent and effort with social advancement; specifically, the idea that education recognises and gives qualifications to the most intelligent people, assigning them to the most important jobs with the biggest rewards. The opposite is **social reproduction**.

Methodological pluralism: using a mixture of methods to create richer and more detailed data.

Moral Panic: process where the Media identifies a group as a threat, exaggerates its importance, arouses public concern and brings about new policies and social change

Neoliberalism: economic and political theory that restrictions on business should be lifted and the role of the state reduced in order to encourage independence and entrepreneurialism; supported by the **New Right**

Neo-Marxism: several new interpretations of **Marxism** that emerged in the 1970s and became mainstream in the 1990s, incorporating elements of **Interactionism** and later **Postmodernism** to traditional Marxist thought

New Right: a sociological Perspective that proposes we are experience social collapse brought on by a welfare culture that rewards worklessness and deviance in the **Underclass**

Norms: ways of behaving seen as acceptable or expected in society; based on underlying **values**

Nuclear family: family of two parents and their children, without grandparents, in-laws or extended family; considered by **Functionalists** and the **New Right** to be the ideal family type

Objectivity: Being detached and unbiased; not allowing your values or preferences to influence the research – see **value-freedom.**

Observation: a research tool involving watching participants' behaviour over a period of time

Operationalisation: defining the important concepts in your research in a way that makes it clear how they are being measured

Patriarchy: The way society is structured around the interests of males, giving status to masculine behaviour and values and systematically subordinating women; masculine **hegemony** in society

Peer review: a process in scientific reporting where a piece of research has to be checked by other independent scientists before it is published

Pilot study: a small practice version of a study carried out to identify potential problems

Positive action: removing obstacles for disadvantaged groups so they can compete equally with privileged groups

Positive discrimination: discriminating in favour of disadvantaged groups in assigning funding, jobs or places on courses; illegal under the UK's Equalities Act (2010)

Positivism: a methodological Perspective that aims for scientific standards, **objectivity** and **value-freedom** and the discovery of **social facts.**

Primary data: information the researcher gathers personally

Privilege: the advantages a person has, perhaps without realising it, because they belong to high-status groups or have Identities that are respected in society

Qualitative: expressed in words or descriptions

Quantitative: expressed in numbers or statistics.

Questionnaire: a self-report tool containing written questions that respondents answer in writing.

Quota: a form of **positive action** to ensure a certain number of staff or members are from disadvantaged groups

Rapport: trust and intimacy between researchers and the people they study

Reflexivity: the process of reflecting on the way the researcher influences the people they are studying and vice versa; reflecting about your own biases in research

Reliability: consistency in research; when the research gets the same results every time

Representativeness: how closely the makeup of a **sample** resembles the **target population** it is taken from

Researcher imposition: when the researcher imposes their own views onto the research.

Reserve Army of Labour: the **Marxist** idea that Capitalism goes through booms and busts and needs a surplus workforce (e.g. women, the elderly, ethnic minorities) that it can hire and fire as the need arises

Respondent validation: asking the people who took part in research to evaluate the findings and confirm they agree with them.

Right Wing: a political tendency to value privacy, freedom and family values highly

Ruling class: A **hegemonic** group in society that controls the wealth and power, supported by an ideology that either hides or justifies their influence; Marx termed the ruling class 'the bourgeoisie' but **Neo-Marxists** often term it the **Hegemony**

Ruling class ideology: a set of beliefs promoted by the ruling class to preserve their power over the working class; ideology hides the injustice in society and justifies it when it cannot hide it

Sample: a small group of people in a study whose behaviour is studied for what it tells you about the **target population** they are taken from

Secondary data: information that already exists because it was gathered by someone else but the researcher makes use of it.

Semiotics: the study of signs and symbols; a technique for interpreting the deeper meaning in **qualitative data**.

Social Action: sociological theory that focuses on freewill and micro behaviour, such as **interactionism** or **Weberianism**

Snapshot: the opposite of a **longitudinal study**; research that measures social behaviour at one time and in one situation.

Social class: A system for separating people based on their economic position (wealth, income, status); originally a split between the **ruling class** and **working class**, but later admitting of a middle class in between and now many more classes

Social closure: a **Weberian** concept that groups with social status make sure other groups cannot achieve the same status in thew same way

Social fact: an underlying rule or law of society that can be used to formulate accurate predictions about social behaviour – a key concept for **Positivism**

Socialisation: The process of acquiring norms and values due to upbringing (primary socialisation) and education/experience (secondary socialisation)

Social mobility: the ability to go up (or down) in social class based on hard work, talent and qualifications, usually between one generation and the next (i.e. children being a higher class than their parents)

Social reproduction: the opposite of **Meritocracy**; the idea that social divisions are reproduced each generation despite the education people receive

Social solidarity: The experience of 'belonging' in society, linked to **value consensus**; it is the opposite of **anomie**

Structuralism: sociological theory that focuses on how individuals are controlled by social structures, such as **Functionalism**, the **New Right**, **Marxism** and most forms of **Feminism**

Subculture: a group within society that shares some of the **norms and values** of mainstream society but also has distinctive norms and values of its own

Subjectivity: viewing situations from your own unique perspective rather than trying to be detached and unbiased

Target population: the original group the research is investigating from which a **sample** is taken.

Triangulation: using two methods so that the second one can check the **validity** of the first one.

Underclass: term used by the **New Right** for a class below the working class, characterised by single mothers on benefits, poorly socialised children and irresponsible, workless and crime-prone adult males

Validity: truth and authenticity in research; when the research shows what the researcher claims it shows

Value-freedom: an **objective** standard for research that is practised by **Positivists**.

Values: powerful ideas shared by people in a culture about what is right and desirable and what is shameful or wrong; often expressed in behaviour as **norms**

Verstehen: A term used by **Max Weber** to mean 'empathic understanding' rather than studying social behaviour in a purely detached and scientific way

Warm Bath Theory: theory proposed by Parsons (1959) that the family stabilises adult personalities, enabling men to de-stress after working in Capitalist society and wives acting as an 'emotional safety valve'

Weberianism: sociological Perspective based on the ideas of Max Weber and mixing **Marxist** ideas about Capitalism with a **Social Action** theory

Welfare State: aspect of modern societies that looks after citizens through free or subsidised healthcare and education along with benefits for the unemployed; funded through taxation of the wealthier citizens

White Privilege: Unearned advantages that people enjoy because they are White but do not consciously appreciate

Windrush Generation: Immigrants from the Caribbean who settled in the UK in the 1950s and 1960s

Working class: The majority group in society that is systematically excluded from access to wealth and power; controlled by **ideology** and the threat of force by the **ruling class**; Marx terms the working class 'the proletariat.'

ABOUT THE AUTHOR

Jonathan Rowe is a teacher of Religious Studies, Psychology and Sociology at Spalding Grammar School and he creates and maintains **www.psychologywizard.net** and the **www.philosophydungeon.weebly.com** site for Edexcel A-Level Religious Studies. He has worked as an examiner for various Exam Boards but is not affiliated with OCR. This series of books grew out of the resources he created for his students. Jonathan also writes novels and creates resources for his hobby of fantasy wargaming. He likes warm beer and smooth jazz.

Jonathan has created the **Sociology Robot** YouTube channel with video lectures supporting the material in this Study Guide.

Printed in Great Britain
by Amazon

82133997R00113